Critical Perspectives on Canadian Theatre in English

General Editor Ric Knowles

PLAYWRIGHTS CANADA PRESS

Theatre in Atlantic Canada

Critical Perspectives on Canadian Theatre in English

volume sixteen

Critical Perspectives on Canadian Theatre in English

volume sixteen

Theatre in Atlantic Canada

Edited by
Linda Burnett

Playwrights Canada Press
Toronto • Canada

Playwrights Canada Press

215 Spadina Avenue, Suite 230, Toronto, Ontario CANADA M5T 2C7
416-703-0013   fax 416-408-3402
orders@playwrightscanada.com • www.playwrightscanada.com

The publisher acknowledges the support of the Canadian taxpayers through
the Government of Canada Book Publishing Industry Development Program,
the Canada Council for the Arts, the Ontario Arts Council,
and the Ontario Media Development Corporation.

Cover image: Jin-me Yoon, between departure and arrival, 1996/1997.
Partial installation view, Art Gallery of Ontario.
Video projection, video montage on monitor, photographic mylar scroll,
clocks with 3-D lettering, audio. Dimensions variable.
Courtesy of the artist and Catriona Jeffries Gallery, Vancouver.
Typesetting/Cover Design: JLArt

Library and Archives Canada Cataloguing in Publication

Theatre in Atlantic Canada / Linda Burnett, editor.

(Critical perspectives on Canadian theatre in English ; 16)
Includes bibliographical references and index.
ISBN 978-0-88754-890-1

1. Canadian Drama (English)--Atlantic Provinces--History and criticism.
2. Canadian drama (English)--20th century--History and criticism.
3. Canadian drama (English)--21st century--History and criticism.
I. Burnett, Linda Avril II. Series: Critical perspectives on Canadian
theatre in English ; 16

PS8177.5.A8T54 2010   C812'.54099715   C2010-902255-6

Mixed Sources
Product group from well-managed
forests and other controlled sources
www.fsc.org Cert no. SW-COC-003438
© 1996 Forest Stewardship Council

First edition: May 2010
Printed and bound by Hignell Printing at Winnipeg, Canada.

This volume is dedicated to Dr. Leanore Lieblein
for being so wonderful a mentor over so many years.

Table of Contents

General Editor's Preface

Canadian Theatre Studies, as a formal discipline, is barely thirty years old, yet already it has moved through empiricist, nationalist, regionalist, particularist, materialist, and postmodernist phases, each of which has made significant contributions to the almost simultaneous construction and deconstruction of the field's histories. This series, *Critical Perspectives on Canadian Theatre in English*, was founded in order to trace these histories in volumes focusing on specific topics of significance to the still emerging discipline.

The series was launched in 2005 with the intention of making the best critical and scholarly work in the field readily available to teachers, students and scholars of Canadian drama and theatre. It set out, in individual volumes, chronologically to trace the histories of scholarship and criticism on individual playwrights, geographical regions, theatrical genres, themes and cultural communities. Over its first five years the series published fifteen volumes, collecting work on *Aboriginal Drama and Theatre*, *African Canadian Theatre* and *"Ethnic," Multicultural, and Intercultural Theatre*; on playwrights *Sharon Pollock, Judith Thompson* and *George F. Walker*; on *Feminist Theatre and Performance* and *Queer Theatre in Canada*; on *Theatre in British Columbia* and *Theatre in Alberta*; on *Environmental and Site-Specific Theatre*; *Collective Creation, Collaboration, and Devised Theatre*; *Space and the Geographies of Theatre*; *Theatre Histories*; and *Design and Scenography*. I am very proud of this achievement, proud that these volumes have already been widely cited in subsequent scholarship, and proud that, although this is primarily a reprint series, essays newly commissioned for individual volumes have been nominated for and have won scholarly awards.

As the series continues, so do its original objectives. Each volume is edited and introduced by an expert in the field who has selected a representative sampling of the most important critical work on her or his subject since the 1970s, ordered chronologically according to the original dates of publication. Each volume also includes an introduction by the volume editor, surveying the field and its criticism, and a list of suggested further readings which recommends good work that could not otherwise be included. Where appropriate, the volume editors commission new essays on their subjects, particularly when these new essays fill in gaps in representation and attempt to correct historical injustices and imbalances, particularly those concerning marginalized communities. The volume topics have also been chosen to shed light on historically marginalized communities and work, while individual volumes have resisted the ghettoization of such work by relegating it to special topic volumes alone.

Volumes 16 to 21 bring the series to its conclusion by carrying on the work of the first fifteen volumes. They continue to address specific geographical regions, including the Atlantic Provinces and the "region" of Toronto; particular genres, including political, popular, and community-based theatre and the Canadian phenomenon of solo performance; and they focus on Canada's vexed relationship with "Shakespeare." The series' final volumes will be launched in Spring 2011, at which point they will be succeeded by a new series, New Essays on Canadian Theatre, which will make its own contributions to the development of the discipline. Already in the planning stages are volumes of new essays on Asian Canadian theatre, on new Canadian realisms, and on Latino/a Canadian theatre.

It is my hope that these series, in conjunction with the publications of Playwrights Canada Press, Talonbooks and other Canadian play publishers, will facilitate the teaching of Canadian drama and theatre in schools and universities for years to come. I hope that, by making available and accessible comprehensive introductions to some of the field's most provocative figures and issues, that they will contribute to the flourishing of courses on a variety of aspects of Canadian drama and theatre in classrooms across the country. And I hope that they will honour the work of some of the scholar/pioneers of a field that is still, excitingly, young.

Ric Knowles

Acknowledgements

In editing *Theatre in Atlantic Canada*, I have been helped by a number of individuals whom I would like to acknowledge and thank here: Ric Knowles, who has responded always in a timely fashion to my questions and offered much appreciated advice; Annie Gibson, another quick responder to questions asked; and Jason Woodman Simmonds, Maureen Moynagh, Renée Hulan, Len Falkenstein, Greg Doran, and Jennifer Andrews, who assisted me in my search for published academic work on Aboriginal theatre/theatre artists of Atlantic Canada. I am especially grateful to Len Falkenstein for offering to write an essay on John Barlow's *Inspiration Point* for this volume. I would also like to thank Emilia Vernelli, faculty secretary, for re-typing a number of the essays reprinted here, and Megan Chamberlin, student assistant in the department of English, Fine Arts, and Music at Algoma University, for proof-reading the re-typed essays. Finally, I would like to thank all of the individuals who generously granted permission for their essays to be included here, as well as the institutional holders of copyright who granted permission to reprint.

Donna E. Smyth's "Mermaid Theatre: The Mythic Dimension" was first published in *Canadian Theatre Review* 18 (1978): 28–32; Brian Parker's "On the Edge: Michael Cook's Newfoundland Trilogy" in *Canadian Literature* 85 (1980): 22–41; Alan Filewod's "The Political Dramaturgy of the Mummers Troupe" in *Canadian Drama/L'art dramatique canadien* 13.1 (1987): 60–72; Bryden MacDonald's "Not Leaving Home: Growing up Artistically in Atlantic Canada" in *Theatrum* 21 (1990/91): 14–18; Robert Nunn's "The Subjects of *Salt-Water Moon*" in *Theatre Research in Canada/Recherches théâtrales au Canada* 12.1 (1991): 3–21; Ric Knowles's "AnOther Story: Women's Dramaturgy and the Circulation of Cultural Values at Mulgrave Road" in *Atlantis: A Women's Studies Journal/Revue d'Etudes sur la Femme* 20.1 (1995): 169–81; Mary Elizabeth Smith's "On the Margins: Eastern Canadian Theatre as Post-colonialist Discourse" in *Theatre Research International* 21.1 (1996): 41–51; Bruce Barton's "Too Distant Voices: The Publishing of Dramatic Texts in the Maritimes" in *Canadian Theatre Review* 98 (1999): 4–8; Denyse Lynde's "*Icycle*: New Languages. Newfoundland's Artistic Fraud Creates New Languages for Theatre, New Languages for Icebergs" in *Canadian Theatre Review* 115 (2003): 12–16; Michael Devine's "Cultural Evolution in Newfoundland Theatre: The Rise of the Gros Morne Theatre Festival" in *Theatre Research in Canada/Recherches théâtrales au Canada* 25. 1–2 (2004): 67–88; George Elliott Clarke's "Afro-Gynocentric Darwinism in the Drama of George Elroy Boyd" in *Canadian Theatre Review* 118 (2004): 77–84; Jerry Wasserman's "'God of the Whiteman! God of the Indian! God Al-fucking-mighty!':

The Residential School Legacy in Two Canadian Plays" in *Journal of Canadian Studies* 39.1 (2005): 23–48; George Belliveau, Josh Weale and Graham Lea's "TheatrePEI: The Emergence and Development of a Local Theatre" in *Theatre Research in Canada/ Recherches théâtrales au Canada* 26.1–2 (2005); Glen Nichols's "Building Bridges: English & French Theatre in New Brunswick" in *Theatre Research in Canada/ Recherches théâtrales au Canada* 26.1–2 (2005): 4–18; Maureen Moynagh's "Can I Get a Witness? Performing Community in African-Nova Scotian Theatre" in *Canadian Theatre Review* 125 (2006): 41–46; and Roberta Barker's "Crossing the River: Zuppa Circus's *Penny Dreadful*" in *Canadian Theatre Review* 135 (2008): 14–16. "On the Edge of the Eastern World: John Barlow's *Inspiration Point* and Atlantic Canadian Aboriginal Theatre," by Len Falkenstein, was commissioned for this volume and is published here for the first time.

Introduction: Theatre in Atlantic Canada

by Linda Burnett

One mandate of *Critical Perspectives on Canadian Theatre in English*, as Ric Knowles makes clear in his General Editor's Preface to Volume 3 of this series, is to publish "the work of scholars and critics who have, since the so-called renaissance of Canadian theatre in the late 1960s and early 1970s, traced the coming-into-prominence of a vibrant theatrical community in English Canada." It is also to highlight "important work from and about marginalized communities," work by and about women, First Nations people, people of colour, and Gay, Lesbian, and Bi/Trans-sexual people.[1] With respect to *Theatre in Atlantic Canada*, this mandate has proven a challenge, one that has left me with more questions than answers.

Certainly, it has been recognized that theatre in Newfoundland, in the words of Donna Butt, founder and Artistic Director of Rising Tide Theatre, and a driving force in Newfoundland theatre for over thirty years now, experienced a "cultural 'renaissance'… circa 1973" (qtd. in Jones 93–94).[2] In 1967, Michael Cook arrived in Newfoundland and at Memorial University, as Michael Devine remarks in "Cultural Evolution in Newfoundland Theatre: The Rise of the Gros Morne Theatre Festival," and "began to influence a younger generation of students who had been touched, like other students across Canada, with a new nationalism." In 1972, Chris Brookes and Lynn Lunde founded the Mummers Troupe, a St John's theatre collective that," in Terry Goldie's words "must be seen as […] the first company to devote itself to providing professional productions on Newfoundland subjects, performed by Newfoundlanders." Rising Tide, which Goldie refers to as "the 'child' of the Mummers Troupe" (97), was founded in 1978. CODCO burst on the scene in 1973. British-born Maxim Mazumdar moved to Newfoundland in 1978 and established the Stephenville Festival in 1979, Theatre Newfoundland Labrador (TNL) in 1981. In less than a decade, theatre in Newfoundland was reborn.

Theatre in the Maritimes also experienced a renaissance during this period and into the 1980s. In Nova Scotia, Mermaid Theatre was founded in 1972 by Evelyn Garbary in Wolfville, Mulgrave Road Co-op Theatre in 1977 in Guysborough. By the fall of 1981, according to Richard Perkyns, there were "five professional N.S. theatre companies touring the province, four of them with N.S. plays" (110). By 1984, The Ship's Company Theatre was established in Parrsboro. In Prince Edward Island, TheatrePEI, "inaugurated in 1980," according to George Belliveau, Josh Weale, and Graham Lea in "TheatrePEI: The Emergence and Development of a Local Theatre," represented "the first formal theatre organization dedicated to the development of distinctly local theatre" on the island. In New Brunswick, the self-named "provincial" company, Theatre New Brunswick (TNB) was founded in Fredericton in 1969, Live Bait Theatre in 1988. With respect to Acadian theatre, as Glen Nichols details in "Building Bridges: English & French Theatre in New Brunswick," Théâtre populaire d'Acadie was established in Caraquet in 1974, Théâtre l'Escaouette in Moncton in 1978.

What Knowles describes as "steady growth in and development of theatre in Atlantic Canada" culminated with two theatre conferences in 1985. In Halifax, "[t]wenty-one professional theatre companies from the Maritimes and Newfoundland met at Neptune Theatre on 26–28 April 1985 [...] at the first ever Atlantic Theatre Conference" ("Halifax" 126). Then the following year, in April of 1986, theatre companies met at Mount Allison University, this time with playwrights, performers, students, academics and other theatre devotees from across the country, to participate in Theatre in Atlantic Canada, a symposium sponsored by the Anchorage Series in Canadian Studies. As Knowles has written, this conference marked a high point for theatre in the region—"the overwhelming atmosphere... was celebratory, and visitors from outside the region expressed surprise and pleasure at the range and quality of the work performed over the three-day meeting, as well as at the dedication, interest and numbers of participants." More importantly, the "mood" of the symposium was shown to be "justified" when a survey conducted by the Playwrights' Union of Canada "showed that, in spite of regional disparities and economic hardships, Atlantic Canada produced a higher percentage of Canadian work in the 1985–86 season than did any other region in the country" ("Atlantic Theatre" 140). The "coming-into-prominence of a vibrant theatrical community" in the region appeared well underway by the mid-1980s.

Further, since then there have been lots of reasons for optimism. Yes, some theatre companies have closed shop, including CODCO, The Mummers Troupe, TheatrePEI, Mermaid Theatre, Jest in Time, and the Atlantic Theatre Festival. Yes, as Mary Vingoe points out, "so many theatre companies [have] gone down without a trace" in Nova Scotia's capital city that" Paul Thompson "once named Halifax as 'the Bermuda triangle' of theatre" (xvii). But others continue to produce plays, including TNL, Rising Tide, Mulgrave Road, Ship's Company, TNB, Live Bait, Théâtre populaire d'Acadie, Théâtre l'Escaouette, and the Victoria Playhouse, "which traditionally produced a typical mix of light summer stock fare," according to Belliveau, Weale, and Lea, but which "has had at least one locally created play in each year since TheatrePEI stopped producing." And still others have emerged: Newfoundland's Artistic Fraud (1994); New Brunswick's Moncton-Sable (1997); and Nova Scotia's Irondale Ensemble Project (1990), Two Planks and a Passion Theatre (1992), Zuppa Circus (1998), and Onelight Theatre (1999). Determined to prove Thompson wrong about Nova Scotia's capital city, Mary Vingoe, Gay Hauser, and Wendy Lill established Eastern Front Theatre, now in its 17th year, in Dartmouth in 1993. Finally, many of the region's summer theatre festivals continue to thrive, including Festival Antigonish and the SuperNova Theatre Festival (NS); the Gros Morne Theatre Festival, the Stephenville Festival, and the Grand Bank Regional Theatre Festival (NL); and the NotaBle Acts Summer Theatre Festival (NB).

Other good things have happened since 1986. The Playwrights Atlantic Resource Centre (PARC) was formed in 1991 by Wanda Graham to serve the playwrights of the region at a time when there was little opportunity for the development of new plays and few opportunities for young actors, playwrights and directors in this region. The dream was, says Graham, "that one day our Atlantic plays and playwrights would not only feature on our regional stages regularly, but on national and international stages, in collections, on shelves of libraries, in bookstores, and in University Theatre programs around the world" (qtd. Munday 9–10). That Nova Scotia now has the Merritt Awards to recognize excellence in theatre, and Halifax now has both the Mayor's Award for Achievement in Theatre and the Mayor's Award for Emerging Theatre Artist are an indication that progress towards the realization of this dream is being made. So are Jenny Munday's words in 2006: "More young theatre artists find it possible to stay in the region or to return to work here. More new plays are written and developed and produced. This has led to the emergence and survival of an astounding number of new companies, an astounding amount of new work, and a pretty healthy theatre community" (10).

That the theatre community of Atlantic Canada appears as "pretty healthy" of late to Munday and others has much to do with the strength of the region's theatre companies and festivals, Munday suggests, and with the "profound impact" that PARC has had (10). But the theatre community's "strongest card," Vingoe claims, is the "quality" of its playwrights, whom Vingoe refers to as "the finest poets of the Canadian stage"—"George Elliott Clarke, Bryden MacDonald, Don Hannah, Mary-Colin Chisholm, Des Walsh, Daniel MacIvor, Kent Stetson, Wendy Lill, Berni Stapleton, Robert Chafe, Andy Jones" (xx). I agree with Vingoe and would add more names to her list of "poets": Melissa Mullen, Louise Delisle, Michael Melski, George Boyd, Walter Borden, David Woods, Michael Cook, David French, Charlie Rhindress, Lance Woolaver, Norm Foster, John Barlow, Cindy Cowan, Jenny Munday…. My list continues to grow.

Ever since hearing Vingoe remark, during her "Opening Words" at the Shifting Tides conference, that Atlantic Canada is the home "of the true poets of the stage," I have pondered why this might be. Vingoe wonders if "the price of depth is isolation," but I think that she comes closer when she quotes the words of Sarah Stanley: "there is so much here" (xx). Playwrights from Atlantic Canada possess in their stories, as David Ferry commented at Shifting Tides with respect to the situation in Newfoundland, an "endless mine of material." And as Michael Melski put it when I interviewed him, "there is an enormous resource in the East of stories. I'm always finding them." Melski himself draws on these stories in his plays. In *Miles from Home*, for example, he tells the story of Cape Breton's Johnny Miles, a child-miner and grocery-cart delivery boy who won the Boston Marathon twice, the first time in 1926, when he demolished world and Boston record marks. Robert Chafe also draws on local stories. In *Tempting Providence*, he tells the story of Myra Bennett, a British-born nurse, who came in 1921 to the isolated community of Daniel's Harbour on the Great Northern Peninsula on a two-year nursing contract and stayed for more than fifty years, coming to be known to Newfoundlanders as the Florence Nightingale of the

North. Another example is provided by Kent Stetson, whose *The Harps of God*, in the words of Knowles, "*is* a kind of historical documentary" of the Newfoundland sealing disaster of 1914 ("Of Mortality" 171).[3]

While many would agree with Chris Brookes, who at Shifting Tides suggested that the theatre of Atlantic Canada responds to the "need to reflect ourselves to ourselves," the playwrights of this region are doing far more than simply *telling* their stories, however; they are *retelling* them. They are engaged in a complicated and self-conscious revisionist rewriting of their culture, what Bruce Barton refers to as "myth-making and myth-challenging" (iii). Examples of this revisionist rewriting are offered by the work of Wendy Lill and George Elliott Clarke. Lill's *The Glace Bay Miners' Museum* is "a profound, hard-edged work that examines 'culture versus the onslaught of industrialization' and radically challenges [the] 'misty romanticism' that has often 'cloaked' the stories of coal mining families" (Globe Theatre). Clarke's *Beatrice Chancy*, a slave narrative set in 1801 on a plantation in the Annapolis Valley of Nova Scotia, challenges the notion that the story of slavery belongs not to us, but to others, to the United States, the Caribbean, South America.

Finally, in addition to making full use of the "so much here," the theatre artists of Atlantic Canada display an openness to outside influence and to alternative theatrical forms. Newfoundland's Jillian Keiley, as Michael Devine points out, is an excellent example of "an artist firmly grounded in her own culture, determined to integrate that culture with outside influences, and [...] to carry the resonance of her culture far and wide" (35–36). George Elliott Clarke's *Beatrice Chancy*, as David Sealy notes, draws not only on "the apocalyptic tradition of song, story, and sermon which, according to Clarke, constitutes the literary production of Black Nova Scotia," but on "the romantic tradition of Shelley, Byron, and Wordsworth" (117). And Nova Scotia's Zuppa Circus, New Brunswick's Moncton-Sable and Newfoundland's Artistic Fraud are three highly innovative theatre groups that experiment with form. A wonderful example of the sort of work they are producing is provided by Artistic Fraud's *Fear of Flight*, a creative and visually stunning ensemble piece containing monologues written by playwrights Berni Stapleton, Judith Thompson, Marie Clements, Guillermo Verdecchia, Bryden MacDonald, Daniel MacIvor, and Denise Clarke, which was performed in St. John's at Magnetic North in 2006 by students of the Sir Wilfred Grenfell College's theatre program.

From where, then, comes the "sense of reticence" about the state of theatre in Atlantic Canada that Wendy Lill describes so well in an interview that was published in 1991: "In the East, I find [...] a sense of reticence. It's not insecurity, because there's certainly a great deal of pride here: people who are here want to be here. It's more a feeling that's been drummed into Easterners for decades that historically "East is Least" and that their stories aren't as interesting as those from the West" (Rudakoff 37).

This "sense of reticence" lingers still. Thus, when Nova Scotia playwright George Boyd's *Wade in the Water* premiered in Montreal in 2003, Toronto's *The Globe and Mail*, as Ron Foley MacDonald notes, "published a major review," while "no Nova

Scotian media outlets seemed to notice." Thus, no university in Atlantic Canada has sponsored a major conference on theatre in Atlantic Canada since the Mount Allison symposium in 1986. When a long overdue national conference on the theatre and drama of the Atlantic region took place in 2004, this conference—"Shifting Tides: Atlantic Canadian Theatre Yesterday, Today, and Tomorrow"—took place, not at Dalhousie University, not at Memorial University, not at the University of New Brunswick, not at the University of Prince Edward Island, but at the Graduate Centre for the Study of Drama at the University of Toronto.

Why, with so many exciting theatre companies and festivals, so many wonderful playwrights in Atlantic Canada, are the region's media outlets seemingly reluctant to publish reviews of the productions of its playwrights, the region's universities to focus on the work of its theatre artists? Why are plays by local playwrights that are published by Maritimes and Newfoundland publishers as "rare" as "woodland sprites," as Bruce Barton shows in the Maritime context in "Too Distant Voices: The Publishing of Dramatic Texts in the Maritimes," reprinted here, and Denyse Lynde in the Newfoundland context in "Writing and Publishing: Four Newfoundland Playwrights in Conversation" (Lynde). Why must so many theatre artists from the region spend so much time in Toronto or Montreal in order to achieve the recognition they deserve? Len Falkenstein points out in "On the Edge of the Eastern World: John Barlow's *Inspiration Point* and Atlantic Canadian Aboriginal Theatre," an essay commissioned for this volume, that there is no "Maritime equivalent of an Aboriginal developmental company" like Toronto's Native Earth Performing Arts. Why is this?

There are no easy answers to these questions, but surely, as Knowles, Vingoe, Munday, Barton and others have suggested, money, or the lack thereof, offers one answer. As Vingoe puts it, "Government and corporate support, infrastructure and training, audience development and critical support, all contribute to a theatre community's sustainability. These are all things that Atlantic Canada has lacked and still lacks" (xviii). Mary Elizabeth Smith points to another answer in her discussion of the cultural imperialism that persists after Confederation reprinted here. She remarks, "Recruiting of theatrical personnel is now done in Toronto instead of New York. Some people would say that the new cultural, economic and political imperialists are Ontario and Quebec, as the opponents of Confederation feared they would be."

For now, however, I wish to leave such answers and return to the two-part mandate of the Critical Perspectives series. Arguably the work of scholars and critics has done much to document the development of a flourishing theatrical community in Atlantic Canada. Included in this volume are essays by Donna E. Smyth, Alan Filewod, Ric Knowles, Denyse Lynde, Michael Devine, George Belliveau, Josh Weale, Graham Lea, and Roberta Barker on a number of the region's important theatres and festivals (Mermaid Theatre, the Mummers Troupe, Mulgrave Road Co-op, Artistic Fraud, the Gros Morne Theatre Festival, TheatrePEI, and Zuppa Circus); essays by Brian Parker, Robert Nunn, George Elliot Clarke, Jerry Wasserman, and Len Falkenstein on the work of key playwrights of the region (Michael Cook, David French, George Elroy Boyd, Wendy Lill, and John Barlow); and essays by Bruce

Barton, Bryden MacDonald, Glen Nichols, Maureen Moynagh, and Mary Elizabeth Smith on the publishing of dramatic texts in the region, the difficulty in surviving as an artist in Eastern Canada, English and French theatre in New Brunswick, African-Nova Scotian Theatre, and the theatre of the region as post-colonialist discourse.

However, while it was relatively easy to satisfy the first part of the mandate, it has been difficult to satisfy the second part, which calls for titles in this series to foreground "important work from and about" the region's "marginalized communities." When he first saw my working bibliography for this book, Ric Knowles observed in an email note that it did not include anything "from gay or lesbian perspectives." This was not news to me, as I had searched hard for an essay on the work of one of the region's gay/lesbian theatre artists from a queer perspective, but with no success. I asked Knowles if he could help and he, too, had no luck. I finally had to accept that scholarly work on theatre artists from Atlantic Canada from this perspective simply did not exist.

The situation with respect to work from and about Aboriginal theatre artists from the region was no better. In his email, Knowles said that he and Monique Mojica "were unable to come up with anything for *Staging Coyote's Dream.*" And the only essay that I could find was on Yvette Nolan's *Annie Mae's Movement*—and while Annie Mae was from Nova Scotia, Nolan was born in Manitoba and is now best known as the Artistic Director of Native Earth Performing Arts, in Toronto. So I asked colleagues for the names of academics working in this field and Aboriginal artists on the east coast. They all replied by email: Renée Hulan, of Saint Mary's, said that "though there are a number of people working on Atlantic Canadian literature," she could not "think of anyone who is studying First Nations drama specifically"; Jennifer Andrews, of the University of New Brunswick (UNB), told me about her "student, Jason Simmonds [...] who is writing on Aboriginal adaptations of Shakespeare in Canada," but added that she was "certain that none of those is by an Atlantic Canadian writer"; Greg Doran, of the University of Prince Edward Island, replied that he knew of no "article on the topic" and that "the only play that comes to mind is Yvette Nolan's *Annie Mae's Movement*"; Maureen Moynagh, of St. Francis Xavier, passed on the information, from a colleague, that Glen Gould, the Mik'maq playwright and actor, is "someone who is doing work in the theatre"; and Jason Simmonds, Ph.D. Candidate at UNB, wrote to say that he had "not come across anything in this area," and that he could not "think of any Native theatrical productions in Atlantic Canada." Needless to say, I was thrilled when I received an email from Len Falkenstein offering to write "something on a play by New Brunswick Miq'mac playwright John Barlow called *Inspiration Point.*" In that essay, which appears in this volume, Falkenstein considers, among other things, some reasons why "few Native playwrights have emerged from the region."

Work from and about women and people of colour also presented a challenge. Much less has been published by women or on the work of women than has been published by men or on the work of men in the area of theatre in Atlantic Canada. This is reflected in this volume, where, of the seventeen essays included, only five are by women. It is also reflected in the subjects of some of those essays as, of the five essays that focus on the work of an individual playwright, only one, Jerry Wasserman's essay, focuses on the work of a female playwright, Wendy Lill. Further, of the six African-Nova Scotian playwrights discussed by Maureen Moynagh in her essay, only one is a woman, Louise Delisle.

As for people of colour, I agree completely with George Elliott Clarke who, in an email exchange with me, suggested "that 'race' is one reason" (he agreed that gender was another) that minority playwrights "have been ignored/overlooked/undertheorized," and that "we are only slowly, painfully, beginning to think of CanLit as NOT being the province of only a couple of ethnicities and one 'race'" (2 November). Few scholarly essays have been published on Clarke's two plays that are set in Nova Scotia—*Whylah Falls: The Play* and *Beatrice Chancy*. On *Beatrice Chancy*, Clarke saw only "three" essays that focused on his play and a few "others that discuss B.C. along with other writers' works," and "[u]pon reflection," he realized, "that there is no academic essay on *Whylah Falls: The Play*" (6 November). Since Clarke's work has received more critical attention than the work of most other African-Nova Scotian or Africadian writers, this is telling. In this volume, an essay by Clarke on the drama of George Boyd is included.

I am not sure, however, that the *only* reason for the dearth of scholarly essays in the field of theatre from and about the marginalized communities of Atlantic Canada is that the work of minority artists has been, as Clarke puts it, "ignored/overlooked/undertheorized." Certainly, some mainstream artists and institutions have received more critical attention than those from groups that have been historically excluded. Neptune Theatre and the plays of Michael Cook, which come about as close to mainstream as it is possible to get in this region, have received a fair bit of attention from scholars. But so have the Mummers Troupe, Acadian theatre companies in New Brunswick, and Mulgrave Road Co-op Theatre, none of which can be viewed as mainstream. That we have a small body of important work on each of these groups, it seems to me, is more a reflection of the specific interests of a few exceptional scholars—Alan Filewod, Glen Nichols, and Ric Knowles—than anything else.

In the process of editing *Theatre in Atlantic Canada*, what came as a real shock to me was that it is not just the work of minority theatre artists, but the work of most theatre artists from the region that has received little or no attention from scholars. I was astounded to discover that nearly no academic essays have been published on the work of most of the region's playwrights. For example, Daniel MacIvor, who has had fourteen volumes of his plays published, has received no critical attention. The *MLA International Bibliography* lists just two reviews of MacIvor's work. *The Association for Canadian Theatre Research Bibliography* lists four short essays on MacIvor's work that were published in *Canadian Theatre Review* or *Theatrum*, three short pieces by MacIvor himself, and four reviews or interviews that make reference to MacIvor's work. I was unable to find a single essay on any of MacIvor's Atlantic Canadian plays. The situation is not much better in the case of Wendy Lill, who, according to Shelley Newman and Sherrill Grace, "has created a substantial body of work that has received professional production but little critical analysis to date." Both

MacIvor and Lill can be counted among Canada's most important playwrights. They have been recognized internationally, their productions reviewed, themselves interviewed. So why is it that their work, and that of so many other playwrights from this region, has been disregarded by scholars and critics? Surely the work of "the finest poets of the Canadian stage" deserves better.

(2010)

Notes

¹ Knowles, *Judith Thompson* iii.

² This Introduction will not provide parenthetical citations or Works Cited listings for essays published in this volume.

³ I have discussed some of what I say in this and the following few paragraphs in "Myth-Making and Myth-Challenging" (Burnett).

Works Cited

Andrews, Jennifer. Email. 4 Aug 2009.

Barton, Bruce. "Performing Culture: The Maritime(s) Way of Life." *Marigraph: Gauging the Tides of Drama from New Brunswick, Nova Scotia, Prince Edward Island.* Toronto: Playwrights Canada, 2004. iii–vii.

Burnett, Linda. "Myth-Making and Myth-Challenging: The Theatre of Atlantic Canada." *Canadian Theatre Review* 128 (2006) 4–6.

Clarke, George Elliott. Email to the author. 6 November 2009.

———. Email to the author. 2 November 2009.

Devine, Michael. "Keileydography: The Symphonic Theatre of Jillian Keiley." *Canadian Theatre Review* 128 (2006): 31–36.

Doran, Greg. Email to the author. 5 August 2009.

Falkenstein, Len. Email to the author. 5 August 2009.

Ferry, David. "A Point of View of the Development of Post-1960's Professional Theatre in St. John's." Paper presented to Panel 1: Discovering Newfoundland and Labrador. Shifting Tides: Atlantic Canadian Theatre Yesterday, Today, and Tomorrow. Graduate Centre for the Study of Drama, University of Toronto. 25–28 March 2004.

Globe Theatre. *Study Guide for The Glace Bay Miners' Museum*. 14 June 2006. http://www.globetheatrelive.com/19992000season/studyguideglacebay.htm.

Goldie, Terry. "Newfoundland." *Contemporary Canadian Theatre: New World Visions*. Toronto: Simon & Pierre, 1985. 96–100.

Hulan, Renée. Email to the author. 13 July 2009.

Jones, Heather. "Rising Tide Theatre and/in the Newfoundland Cultural Scene." *Canadian Theatre Review* 93 (1997): 38–41.

Knowles, Ric. "Atlantic Theatre: a Review Article." *Journal of Canadian Studies* 22 (1987): 135–40.

———. Email to the author. 6 July 2009.

———. "Halifax: the First Atlantic Theatre Conference." *Canadian Theatre Review* 44 (1985): 126–27.

———, ed. *Judith Thompson*. Toronto: Playwrights Canada, 2005.

———. "Of Mortality and Men." *Canadian Literature: A Quarterly of Criticism and Review* 187 (2005): 171–72.

Lynde, Denyse. "Writing and Publishing: Four Newfoundland Playwrights in Conversation." *Canadian Theatre Review* 98 (1999): 28–46.

MacDonald, Ron Foley. "East Coast Playwrights Keep Goin' Down the Road." 7 December 2009. http://aco.ca/a_e/play.html.

Melski, Michael. Personal interview. 2 February 2004.

Moynagh, Maureen. Email to the author. 17 August 2009.

Munday, Jenny. "PARC and Me and Middle Age." *Canadian Theatre Review* 128 (2006): 7–10.

Newman, Shelley and Sherrill Grace. "Lill in Review: a Working Bibliography." *Theatre Research in Canada* 21 (2000): 49–58. 17 Dec 2009 http://www.lib.unb.ca/Texts/TRIC/bin/get.cgi?directory=vol21_1/&filename=Lill_bibliography.htm.

Perkyns, Richard. "Nova Scotia." *Contemporary Canadian Theatre: New World Visions*. Toronto: Simon & Pierre, 1985. 106–11.

Rudakoff, Judith and Rita Much. *Fair Play: 12 Women Speak—Conversations with Canadian Playwrights*. Toronto: Simon & Pierre, 1990.

Sealy, David. Rev. of *Beatrice Chancy* by George Elliott Clarke. *Canadian Review of American Studies* 30.1 (2000): 116–18.

Simmonds, Jason Woodman. Email to the author. 11 August 2009.

Vingoe, Mary. "Opening Words." *Shifting Tides*: Atlantic Canadian Theatre Yesterday, Today, and Tomorrow. *Theatre Research in Canada*. 26.1–2 (2005). xv–xx.

Mermaid Theatre:
The Mythic Dimension

by Donna E. Smyth

Ulgimou, a Micmac chief, pursues his dead son's soul to the Spirit World. He gambles with the Chief of Spirits and wins not only his son's soul but seeds of corn and tobacco for his people. Triumphantly carrying the soul in a pouch, he returns to the tribe. But in the midst of his dance of celebration, he hands the pouch to an old woman. She wants to see the soul. She opens the pouch. The soul escapes and can never be won again.

Dramatically, that moment is unforgettable. We, as audience, hear an unearthly cry. We see the masked figures frozen, Ulgimou desperately reaching out. At the same time as we feel the intense human grief of the father who has twice lost his son, we also see an incredible thing—a soul taking flight.

This is dramatic recognition in the fullest sense of the word. It is drama and myth interfused. We are startled out of ourselves; we transcend a particular time and place so that this legend no longer belongs only to the Micmac Indians, the original inhabitants of Nova Scotia. What we are recognizing is the mythopoeic truth: our own souls are reflected here. We remember Orpheus grieving for Eurydice and all that passionate intensity of the living for the twice dead, forever dead. Irrevocable loss through a moment's carelessness.

This narrated mime is the type of drama being offered for young audiences by the Mermaid Theatre of Nova Scotia. Founded six years ago by Evelyn Garbary, artistic director and principal writer, and Tom Miller, resident director and puppetmaster, Mermaid has forged for itself a distinctive style and aesthetic.

To dramatize myth is a demanding task. W.B. Yeats, in his many experiments, knew the problems and wrestled with many versions of *The Shadowy Waters* before realizing that, paradoxically, myth cannot be treated subjectively. The shadowy "soul images" must become bright and clear, must be objectified until they are filled with their own life and move of their own accord. Mermaid accomplishes this movement toward objectification through the use of masks, dance, mime, puppets and a sparse, clean style of playing. This clean style, without superfluous movement, effectively counterpoints the visual extravagance of Tom Miller's masks and costume design. It is the same combination of hieratic gesture and ritual costume that we see in Aztec art or the Kathakali dance troupe.

Mermaid has learned economy in every aspect of design. The settings are simple, functional and abstract: one tree can be a forest and the same flat rotates to become a wigwam. Details of costume and stage props are carefully researched. If Glooscap, the God whose power centre was Cape Blomidon, wears an amulet, then that amulet is as authentically Micmac as possible. Basic research begins with the original legends collected and translated by Silas Rand, a Baptist missionary of the 19th century. At this point the legends are simply stories or episodes which have to be transmuted by Evelyn Garbary into dramatic, mythic material. This process also involves a study of the Micmac culture in order to understand the significance of attitudes, locale and tribal history. Characters have to have authentic names, chants in Micmac have to be pronounced correctly. Meticulous attention to such detail creates the initial, literal level of credibility.

Myth always springs from a particular culture and, while timeless in its use of archetypes, is coloured by a specific time and place. Again, Yeats's use of Irish mythic material is a good comparison. Cuchulain is a sun-hero/god but also an Irish chief, one of the great Kings of the warrior culture of pre-historic Ireland. The mythic dimension must be approached through the particular human experience.

But where Yeats eventually concluded that his plays were fit only for a small knowledgeable audience, Mermaid has played to 1,000 schoolchildren at one time, perhaps half of whom have never seen live theatre before. Clearly there is a division in the assumed use and value of mythic drama. Yeats, influenced by the *Noh* and his own personal mythology, aimed for an aristocratic ideal. He chose to ignore the traditional popular appeal of dramatized myth in many cultures.

The Balinese puppet theatre, for example, used to perform for all age groups all day and night. Far from being esoteric, the multi dimensional nature of mythic drama "leaps" over assumed age/experience categories. A literal story line and lively entertainment appeal to children of all ages. Mermaid's *Bullfrog*, for example, is a comedy about a greedy, despotic Frog Chief who has to be taught a lesson. Bullfrog is played as a giant puppet, huffing and puffing about the stage. He is, in very truth, a frog and yet, as we watch him, we realize he is also a certain type of politician—the *Man*, the *Boss-Boss*. The possibilities for caricature and satire are endless.

Young people may or may not understand these other levels of the play but the theatrical experience can operate at inarticulate levels which are in themselves perhaps more powerful for being as yet inarticulate. Here begins the sense of wonder. When the mind encounters something it cannot rationally explain, imagination is liberated. A man being transformed into a turtle is no longer an impossibility. The limitations of conscious logic have been left behind. We claim that intuitive, emotional dimension of our being which, according to Ionesco, makes us a whole being:

> The non-metaphysical world of today has destroyed all mystery; and the so-called "scientific" theatre of the period, the theatre of politics and propaganda, anti-poetic and academic, has flattened mankind out,

alienating the unfathomable third dimension which makes a whole man. (47)

One of the fascinating things about the Micmac legends is that they take this spiritual dimension for granted. They speak of a time when man and gods conversed as easily as man and man, when the world was alive, every rock and tree animated with its own flickering reality. Yeats found a similar attitude among the Irish peasants and spent the rest of his life trying to encompass that vision: "Natural and supernatural by the self-same ring are wed." (284)

The unselfconscious nature of this intercourse between the human and the divine means that theatre audiences can respond on a level which neatly sidesteps skepticism and cynicism. Once the stylized conventions are accepted, the resurrection of the Invisible Hunter, in Mermaid's *The Invisible Hunter*, is the inevitable consequence of the events. The once-benevolent Hunter is now the Spirit of Vengeance swooping down upon an uncaring and careless world:

> …because you did not care; care for the young of your own blood, the fish shall rise from the sea and the clouds shall be their habitation. Because you did not care, birds shall bury themselves in the earth and serpents grow wings.

And the stage darkens as the spirits of fish fly through the air, strange noises are heard, monstrous creatures appear. This is apocalypse.

It is also powerful theatre. Mermaid never patronizes young audiences by the dilution or playing down of material. Nor do they allow a kind of Walt Disney cuteness which instantly familiarizes that which is wild and wonderful. There are occasional exceptions such as the feminization of certain water spirits into giggling girls but such breaks in tone are infrequent. The company assumes that theatre for young people should be of the highest caliber and, on the whole, their repertoire meets that condition.

The native peoples' myth phase of Mermaid's development is both an achievement and a beginning. These plays are cultural vehicles for preservation and transformation. Part of the native peoples' culture and religious beliefs are preserved in a form which allows us to imaginatively understand them. It is one thing to read an anthropologist's collection of myths; it is quite another to dramatize that myth so that its power lives again. We learn that these legends are not simply picturesque stories; they are a paradigm of the human psyche.

We also learn that cultural barriers can be crossed and that one culture can teach another. In a period of diminishing natural resources, the Micmac philosophy of "caring" and "taking care" is obviously a wiser approach to this planet Earth than A.I.B. hearings rolled across Canada like some gigantic snow-ball. [1]

The potential for transformation lies in Mermaid's techniques for dramatizing myth. In a country still creating its culture, mythic images have to be seized and understood. The myth-making process itself becomes a focus of attention. Beyond

The Bush and the Salon we discover another reality which does not diminish the documentary but seeks pattern in the detail and demonstrates the continuity of human experience.[2] Mermaid is developing a style, an approach to material which offers exciting possibilities for Canadian theatre and Canadian dramatists. It is just possible that this company may achieve what Yeats so ardently wished for but failed to accomplish: a mythic theatre which springs from the common history and experience of a people.

(1978)

Notes

[1] "A.I.B." refers to the Anti-Inflation Board, established by an Act of Parliament in 1975 to administer a wage-and-price-control program. It ceased operations in 1979. Thanks to Don Jackson, Political Science, Algoma University for recognizing this reference—Ed.

[2] *The Bush and the Salon* was a CBC radio documentary drama series that ran from 1971–1977, each episode of which focused on a different "pioneer" of early Canadian life—Ed.

Works Cited

The Invisible Hunter. Script by Evelyn Garbary. Designed by Tom Miller. Mermaid Theatre, Wolfville, Nova Scotia. 1975.

Ionesco, Eugene. "The World of Jonesco." *The Tulane Drama Review* 3.1 (1958): 46–48.

Yeats, William Butler. "Supernatural Songs." *The Collected Poems of W.B. Yeats.* Ed. Richard J. Finneran. NY: Simon & Schuster, 1996. 283–92.

On the Edge:
Michael Cook's Newfoundland Trilogy

by Brian Parker

Michael Cook has weaknesses as a dramatist that have drawn down upon him the obloquy of critics, and it is perhaps as well to consider these first. He thinks of himself basically as a poet, and has explained that plays occur to him not in the form of Aristotelian "action" but poetically as "a series of images, dramatic scenes, and circumstances" (Anthony 215, also 211, 222). The obvious difficulty he has in organizing his work, perhaps his most serious defect as a dramatist, reflects this centrifugal habit of imagination. None of his plays has much conventional plot and all tend to be wordy and overwritten. At one extreme, he uses overlong "realistic" monologues, as in *Quiller* and *Thérèse's Creed*, which reveal the effect of his apprenticeship to radio drama; at the other, he throws heterogeneous materials loosely together in quasi-historical Brechtian [1] structures with huge casts, like *Colour the Flesh the Colour of Dust*, *The Gaydon Chronicles*, and *On the Rim of the Curve*, where social caricature, historical or regional realism, and poetical philosophizing all clash. He compensates for his plays' verbosity with rather obvious stage effects: either by the detailed recreations of everyday routines—cooking, washing, net making—or by vaudevillian songs, dances, and allegorical tableaux, according to whether the bias of a particular play is realistic or presentational. His work can be thematically confusing because it combines an almost reflex sympathy for any underdog with a more existentialist concern with the strain isolation imposes on human relationships. And these imprecisions are reflected in unevennesses of rhetoric. Cook is capable of genuine poetic intensity, but too frequently he falls into philosophical overexplicitness or poetical overwriting, both of which can strain characterization.

Nevertheless, Michael Cook remains an important dramatist, because beneath the technical crudities, at the poetic heart of his work, lies an intensely imagined experience of Newfoundland life, presented with such integrity that at its best it rises to comment on the human condition.

Paradoxically, Cook is helped in this because he is not a Newfoundlander by birth, but a Briton of Anglo-Irish descent who arrived in Canada as recently as 1965. [2] Thus he brings to Newfoundland an outsider's eye like that of the original settlers. What he sees is the "survival" experience which critics such as Northrop Frye and Margaret Atwood have argued is the central Canadian literary theme: confrontation with a relentlessly hostile environment which undermines all confidence in human institutions and even in identity itself. By its very nature drama finds it more difficult to represent this experience than poetry or the novel because it can only represent reactions to the experience, not the confrontation itself, and Cook is perhaps the most successful dramatist so far in conveying the experience in stage terms. He says specifically that our drama needs

> to try and come to terms with the landscape, the environment, and the people like any stranger walking new in the land. Like any immigrant, either now or four hundred years ago… we have never developed a theatre of character in conflict with environment. Which also implies, the environment being what it is, a theatre inhabited by Gods and Heroes. ("Why Did I Write" 76)

Hence one of his attractions to historical drama, to which he says he returns in order to reactivate his own original experiences ("An Interview," Lister 179).

Newfoundland seems to Cook "the last human frontier" (*Toronto Star* 9 February 1974)[3] and it has given his work "focal identity" because he found surviving there a tragic and heroic individualism: "a way of life in which individuals struggle with timeless questions of worth and identity against, an environment which would kill them if it could" (*Guide* 24). Newfoundland experience strikes him as "essentially Greek, profoundly tragic" (Interview, CTR 74), with

> a kind of mythic quality, a kind of elemental quality, very primitive, very brutal, and yet with immense community and tribal strength which we have just about lost everywhere else. ("An Interview," Rubin 52)

"The experience of such a people," he says in *CTR* in 1974,

> teeters between private suffering and defiant joy. Their expression is essentially artistic, a Satanic struggle to impose order upon experience rendered frequently chaotic by a blind and savage nature. (74)

This "essentially artistic" mode of life takes several forms. It can be manifest in the rituals of work and celebration of *The Head, Guts and Sound Bone Dance*, or in the very houses themselves, as climactically in *Jacob's Wake*:

> Their craft is manifest in the work of their hands, the boats made from wood, cut and hauled laboriously during the dark winter months; the houses whose simple design often deceives visitors, for they are built with absolute economy… in addition to acting as the prow of the ship in the teeth of Atlantic gales.

But pre-eminently for Cook, artistry is to be found in the Newfoundlanders' retention of "a language colourful, new, musical, scatalogical… full of the power of ancient metaphors" (*Guide* 24).

Experience on this primitive, existential plane appeals, Cook thinks, to men who have come to realize that "somewhere in the transition between rural and industrial man they left behind a portion of their souls" (*Guide* 24). His main purpose as a playwright is thus twofold: to reaffirm the validity of the traditional Newfoundland way of life, while also exploring the tragic cost of such "Satanic" assertions of order, and, at the same time, to record its demise beneath the pressures of a shallow, regimented, urbanized civilization with which Cook has little patience. He has explored these themes in some forty plays,[4] but his strengths and weaknesses and the range of his technique can be discovered by looking in some detail at his so-called "Newfoundland Trilogy"—*Colour the Flesh the Colour of Dust* (1972), *The Head, Guts, and Sound Bone Dance* (1973), and *Jacob's Wake* (1975)—recognizing, however, that they are not strictly a trilogy at all, since there is no continuity of action or characters between them and they are written in wholly different modes. (Indeed, Cook seems originally to have envisaged *Colour* as the second play of the trilogy, to be preceded by a play on Sir Humphrey Gilbert which eventually became *On the Rim of the Curve* [*Ottawa Citizen* 14 October 1972].) What binds the plays together is their common concern with unmediated experience "on the edge of the world" ("Why Did I Write" 74).

    Colour the Flesh the Colour of Dust was Cook's first stage play and is something of a mess. Ostensibly it is a Brechtian "epic" about the surrender of St. John's to the French in 1762 and its subsequent recapture by the English. However, as the "Spokesman" character in the plays points out, "Historically, this has been a pretty inaccurate play" (D42). Its interest lies in Cook's reactions to Newfoundland, but the overall effect is incoherent because he has tried to cram too much into it without a clear sense of priorities.

    Perhaps the simplest element—the one that the reviewers seized on with relief—is the broad satire directed against a hypocritical merchant called Tupper and his ally, magistrate Neal, who manipulate the political situation for their own advantage ("Wars may come and wars may go, Tupper—but trade—" [D15]). This concentrates in two main scenes. In Act I Tupper adulterates his flour with sawdust only to discover that he must now purify it again in order not to antagonize the French, and in Act II he tries to learn French in order to trade with the new garrison and insists on teaching his shopboy what he does not know himself. But the comedy of these situations is complicated by other elements. In the first act a more savage level of satire comes into play when Tupper cheats the pathetic Mrs. McDonald whose family is starving, and justifies himself with selfconsciously villainous irony:

> It wouldn't be right now, for me to give you something and you worrying about whether you'd ever pay it back… it's a terrible thing in these times to have a working conscience, Mrs. McDonald; and I'm afraid yours will drive you to the grave. (D12)

Later we hear that Mrs. McDonald is dead. Moreover, in each scene there is an episode with the shopboy in which the action overlaps with another, more complicated concern of the play. In a dumbshow at the end of the flour scene the Boy encourages starving urchins to loot his master's stores, and during the French lesson in Act II he reveals an unexpected (and implausible) command of idiomatic French and menaces his master with a knife. Both incidents remain comic within the context of the scenes, but their suggestion of hidden violence relates also to a more complex aspect of the play—its presentation of the populace of St. John's, towards whom Cook's attitude seems ambiguous.

Basically, *Colour the Flesh* conveys a sympathetic awareness that history does not interest or affect ordinary people except for the worse. Their concern is always for survival: whichever side governs, the drudgery of work must go on; social inequalities will continue; at most, war provides a break in bleak monotony and perhaps the chance of a cathartic outburst of violence. This attitude is made explicit in speeches by the Spokesman. He refuses the Lieutenant's challenge to personal combat in Act I (and encourages the mob to overwhelm him) with the explanation,

> You need time and money to uphold honour. And you need to think of yourself as being someone with a place in life, as having a situation, you see. But us now—we're scum. (D17)

And in Act II he elaborates on this directly to the audience in a speech which seems to have been influenced by the Common Man of Bolt's *A Man for All Seasons*, claiming that concern for survival represents the natural truth of humanity: "We are the nature you try to subvert, divert, convert, and in general screw up in a lot of ways" (D42).

This basic attitude is complicated and confused by several factors. Reminders of the Irish antecedents of the populace, for example, while serving to emphasize the gap between them and their governors tend to shortcircuit their more basic position by popular jokes against the English, or to suggest that ambiguities in their attitude are typically and exclusively Irish. Thus, the Woman criticizes their adulation of her lover Sean, who has already been hanged at the opening of the play for distributing stolen bread, by complaining that

> you made a hero of the fool and you didn't lift a finger—Jesus Christ, isn't that Ireland all over—To make heroes of fools and every fool a hero. (D18)

In fact, the crowd shows no tendency at all to foolish heroics, so her generalization is confusing.

The crowd's actual behaviour also has its contradictions. The idea that ordinary people have no stake in war is challenged by a scene in which a deputation of loyal fishermen try to persuade the demoralized Captain to defend St. John's. Yet Cook also recognizes a viciously destructive side to the populace, an appetite for senseless violence. The Woman (speaking as Girl) tells how her trapper husband gratuitously killed an inoffensive Indian ("and it seemed as if nothing had happened" [D30]);[5] and the play presents in sadistic detail what Cook's stage direction calls the "communal orgasm" (D27)of the mob's killing of an English soldier, the nihilism of which is later directed at the audience itself when the Spokesman threatens that "one day, we'll kill you all. Because there'll be nothing else left to do" (D43).

The murder is explained (a little too glibly) by one of the soldier's comrades: "In a funny way, Willie, you've saved us all—I mean—It was like you were a bleeding sacrifice" (D28), and its specifically sexual nature—impalement through the groin with a hook—seems intended to reflect relationships between potency and survival, imperialism and sexual exploitation that Cook has not really managed to make clear. Respect for a vitality that is destructive yet at the same time necessary for survival is an important motif in Cook's tragic vision, but in *Colour the Flesh* he is not sufficiently in command of its contradictory implications.

A result of this is that the play's imaginative force is concentrated on the negative aspect of Newfoundland experience—the spiritual defeat created by life on a barren rock hemmed in by the sea, where, as the Captain explains, nothing human seems able to endure:

> People build. Then fire. Or drowning. Or famine. Or disease. Or just—
> failure of the spirit. [...] The thin scrub marches back across the cleared
> land—The flake rots into the sea [...] I tell you [...] nothing will be
> remembered here—That people will be born and live and die and their
> passage will go unnoticed. That their buildings will fall and rot back to
> the land. That their history will die in their children. [...] It belongs to
> the bottom of the sea ... to secrecy and silence. (D36)

The play shows this spiritual demoralization in various ways. At its simplest it is seen in the British soldiers of the opening scene, who have lost all hope for the future and all pride in their profession, yet at the same time hate the pointless brutality they have fallen into. More thoroughly, this state of mind is explored in the characterization of Captain Gross, the garrison commander. Gross tells Lieutenant Mannon that he was just as keen for "law" and "honour" (D22) as the Lieutenant once, "But this rock now... something in it defeats the spirit" D35). Squalor, insubordination, separation from his family, sexual infidelity, a growing sense of isolation, the harshness of the land, and the drink with which he has tried to dull his sensibility, have eaten away his self-respect.

At first the remnants of the man he was are reflected in a rather dandyish, epigrammatic turn of speech, reminiscent of Shaw's General Burgoyne: "Honour is an expensive luxury, reserved for naval battles and campaigns mounted for Imperial gain" (D22); but when a whore breaks in to shame him with her scolding, this brittle elegance snaps and Gross drops abruptly into a more symbolic mode of speech: "I see icebergs in my sleep. All the time" (D23). The switch of rhetorical levels is shocking but quite deliberate: it reflects Gross's surrender to a different plane of experience; and this poetic style becomes his norm for the rest of the play. At times it seems a bit self conscious, as when he answers Tupper, who has said he tries to avoid the sea:

> But we are at sea, Tupper. At this moment [...] Listen—can you hear it?
> We're adrift, man. Helpless. The whales and ice thrash about us. [...]
> Without a rudder, what can a man do? Drifts, Tupper. Only his head
> above the wave. Limbs, loins—ice cold. (D38)

Here poetry and dandyism seem to mix. But this, too, may be deliberate, since there is always a certain posing quality in Gross, a need to have his situation appreciable by others.

Gross's speeches play a large part in establishing the special Newfoundland *angst* of *Colour the Flesh*, as in the lines already quoted where he describes his pain at human impermanence, evoking despair in terms of the environment that caused it; and in that particular scene, which is a key one, the setting strengthens the link, because Gross speaks the lines to the Lieutenant when the two meet in a fog. Like the tattered uniform that he insists on wearing even after St. John's has been recaptured, the fog becomes a conscious symbol for the Captain. It represents his sense of isolation and spiritual drift, but at the same time, as he recognizes, it provides comfort by insulating him from reality ("The fog, I find, always makes life more bearable" [D36]); moreover, it also leads to greater self-knowledge ("a man learns things walking alone in the fog" [D35]), since it is in the fog that he recognizes that the seed of his collapse was already in him before he came to Newfoundland: "[My spirit] was defeated before I got here" (D35).

What that seed was is illustrated by his reasons for not defending St. John's. His initial explanation, that the garrison is outnumbered, is immediately (and a little too patly) contradicted by the arrival of the contingent of loyal fishermen. This drives him back to the real reason, his inability to take moral responsibility for the loss of life that a battle will entail. Our reaction to this is meant to be ambivalent. Gross's reluctance to take life agrees with the play's conclusion that just being alive, mere existence, is man's basic value; but it also relates to the idea, recurrent in Cook's drama, that feelings of humanity may be weakness in a savage environment—a point the Lieutenant's Woman later states explicitly. The play returns to a similar ambivalence at the end, when Gross tries to comfort the Woman for the Lieutenant's death by emphasizing the fact that she and the child she carries are still alive. This is very close to the Woman's own position, yet she rejects the Captain's support because from it he extrapolates a sentimental justification for his own collapse, appealing to authorities the Woman does not recognize: "I will tell them that you live here—That I did what I did because you live here" (D46). As in his pathetic consolation that the official report of the debacle will secure for him some measure of remembrance, Gross shies away from the isolation of his position. He cannot dispense with an external source of notice and justification, even if it condemns him.

The Captain's breakdown is interestingly complex but not quite clearly worked out, and as he is not the play's protagonist, he is slightly off centre in our interest anyway. Potentially more interesting than Gross, though even less developed, is the character of Lieutenant Mannon. He, too, feels the isolation of their position:

> We are stranded on some island at the edge of time. There's the sea. And the fog [...] We can't gentle it in any way—impose an order or a universal design upon it [...] Ultimately we respond to the ferocity of the sea. And the impermanence of life. (D19)

His hobnobbing with the common soldiers in scene one suggests that this experience has already begun to corrupt the Lieutenant's concern for "spit and polish," but the challenge of the French invasion apparently revitalizes his sense of "duty" and "honour" (D22). During the action, however, he discovers that he does not believe in these values for their own sake but because, without them, he, too, would face a moral collapse: "It's all I've got, see. Certain loyalties. Certain obligations and contracts" (D42). The strained nature of such ideals forces him into unnecessary rashness and falsifies his relationship with the Woman. Significantly, at the end he is shot in the back by one of his own men. A major flaw in the dramaturgy is that the reason for this killing is never made explicit, but there are sufficient hints for us to assume that it must be because of the pressure that the Lieutenant's idealism puts on others, a certain self-serving quality in his "honour" that Cook would later develop more fully in the monomaniacal skippers of *The Head, Guts, and Sound Bone Dance* and *Jacob's Wake.*

Cook explores the nature of the Lieutenant's failure through his love for the Woman, who began the play mourning for the hanged Sean, another "fool" killed for resisting things as they are. The affair has been condemned as a misleading cliché (Kareda), but it seems to me quite central to Cook's purpose. At one level, it can be seen as a further stage in the Lieutenant's corruption, since, like Captain Gross and the common soldier, he is betraying the wife he left behind. Certainly, the Captain associates the Lieutenant's idealism with sexual guilt: "It's your conscience then and not our impossible position that's exciting you" (D23); and the Lieutenant himself admits he is tempted to settle down as a Newfoundlander, but recoils from the "rot" (D42) he thinks this will involve. More complex than this suggestion of corruption is the confrontation the love affair establishes between rival alternatives to the Captain's surrender to despair, nicely emblematized in a tableau where the Woman, having rescued the Lieutenant from the mob, holds him prisoner by a noose around the neck.

The Woman says she is attracted to the Lieutenant by two factors: by "the life that runs in my loins" (in contrast to Gross's image of frozen loins, cited earlier), but also by an element she sees in him that she calls "dignity," which he shares with her previous lover, Sean: "You have been gifted with a sense of yourself that nothing can break—Sean had that" (D19).

It turns out that she is wrong: the Lieutenant relies on the external order of "honour," not the internal strength of "dignity." After she finds she is pregnant, this leads the Woman to retreat to the other, more basic need to "be." She now condemns her previous "humanity" because "It's not possible to live very long once you accept that" (D19)—a sentiment adopted more cynically in the Magistrate's advice about controlling the populace: "No matter how much they hate you—at the moment of violence, weaken—be generous—it destroys the flame of their spirit" (D34). The Woman (speaking as Girl) pleads for the value of mere existence ("You want to begin and end things—we exist" [D42]). In contrast to Gross's reliance on his written report, she insists that her unborn child will be "the only testament we can scribble"; and her position is summed up with the simple, almost banal comment: "the bravest people I know are the ones who endure" (D42).

This is the stoic note on which the play concludes, though not without some further nuances. *Colour the Flesh* ends as it began with the Woman mourning a dead lover, but whereas the first death was emblematized by a tableau in which she cradled

Sean's body like a *pietà*, at the conclusion of the play the stage direction tells us she hugs her pregnant belly: an image of life has replaced the opening image of death. She comments to the dead Lieutenant:

> You were nothing to anyone, but me; and your sense of honour, your King and Country. Now you're dead. And the honour and the King and the Country lie dead with you. And there's only me left—me and him— me and her—what's it matter? (D46)

This is an affirmation, if a very bare one; but "What's it matter?" is ambiguous, meaning either "What does it matter whether the child be a boy or a girl?" or, more bleakly, "What does it matter that the child and I survive?" This shadowing even of stoicism is also reflected in her repudiation of the Captain's attempts to console her because "there's life in you yet"; and is expressed in the "Woman's Song" that gives the play its title and is returned to at the end:

> But to you I gave,
> As give I must
> to colour the flesh
> the colour of dust
> [...]
> But it's a fool
> Who doesn't trust
> to give himself
> because he must... (D7)

Dust colours the flesh; love ends in death. Nevertheless, it is foolish to deny them.

As a work of art *Colour the Flesh* is exasperating yet memorable. There are striking scenes, passages of vividly evocative poetry, and some shrewd insights into behaviour; but the overall structure is incoherent, as Cook himself recognizes ("*Colour the Flesh* is a lousily structured play" ("An Interview," Lister 179). The presentational elements—the Spokesman's address to the crowd and a voice-over reading of the official report of the surrender (which was cut in production)—are not adequate to establish a truly "epic" mode; the songs can be tangible (as in the ballad of "Old Noll Cromwell" [D27]) and sink sometimes to pretentious doggerel; the rhetoric is uncertain, with no attempt at the Newfoundland dialect used so effectively in the other two plays of the trilogy; and the symbols of the hanged man, the fog, and the *pietà* (made more explicit in the original draft by comparisons to Christ, the Romans, and Mary) are all rather too obvious.

Nevertheless, for all its faults, *Colour the Flesh* stays stubbornly in the mind because it does manage to convey Cook's intuition of a double-edged vitality in existence itself, destructive yet enduring, and his sense that this may be our last defence against spiritual collapse. These intuitions are developed further in *The Head, Guts, and Sound Bone Dance*, which is his most powerful stage play to date.

Whereas *Colour the Flesh* is very loosely organized, *Dance* has a form that is almost perfectly suited to its theme. At its core is the same harsh Newfoundland experience, but confrontation with it is now more active and heroic. Moreover, the focus has been shifted to the tragic price exacted for such heroism, and the main threat is no longer nature itself but the modern world that renders heroism obsolete. Cook summarizes the plot as "Two old men trying to keep the past alive to the exclusion of the rest of the world" (*Saskatoon Leader-Post* 5 December 1977*).

The action centres on a Newfoundland fisherman, Skipper Pete, an "Ancient leader of a savage pack with the instincts still there but the ability in pitiful repair," [6] who in his "splitting room" on a fishing stage jutting into the Atlantic tries to keep tradition alive by remembering past glories and ritualistically making preparations for "one more trip" (26). Pete stands uncompromisingly for

> The old way. The only way. The proper way to do things. Greet the day at cockcrow. The sea, no matter the weather. Stack the gear. Mend the nets. Make the killick [a stone anchor]. Keep the store in order. They's nothing without it. (18)

His son-in-law, Uncle John, once the cook on the Skipper's fishing boat, aids him, and so does his simple-minded son, Absalom, a sixty-year-old who is the only one of the three still physically able to go fishing. For most of the play, John's wife tries unavailingly to free her husband from the Skipper's domination, until a fatal accident convinces him she is right.

Our attitude to the Skipper is contradictory. He is admirable in his intransigent insistence on natural truths that lie beneath the surface of contemporary society; but, at the same time, he is a monomaniac like Melville's Ahab, [7] who refuses to recognize change or alternative styles of life and is prepared to sacrifice everyone to his own stark vision. Though in the past he was famous for never losing a man, Uncle John accuses him of tyrannizing over his crews for self-aggrandizement—

> Ye saved 'em all right. But not to stand up. Not to walk the world. Crawl! Ye made 'em crawl. Ye made me crawl [...] We escaped the rule of others. And exchanged it for the rule of our own kind. (13)

—and he reminds the Skipper that (like the Magistrate in *Colour the Flesh*) he never showed humanity except to disarm men on the brink of mutiny. This same brutal imposition of personality continues into the present with the Skipper's vendetta against seagulls; his sneer that, if John had gone to the war, "You'd never have survived there. Unless I was wid yer" (11); and, more comically, with his insistence that his son-in-law must urinate decently, as though he were still on board his ship. Most strikingly, it is shown in the elaborate work rituals—preparing equipment, cleaning, salting, and cooking the fish, and careful cleaning up afterwards—that he enforces before he will allow his companions to celebrate, also ritualistically, his son Absalom's "end of voyage" and miserably small catch.

The Skipper sees these rigid codes as necessary to impose order upon chaos:

> I 'low the sea's a big place. Now a man's a small place. You've got to have
> order. Decency. There 'as to be a way of doing things. A man's way. That's
> why we're here, isn't it? They's only we left. (11)

And according to the opening stage direction, this tension should be reflected in the
play's set. The "splitting room" is crammed with

> an immense variety of gear representing man, and fish, and the sea in a
> tottering, near derelict place, and yet also reveal[ing], as we become
> accustomed to it, an almost fanatical sense of order. (5)

The egotism of the Skipper's need to impose order is qualified, however, by a strain of
mysticism in him. He holds that it is useless to demand meaning, as Uncle John does
at one point; life can only be accepted: "It doesn't matter what it means. It's enough
that it's there" (13). Fishermen in the past knew their proper place in nature: "We
understood each other—the sea, the cod, and the dog fish, and the sculpin, and the
shark, and the whale. They knew us and we knew they" (25).

And in spite of the fish's disappearance, Skipper Pete believes—or wishes to
believe—that this state of things will return, ousting the modern world of relief,
welfare, and education, for which he has total contempt: "we waits [...] And one day,
they'll come back, in their t'ousands. [...] They's waiting for the old days like we
is" (25).

These two sides to his attitude—the "Satanic" compulsion to an order based on
egotism and his mystique of man's relation to nature—are given religious overtones,
which are handled much more skillfully than the hanged man and *pietà* devices of
Colour the Flesh. On the surface, the Skipper is an intolerantly conservative Catholic
who will not attend his sister-in-law's funeral because it is to be held in a Pentecostal
church, nor welcome the visiting bishop because he has come by car instead of boat
and the traditional floral arches have not been built to welcome him. The Skipper's
orthodoxy is wholly superficial, however. He warns Uncle John that "God is not
merciful. Don't ye ever forget that," and seems to substitute his own authority for the
bishop's when he defends the sternness of his regime by claiming "I made an arch for
ye" (13). When the Skipper boasts of never changing a habit or opinion, Uncle John
replies with irony: "You and the Pope 'as got something in common after all then,
Skipper" (21), and John's wife pushes the implications of this a stage further when she
says her father is "Only one breath away from God or the Devil hisself" (16). On the
other hand, the Skipper's reaction to the news of young Jimmy Fogarty's death is
wholly pagan and fatalistic, deifying not himself but the sea: "The sea wanted him. Old
Molly. She took him in her good time" (30).

The set reflects this pantheism. The left wall of the "splitting room" has "a ragged
window, once a church window, saved from an abandoned church somewhere and put
to use by a crude insertion into the room" (5), and it is through this window that the
Skipper gazes as he rhapsodizes about the past and envisions its return. At the end,
when he is left alone, the setting sun dies through it to conclude the play.

For a while, with memories, work rituals, drink, and snatches of song, the Skipper and his two companions manage to create their own reality within the shack, culminating in the drunken dance of triumph that gives the play its title. A stage direction tells us that during this dance "For a moment they are all one. All free" (29); and one implication of the title is, of course, the celebration of a sense of life in the raw, a dance of fundamentals. But as the title also implies, it is a dance of discarded remnants as well, the pieces of the fish that are thrown away: the dance is ultimately a dance of death. All along, the emphasis on heroic individualism has been balanced by a recognition of the sterility of the Skipper's way of life. His is a world with no place for women or children. Though his sister-in-law, we hear, was good to the family, Skipper Pete has no intention of attending her funeral; and he despises his daughter, Uncle John's wife, partly because he wanted to father only sons, but also because he realizes she is a bitter rival for John's loyalty, without which he cannot keep his vision alive: "Memories ain't no good unless you can see someone else working out the same ones" (26).

Uncle John and his wife have only daughters themselves, their son having been stillborn; and John blames this on the Skipper, who, he claims, killed their sex-life by his expectations of a grandson. We hear that when the Skipper's own son, Absalom, was young, his father sent him back into a fifteen-below blizzard to gather five more sticks of firewood and, when the boy's horse returned alone, refused to go to look for him because "Ye know ye had to bring 'em up hard else they wouldn't survive" (9).

Absalom is now retarded, a sixty-year-old with the face of a child, still unable to look his father in the face. When he asks the Skipper to sing, he underlines the significance of his name by repeating the psalmist's cry for the son he has destroyed, "Oh Absalom, my son. Absalom. Absalom" (28)

This destructiveness focusses in the action round the death of Jimmy Fogarty, which alters the relationships within the play. When at the end of Act I another child comes to the shed to beg aid for Jimmy, who has fallen off a wharf and cannot swim, the Skipper and Uncle John ignore him, continuing drunkenly to gaze through the church window, discussing a drowning that happened in the past. This callousness looms behind the subsequent celebration of Absalom's catch, as the noise of the search party is heard increasingly outside; and at the end it is Absalom who finds the body and brings it to his father: "Look what I caught by the side of the boat [...] I nivir caught a boy before. What shall I do wid him, Father? ...Can I have him?" (32–33).

Up to this point Skipper Pete has been insisting that the death must have been fated, that "Old Molly," the sea, touched the boy the day he was born and has taken him in her own good time—"passionately believing what he wants to believe" (30), as the stage direction explains—but confronted by the body in his own son's arms, the tragedy finally touches him:

> Absalom is facing Skipper Pete, the dead boy in his arms. The grandson he might have had! Skipper Pete puts out his hand slowly, traces the blind, wet face with his horny hands. Then, he turns, the hand that

> touched the dead child's face to his throat, as if it is a weight that will choke him. (32)

Uncle John had genuinely not noticed the child's plea, in fact, because the Skipper's arm had kept him turned towards the church window, but now he realizes that Skipper Pete had heard and had deliberately ignored the cry for help. The doubts and rebellions that have worried John throughout the play come to a head, and he breaks at last from his father-in-law's dominion, taking Absalom with him ("he don't know nothing about boys. Only fish" [33]). The play ends with Skipper Pete alone, stubbornly returning to the ritual of his evening chores by lamplight, as the sun dies out in the shack's church window.

Except for the rather forced situation where the child's plea is ignored, *Dance* is remarkably economical and successful in fusing realism and symbolism. Cook admits that the Skipper's disregard of the child's request is "unrealistic," but says, "The scene was intended to drive home the Skipper's character" (*Calgary Herald* 26 October 1974); and the advertisement for a CBC production of the play expands this by explaining that in the Skipper "fatalism reflects an acceptance of tragedy that seems like inhumanity" (CBC). Yet it is less the situation itself that is at fault than the fact that so little of its significance gets into the dialogue. The Skipper's remarks about "Old Molly" emphasize his fatalism retroactively, but his deliberate *willing* of the disaster at the time of the child's plea is left wholly to the actor; the closest the dialogue comes to it is that, at that time, the Skipper and John are discussing the drowning of a young man whose father was restrained from trying to rescue him. Similarly, the Skipper's *anagnorisis*, when the tragedy of Jimmy Fogarty's death at last strikes home to him, is all in dumbshow; Pete does not speak again after he has seen the body in Absalom's arms.

Apart from this particular incident the ingredients of the play are admirably coherent. The characterization of the four main personages—Skipper Pete, Uncle John, Absalom, and John's wife—is sharply individualized; the set, while realistic, has rich symbolic suggestiveness; sounds-off—the sea itself, the mocking cry of seagulls, the bells for Aunt Alice's funeral, and the encroaching noise of the searchers for Jimmy Fogarty's body—all acquire thematic significance; and the elaborate rituals of preparing equipment, feeding the stove, making tea, cleaning and cooking fish, and preparing a celebratory drink, do not substitute for action, mere visual filler, but reflect the old men's attempt to use routines to recreate the past. This culminates in the grotesque dance, which, like the shanties sung by Pete, absorbs "presentational" techniques into the play's realism yet also carries a level of symbolism. The use of a modified Newfoundland dialect which is sparse, proverbial, coarsely comic, and repetitive, gives a sense of authenticity which can rise effortlessly to poetry—as, to give one brief example, Uncle John's comment that Absalom dreams "Of the mackerel thicker'n on the water than moonlight, whispering together" (8). And the result is a powerful, credible picture of the end of an heroic tradition.

[…] [8]

Whereas *Colour the Flesh* is in presentational "epic" form and *Dance*, for all its realistic elements, operates symbolically, in *Jacob's Wake* Cook relies mainly on contemporary realism. He has said, in fact, that "of all the plays I've written, it's the one that is most closely based upon people I know" (Anthony 228). Yet this concern for realism is combined with a variant of the Newfoundland experience that is difficult to present realistically. Cook's object now is apocalyptic. He wishes to convey the destruction of a humanity that has tried to turn its back on nature, evoking

> an environment no longer responsive to the timeless bonding between itself and man which makes communion on this earth possible, an environment with the will for destruction to match our own… an environment which bred E.J. Pratt's *Titanic*-sinking iceberg, a vast neolithic structure created for such a time when man's hubris had made him blind to nature. (Production Notes, *Jacob's Wake* 329)

An absolutely crucial aspect of the staging, therefore, which Cook emphasizes in his "Production Notes," is a sense of the steadily increasing storm outside the outport house which is the setting for the play: "It is essential… that the storm becomes a living thing, a character, whose presence is always felt, if not actually heard, on the stage" (329).

For most of the play, however, this storm is strictly background for the human failings displayed within the house, where the celebration of Good Friday has brought together three generations of the Blackburn family, who represent successive stages of alienation from nature. The traditional heroic fatalism of Newfoundland is represented by Elijah Blackburn, an old sealing skipper very like Skipper Pete of *Dance*, who lies bedridden upstairs, confusedly mingling past and present as he has his log books read aloud and barks out orders as though he were afloat. Elijah shares the Newfoundland attitude which holds that "A house is a ship. Lights agin the night… some adrift… some foundered, some rotting old hulks full of the memories of men.… They's no difference" (362).

Like Skipper Pete, he also has a mystic belief that the vanished seals will return and that somehow he will be able to hunt them again: "They'll come back. The swiles'll come back in their t'ousands and when they do, I'll go greet 'em just like in the old days" (346). But his attitude to nature is "Satanic" ("Swiles is bred and killed in Hell, boy" [345]). He defies the storm like Lear in his madness—and his attraction to sealing lies not in the value of the catch but in the excitement of the hunt itself, the risking of one's own life to have the primitive pleasure of killing.

Like Skipper Pete, he scorns his daughter, Mary, an old-maid schoolteacher whom he wishes he had never begotten, and considers her a "poor substitute" (340) for his second son, Jacob, who was lost while hunting. But Elijah is more complex and sensitive than his predecessor. Offsetting his dislike of Mary is his comfortable rapport with his daughter-in-law Rosie; and he is still remorseful over his dead wife's grief for their son, and distressed by her refusal to believe that he did all he could to save him. Indeed, as the title indicates, Elijah's overriding sorrow is the abandonment of Jacob to the ice, a sacrifice that ended the family's capacity to face nature with traditional defiance.

The Skipper's other son, Winston, and Rosie, his wife, are utterly non-heroic but have a capacity for love which provides an alternative to Elijah's pride. This centres on Rosie, whom Cook presents as an almost too perfect Irish-Catholic mother, loving, undemanding, and self-sacrificing. [9] Rosie lacks grandchildren, however, and like Elijah mourns the death of a child, a daughter Sarah, who might have carried on her kind of values.

Sarah was also Winston's favourite ("Everytime I gits afflicted with me family I thinks of the one that might have been different" [351]), and her birth galvanized him for once to a courage in defying the elements that reminded Rosie of Elijah: "I never seed ye like it. Ye were like a wild man. Like yer fader almost. [...] I believe ye'd 'ave faced the Divil dat night and gone on" (351).

For Winston, life collapsed after his daughter's death ("It was never the same after she died. I doesn't know why," and he has since been left believing in nothing: "They's nothin', Rosie. Nothin'. They's madness and they's death and they's some who work at it and some who wait for it" (351).

Winston, in fact, is the most complex character in the play, to whom our attitude changes radically. At first he seems merely idle, vulgar, and malicious, drinking heavily, hazing his returned sons, and teasing his spinster sister with indecencies. There is a sense of violence in the man, moreover, which culminates in his ineffectual firing of a shotgun after he hears that his son Alonzo has forged his name. His cry on hearing of this—"My name! 'Tis all I've got left" (363)—reveals the damaged self-respect beneath this coarseness. Winston is an Esau figure, an elder son who is aware he has not satisfied his father's expectations ("I wish sometimes that I could have been the son he wanted" [347]); and his self-contempt emerges movingly in a conversation with his wife late in the second act:

> What else could I ha' been, Rosie? What else could I ha' done? [...] It weren't good enough [...] Everything changed afore I knew what to do. The old ones so damned sure [...] Though what about, the Lord knows. An us, Rosie, us.... Like rats in a trap, with the Welfare as bait. I didn't know what to do, so I didn't try. There didn't seem any p'int. (364)

He drinks and curses to cover this sense of worthlessness: "I drinks because it helps me to fergit where I am and I swears because I like it. It sounds good and it protects me from your [Mary's] kind of literacy" (356). As Cook's note on the use of dialect points out, "Winston is a man of considerable experience and education, both of which he seeks to suppress" (329).

Our sympathy for him grows as we realize this sensitivity and note his tenderness not only for Rosie and the dead Sarah but also for the tragic Mildred Tobin, who froze to death with her illegitimate child when her father turned her out into a storm. Moreover, though he knew the culprit was really his own son Brad, Winston loyally kept this quiet even when gossip fathered the child on himself. Though he has proved a disappointment, the Skipper has a liking for him ("But yer'e human. Ye talk to me" [345]), and Winston in return is imaginative enough to appreciate his father despite his feeling of rejection: "I encourage him because beneath that wrinkled old skull and those mad eyes I kin sometimes see a truth about meself which might make some sense o' dying" (359). He therefore resists the move to commit the old man to a mental home, and by the time his sister rejects his offer of reconciliation, throwing beer in his face, our sympathies for the two have switched completely.

In the Blackburns' degeneration Mary has a position between that of Rosie and Winston and that of their children, and our attitude towards her balances exactly our attitude to Winston. Initially, we are sympathetic to her pride in teaching standards, her contempt for her coarse brother and the nephew Alonzo, her opposition to her father's tyranny and to all the men's exploitation of Rosie's good nature, and the pride she shows in her favourite nephew, Wayne. But gradually the narrowness and lack of generosity in her nature emerge. Laudable independence shades into closefistedness, distaste for sexual coarseness becomes a chilling condemnation of the pathetic Mildred Tobin, and pride in Wayne shows itself possessive and even snobbish, as she exults in the impression they will make riding in his car to church. It is she who is ultimately behind the move to put the Skipper in an asylum—a move that denies the values of both Elijah and Winston—though it is Wayne who is her willing instrument in this treachery, just as he has been responsible for the final breakdown of his brother Brad by getting him dismissed from his parish.

The third generation of Blackburns has degenerated completely from the heroism of the Skipper, in fact: the "time of the seal" has given place to "the day of the dogfish" (351). Winston describes their attitudes to Elijah without illusion: "One of 'em pretends ye don't exist and the other wants to save yer black soul. And the third waits fer yer will" (345).

The eldest, Alonzo, is perhaps slightly less unsympathetic than his brothers. He is mainly what Winston pretends to be: drunken, vulgar, and brutal, forever daring his brothers to fight. He has no intention of accepting the responsibility of marriage but is promiscuous himself and the purveyor of lust to others—the proprietor of a roadhouse where he hires prostitutes as strippers—and the original inciter of Brad's affair with Mary Tobin. With his politician brother Wayne he trades business deals for votes, and to get a motel contract is prepared to commit his grandfather to an asylum by forging his father's signature—a cheat he claims to have performed frequently before. Yet just as 'Lonz is the only brother to retain his Newfoundland accent, so too he has some qualms about committing the Skipper and shows at least a vestige of sympathy for both Elijah and Winston. The second brother, Wayne, has no such traces of humanity. His affection for his Aunt Mary is unhealthy self-centred, and he has used the culture she strove to acquire for him merely to become a dishonest politician. Wayne is the furthest removed from nature of them all. Though he expects to become the Minister of the Environment, he has sold the island's last 50,000 acres of standing timber to the Japanese, and his personality collapses when the government he depends on for his power resigns. He becomes "like a man in a trance" (367). Most ruined of the three is the youngest son Brad, who is also the first to be destroyed. His guilt for Mildred Tobin has turned him into a religious fanatic, projecting his self-disgust onto others, and harrowed by fiery visions of an imminent last judgement. This collapse began when, as a child, he was maliciously abandoned to raw nature by his brothers—an incident which not only foreshadows his final destruction, when he goes out into the storm to die like Mildred Tobin, but also shows the brothers' complete lack of sympathy for or trust in one another. As 'Lonz states, perhaps too baldly, "There was never any love here, sure [...] We was too busy survivin' to put up with any o' that foolishness" (361). This lovelessness is reflected in a savage humour that finds its outlet in cheating, hazing and constant malicious joking, like the laughter of the ice which the Skipper swears he heard when Jacob died.

The realism of these family relationships (which have more than a whiff of O'Neill about them) is deepened by religious symbolism. Placing the action on Maundy Thursday and Good Friday not only provides a realistic excuse for the family's reunion but is also meant to relate to Elijah's sacrifice of Jacob on an April 5th many years before. Thus the mourning for Christ is also Jacob's Wake, and their parallelism is driven home by the crucifixion image, borrowed from David Blackwood's striking series of Newfoundland etchings "The Lost Party," in which the Skipper recalls his last sight of his son: "The way dey was, so far away, dey seemed to form a t'in black cross on the ice. Den the ground drift swallowed dem up" (353). This image is recapitulated later as a premonition of disaster: " 'tis the shape of death, boy. I kin see'n jest like that first time, rising out of the drift, moving across the ice widout a sound, a man like a cross growing up into the sky" (363).

The key names are also significant. The Old Testament Jacob was, of course, the favoured son who wrestled with the angel and who, by fathering twelve sons, established the tribes of Israel; thus Jacob's death is clearly the loss of Elijah's hopes for the future. Similarly, Elijah himself was the Old Testament prophet of doom to Ahab's false gods, and his ascent to heaven in a chariot of fire is probably meant to relate to the Skipper's curious apotheosis at the end of the play. A level of religious awareness is also maintained by the Easter hymns coming over the radio, which the Blackburns occasionally join in. Not only do these incorporate Cook's usual device of song realistically into the play, their sentimental rendering makes a point about the religious shallowness of contemporary society, while the particular relevance of several of them to the sea—"Eternal Father," for example, and John Newton's "Amazing Grace"—deepens the symbolic significance of the action, though that significance is far from being Christian.

As usual in Cook, there is also an attempt to use the set to suggest several levels of response. Wayne's type of society is represented by the blandness of the radio's music and its stilted weather forecasts, which gradually give place to the real thing as the storm increases in violence, screaming round the house and finally overwhelming the radio and the lights. Within the house itself a distinction is established between the ground floor and the bedrooms. On the ground floor the ordinary aspects of outport life are conveyed by realistic conversation and methodical processes of quilting, cooking, drying firewood, playing cards, and even preparing drinks—"a traditional part of the family ritual." The bedroom level, by contrast, is appropriately the realm of vision—Brad's nightmares of the last judgment and the Skipper's reliving of his sons' death and premonitions that the house is a ship drifting to disaster

At the end these levels are suddenly reversed. While the apparent corpse of the Skipper is visible on his bed above, his "ghost" enters below to take charge of the house like a ship, impressing his son and grandsons as part of the crew, and heading, he says, defiantly into the truth of the storm: "Comes a time […] When ye has to steer into the storm and face up to what ye are" (368). There is also the sound of seals, and Elijah exults, "The swiles is back. Newfoundland is alive and well and roaring down the ice-pack" (368).

But then the play ends with nature triumphing in "a blackout and the sound of a cosmic disaster […] the final release of the insensate fury of nature that has been building throughout the play." When the lights go up, the fragile house is empty save for the death mask of Elijah, and "All fades into the lone quiet crying of a bitter wind" (368).

This conclusion is certainly not "one of the most ludicrous cop-outs in the annals of Canadian theatre," as one reviewer complained (Ashley). Its significance is clear in the context of Cook's other work; he has mingled realism and symbolism in all his plays; and *Jacob's Wake* itself has a persistent symbolic level, with the identification of house and ship repeated many times before the transformation. Nevertheless, the experiment fails: the reversal of levels is too extreme, and the significance of the end remains unclear. Cook himself tacitly admits this when he suggests that, instead of a realistic set, an "acceptable alternative" might be

> a stark skeletonized set […] as white as bone, stripped of formality, the house equivalent of a stranded hulk of a schooner, only the ribs poking towards an empty sky,

thus freeing the director for "an existential interpretation of the play" (330).

The failure is an instructive one, however, because of its very boldness. The dilemma Cook faces as a playwright is that the experience he wishes to convey arises from an only too actual reality—the awesome environment of Newfoundland—which he cannot present on stage. He is forced to convey its significance poetically, through heightened language and stage symbolism, but this has an allegorical effect, removing the experience from the actuality that is its very essence. Only in *The Head, Guts and Sound Bone Dance* has he found a form to fuse these levels, and even there it is at some cost to the realism. *Jacob's Wake* switches between the levels too abruptly; while the "epic" looseness of *Colour the Flesh* allows realism and symbolism to coexist without a proper fusion. Perhaps the problem is insoluble in stage terms; but unless it is solved, Michael Cook's imagination itself remains "on the edge," its undeniable power denied an adequate dramatic form. [10]

(1980)

Notes

1   John Arden and Robert Bolt are other influences in this direction.

2   For an account of Cook's career, see *Canadian Theatre Review* 16 (1977): 26–28.

3   Full citational information on newspaper articles is unrecoverable. Newspaper titles and dates will appear parenthetically in the text. All page references to *Colour the Flesh the Colour of Dust* are to the Bastet Books (1972) edition; all page references to *The Head, Guts and Sound Bone Dance* are to the U of Toronto P (1993) edition; all page references to *Jacob's Wake* are to the Talonbooks (1993) edition. These page numbers were added to Parker's original essay for this reprinting—Ed.

4   For a full list of Cook's work, see *CTR* 16, 28–31.

5   This concern with the savage murder of Indians who had a proper link with nature is the central theme of *On the Rim of the Curve*. Marie speaks both as Woman and as Girl in the play—Ed.

6   Playscript of *The Head, Guts, and Sound Bone Dance* (1973) 11; a revised text was published in *CTR* 1 (1974). The "sound bone" is the backbone of a fish.

7   Cook makes this comparison himself in the *Calgary Herald* 26 October 1974.

8   Not reprinted here is Cook's brief discussion of two of Cook's shorter plays: *Tiln* (1971) and *Quiller* (1975)—Ed.

9   A fuller portrayal of this type can be found in another of Cook's monologue plays, *Therese's Creed*, published in *Tiln and Other Plays*.

10   I should like to acknowledge the help of Heather MacCallum and Ronald Bryden in getting the data on which this essay is based.

Works Cited

Cook's Plays:

Colour the Flesh the Colour of Dust. 1972. Toronto: Simon and Pierre, 1974; *A Collection of Canadian Plays.* Vol. 1. Ed. Rolf Kalman. Bastet Books, 1972. D1–D47.

The Gayden Chronicles. 1977. Toronto: Playwrights Canada, 1979.

The Head, Guts and Sound Bone Dance. 1973. *Three Plays*, St. John's: Breakwater, 1973; *The CTR Anthology: Fifteen Plays from Canadian Theatre Review.* Ed. Alan Filewod. Toronto: U of Toronto P, 1993. 3–33.

Jacob's Wake. 1975. Vancouver: Talonbooks, 1983; *Modern Canadian Plays.* 3rd ed. Vol. 1. Ed. Jerry Wasserman. Vancouver: Talonbooks, 1993. 325–71.

On The Rim of the Curve. Three Plays. St. John's: Breakwater, 1973.

Quiller. 1975. *Tiln and Other Plays.* Vancouver: Talonbooks, 1976.

Therese's Creed. 1975. *Tiln and Other Plays.* Vancouver: Talonbooks, 1976; *Three Plays.* St. John's: Breakwater, 1977.

Tiln. 1971. *Tiln and Other Plays.* Vancouver: Talonbooks, 1976.

Other Work

Anthony, Geraldine. "Michael Cook." *Stage Voices: Twelve Canadian Playwrights Talk about Their Lives and Work.* Toronto: Doubleday, 1978. 207–31.

Ashley, Audrey M. Rev. of *Jacob's Wake. Ottawa Citizen* 23 July 1975.

Atwood, Margaret. *Survival: A Thematic Guide to Canadian Literature.* Toronto: Anansi, 1972.

Canadian Theatre Review 16 (1977): 26–28.

CBC-TV. *First Choice* 472 (4 October 1974): 2.

Michael Cook. "An Interview with Michael Cook." By Don Rubin. *York Theatre Journal* 5 (1973): 48–54.

———. "An Interview with Michael Cook." By Rota Lister. *Canadian Drama* 2 (1976): 176–80.

———. *Tiln and Other Plays.* Vancouver: Talonbooks, 1976.

———. "Why Did I Write *Head, Guts and Sound Bone Dance*?". *Canadian Theatre Review* 1 (1974): 74–76.

Frye, Northrop. *The Bush Garden: Essays on The Canadian Imagination.* Toronto: Anansi, 1971.

Guide to Special Collections, University of Calgary. Calgary: University of Calgary, 1978.

Kareda, Urjo. Rev. of *Colour the Flesh the Colour of Dust. Toronto Star* 17 October 1972.

The Political Dramaturgy
of the Mummers Troupe

by Alan Filewod

Although known outside of Newfoundland only for the mainland tours of its political documentaries on such subjects as the fishery and the seal hunt, the Mummers Troupe was one of the most innovative Canadian theatres of the 1970s. During its ten-year history the company pioneered indigenous professional theatre in Newfoundland (leaving an enduring legacy in the Resource Centre for the Arts at the LSPU Hall) and became the first company in English Canada to use theatre as a means of political intervention in community development. Although frequently compared to Theatre Passe Muraille, the Mummers Troupe bears more appropriate comparison—theatrically and politically—with such activist Québécois troupes as le Théâtre Euh! and le Grand Cirque Ordinaire.

The frequent comparison with Theatre Passe Muraille is understandable, if reductive. Like Passe Muraille the Mummers Troupe specialized in collectively created localist documentaries. In theatrical technique, ideology and social context, however, the two companies differed significantly. In Ontario and the western provinces the alternative theatre developed as an expression of a nationalist and populist ideology that turned to collective creation and documentary investigation as challenges to theatrical models and dramatic stereotypes that were rejected as colonial in origin. The nationalist revival of the 1970s appropriated the theatrical and atextual performance forms characteristic of the worldwide radical reconstitution of the methods of theatrical production. Consequently the alternative theatre movement in mainland Canada, including Quebec, defined itself in large part by its polemical opposition to an established theatrical system perceived as detrimental to the growth of Canadian theatre.

This was not the case in Newfoundland, which had neither a professional theatre nor an arts council to promote one. The Mummers Troupe found itself in the untenable position of an alternative theatre with no established model to oppose. For the duration of the troupe's life, its founder Chris Brookes argued that the Mummers formed the *de facto* regional theatre in Newfoundland and deserved recognition (chiefly from the Canada Council) as such. When confronted with the argument that the troupe lacked the infrastructure and broad audience base necessary for a regional theatre as defined by the funding bodies, Brookes argued that his theatre was what the regional theatre of Newfoundland needed to be: a popular theatre committed to decentralized art for a predominately rural people in a state of economic and social crisis. The Mummers' commitment to this radical analysis of culture and to a popular political agenda in its plays alienated the provincial government's cultural affairs office, and in the end stood in the way of the troupe's quest for recognition as Newfoundland's authentic regional theatre. Elsewhere I have argued that the crisis over the model of development appropriate for the troupe was in effect instigated by the Canada Council and in the end created the conditions that resulted in the troupe's inevitable collapse in 1982. [1]

The institutional history of the Mummers Troupe was complex and stormy, as Brookes attempted to establish the legitimacy of professional political theatre in the face of official indifference and on occasion outright opposition, and at the same time find solutions to the troupe's constant financial crises. Founded in 1972 by Brookes, Lynn Lunde and John Doyle, the Mummers begins as a nameless street theatre of a type common in the late 1960s. Brookes, who had studied at the Yale School of Drama and had worked in the periphery of the Toronto alternative theatre and with John Juliani in Vancouver, had made his way back to his native Newfoundland with Lunde by performing Punch and Judy shows on university campuses. In St. John's Brookes and Lunde decided to form a radical street theatre, a decision influenced in large part by the revival of regional nationalism and the cultural renaissance that marked the approach of Newfoundland's twenty-fifth anniversary of confederation.

With his genuine delight in popular performance forms, especially puppetry and clowning, Brookes was naturally attracted to the traditional Newfoundland mummers play of St. George and the Turkish Knight, which had been performed in the province within living memory. The mummers play came to be the touchstone for Brookes, and its customary hobby horse became the troupe's familiar emblem. The process of reviving the traditional play and touring it through the streets of St. John's over the twelve days of Christmas transformed the implicitly confrontational ideology with which Brookes had formed his idea of a street theatre troupe. The Mummers may have begun as an anti-establishment expression of the counter-culture, but the mummers play enabled the transition into a populist troupe committed to working class culture and development. As well, the mummers play brought the troupe attention by reviving a celebrated aspect of Newfoundland culture; the good will generated by this affirmation of local culture did much to offset the government's hostility in the troupe's formative years.

The mummers play enabled Brookes to develop a theoretical position which equated popular culture with community struggle, and in the traditional mummers play he claimed a precedent for politically active working class theatre in Newfoundland. [2] At the same time, the mummers play served as a performance lab for the troupe. The apparent artlessness of Brookes' staging, frequently deplored by critics on the mainland, had its origins in the traditional conventions of the mummers play, which was normally performed in living rooms and kitchens. Brookes' seeming disregard for the formalities of conventional staging was derived from the inherently iconoclastic clowning of a folk tradition which emphasized physical energy over mimetic skill. As a general rule, Brookes' shows always worked best when they were close to the audience, when the actors were almost on the audience's laps; the further away the audience was, the more conventional theatrical expectations would intervene and the "worse" the show would seem. This was particularly a problem when the troupe toured the mainland and played in theatres built to a different scale, with different conventions of audience response, than those for which the shows were created originally.

Brookes had in mind from the beginning that his troupe would be committed to political intervention but the methodology of that intervention developed gradually over a decade of work. Beginning as an agitprop troupe, the Mummers began exploring a new form of community intervention theatre in the summer of 1973 in the process which resulted in *Gras Mourn*. This experience led Brookes to the realization that to be effective, political theatre must work in conjunction with community organizations that define the context in which theatre might be useful.

Brookes' published account of his *Gros Mourn* experience summarizes his developing theatrical ideology ("Useful Theatre"). In the summer of 1973, while touring a populist historical revue called *Newfoundland Night* (a show similar in style and technique to Théâtre Euh's *Histoire du Québec*), the Mummers arrived in the outport of Sally's Cove, one of five communities faced with imminent relocation to make way for the newly established Gros Morne park on the island's west coast. In the space of ten days the troupe created an intervention piece blending satire and documentary, which played to the surrounding communities. The show, and the resulting demonstration at the park signing ceremony, brought the Mummers notoriety across Newfoundland and a rebuke from the Canada Council which wrote to Brookes, "as soon as you use real names your theatre becomes political rather than creative" (*Public Nuisance* 99).

That comment may not have been intended as political censure, but it does point to the major problem that continued between the Mummers Troupe and the government institutions upon which its livelihood depended. Brookes' work was perceived as radical and amateurish, as if these two qualities were interdependent, and there was little attempt to define a model of development derived from the troupe's own experience. Instead, the Canada Council defined its expectations of the Mummers' development from its experience of similar troupes elsewhere. The only problem was that the apparent similarities with troupes such as Theatre Passe Muraille were superficial and misleading. In effect, the Mummers Troupe was English Canada's first popular theatre troupe at a time when the phrase was still rarely heard in English and the phenomenon itself unknown. The Canada Council attempted to deal with the troupe fairly by its own terms, and tried to avoid inadvertent political censorship, but its procedures could not cope with the flexible and seemingly *ad hoc* administrative structures that were necessary to the formation of truly popular theatre in the 1970s. The attempt to evaluate the troupe on artistic merits alone, regardless of its political ideology, was itself a misdirected but unavoidable misapplication of a particular set of ideological and aesthetic priorities. Critics and juries who tried to separate artistic merit from political structure failed to realize that for the Mummers political theatre was not a matter of propagandizing a point of view, but of active submersion in a political process.

While the Mummers remained committed to a populist and decentralized analysis of culture and to a political analysis of Newfoundland as a society exploited by multinational capital, the troupe rarely expressed political solutions more extreme than those commonly found in newspaper editorials. The Mummers' political line was similar to that of many "legitimate" community and labour action groups. The Marxist rhetoric that was so much a part of the radical theatre movement in Quebec was notably absent from the Mummers' vocabulary—mainly because the troupe did not define itself in the rigorous ideological terms of a group like Théâtre Euh!, and because in a conservative society like Newfoundland, Marxist rhetoric would tend to alienate the audience the theatre sought to serve.

The opposition of the Mummers from funding agencies and the provincial government was not a response to a perceived Marxist threat but to the more immediate threat of an idea of culture that contradicted the precepts imbedded in government arts policies. That does not mean that the Mummers encountered nothing but hostility from arts agencies; in fact, for most of its life, the troupe's most important patron was the Canada Council. The Council tried to find a meeting ground, but could not in the end reconcile its emphasis on administrative structures with Brookes' declared flexibility of structure and purpose. But if the Canada Council had trouble fitting the troupe into its model, other agencies more readily understood what Brookes was trying to do: some of his most important work was sponsored by such groups as the United Steelworkers of America, the Community Planning Association of Canada, Oxfam, and the Labrador Resources Advisory Council. Ironically, the provincial government was quick to overlook its mistrust of the Mummers' politics when their interests coincided, as they did in 1978 with *They Club Seals, Don't They?* The troupe's lively defence of the seal hunt was funded as part of the Newfoundland government's desperate campaign to win national support for the controversial hunt.

Despite its difficulties, the Mummers Troupe won recognition in the province as an authentic voice of the Newfoundland cultural revival and its shows (chosen in the main by Brookes) explored largely overlooked areas of Newfoundland culture and history. Thus the troupe created shows on mining (*Buchans: A Mining Town*, 1974, and *Dying Hard*, 1976), lumber (*IWA: The Newfoundland Loggers' Strike of 1959*, 1975), inner city neighbourhoods (*East End Story*, 1975), Labrador (*Weather Permitting*, 1977) and even bingo (*Irregular Entertainment*, 1977). It was not until 1976 that the troupe addressed in detail Newfoundland's most famous industry, the inshore fishery, in *What's That Got To Do With The Price of Fish?* After 1975, when the troupe weathered the first of several serious internal crises and had acquired a permanent space in the LSPU Hall in downtown St. John's, the shows changed in theatrical emphasis and dramatic focus. Instead of the documentaries devised for target communities, the shows tended to address topical issues pertinent to the society as a whole. These were the shows by which the troupe was best known to the mainland, especially *They Club Seals, Don't They?* which ranks as one of the most controversial productions in Canadian theatre history.

The Mummers Troupe could have developed as it was expected to, as Passe Muraille did in Toronto, when it moved into its permanent home; it could have begun exploring new dramatic forms and developing new playwrights. In that sense, the troupe did not survive the transition to resident theatre company. When it collapsed in 1982 it had been torn apart by bitter inner schisms and external pressures. The most critical moment came in 1979 when the St. John's arts community challenged Brookes' control of the LSPU Hall. Brookes was a victim of his own administrative gambit; when he started the troupe he had incorporated it as Resource Foundation for the Arts in order to qualify for grants and donations. Having established a legal myth (in the early 1970s this was seen as playing the government game) he promptly put it aside until purchasing the hall. Resource Foundation was the legal owner of the hall; it was a public foundation (although it rarely met to conduct business and elect officers); and in the end it became the centre of the dispute. Using the terms of the foundation's charter, the arts community pushed for a new executive. The fight was long and nasty, and in the eventual arbitration Brookes retained rights to the Mummers Troupe name and some of its meagre assets. But he lost his core group of actors, who went on to form Rising Tide Theatre and to contest the Mummers' Canada Council grant, thus precipitating a major crisis which ended with both groups being placed on project-by-project funding. Although declaring itself a collective company committed to Newfoundland working class theatre, Rising Tide grew into a repertory company resident in the government's Arts and Culture Centre. Brookes struggled on (with reduced funding) until 1981, when he passed control of the troupe to Rhonda Payne and went on to pursue a growing interest in the Nicaraguan revolution and a successful career in radio journalism. Payne kept the troupe afloat— barely—for another season before declaring its death in 1982. Like Brookes, she left Newfoundland to work in Third World popular theatre.

Brookes' problems in sustaining his troupe had serious artistic consequences. His early attempt to create a functional collective developed into a crisis over artistic control of the company. Unwilling to surrender his proprietary interest, and aware of his vaster experience, Brookes encouraged collective creation but practiced centralized management. This led to crises within the company, especially with long-term actors who saw themselves as constituent members of a collective unfairly dominated by Brookes. In 1976 cast members of *What's That Got To Do With The Price of Fish?* presented him with a manifesto in which they complained that he was exploiting them as workers, in contradiction to the basic premise of the troupe. The constant financial crisis prevented Brookes from hiring actors on a charter basis, although in 1975 he did institute a "core group" policy. From 1976 to 1978 Brookes was able to use a basic group of actors in a series of shows, but the promise of a developing ensemble remained unfulfilled. In a company dedicated to collective creation this was a serious handicap: it meant that the troupe was never able to define and expand a theatrical style and vocabulary independent of that provided by Brookes.

Dramaturgical and Theatrical Principles

All of the shows produced by the Mummers Troupe were collectively created (with the exception of the 1973 production of *Once A Giant*, a puppet play by Steven Bush) but at the same time all of them were shaped by Brookes' theatrical style. Even on the rare occasions when Brookes collaborated with a writer (as he did with Rick Salutin on *IWA*), his theatricality was a major element not just of performance but of the text itself. Although transcripts survive of the plays, their textuality is a function of performance and can only be understood in theatrical context.

In all of Brookes' work action builds through gestic units comprised of a montage of documentary narration, storytelling, humorous improvisation, and "mummering," that is, popular performance devices including song, traditional recitation, vaudeville and minstrel show routines, clowning and puppetry. Of equal importance, these elements create a dialectical structure that allows the actors to present the material and comment on it at the same time. Like many Canadian collective documentaries the Mummers' shows invariably authenticate the material by incorporating references to the process of research into the performance text; the "Twenty-five Year Watch" scene in the second act of *Buchans* is an example.

Brookes experimented with a text of signs and signifiers long before the vocabulary of semiotics became fashionable in the theatre. His earliest work was about the process of penetrating working class reality in the theatre: *Newfoundland Night*, his first major show, was little more than a compilation of historical incidents rendered into the Mummers' unique stage vocabulary, counter-pointed by evocative documentary realism: the point of the show was not its polemic message that Newfoundland fishermen had always been exploited, but that a play based on that fact could be toured to isolated outports around the island. In *Gros Mourn* the polemical point became more focused as Brookes attempted to make his theatre of material use to the community. The short time available to create and rehearse the show forced the troupe to develop an effective theatrical language that in effect expanded Brookes' use of popular performance as a political medium. *Gros Mourn* was a semiotic feast, complete with an aminated newspaper, a pedantic lecturer, and numerous references to the park's symbol of an arctic hare. Two recurring vaudeville parodies extended performances signs into dramatic gestures: in the first, "Freddy Federal" and "Percy Provincial" appeared like human puppets and delivered grimly humorous news broadcasts; in the second, two Newfoundland politicians were reviled as low minstrel show comedians:

> **Maynard:** Mr. Doody, Mr. Doody, I wonder if you could tell me who was that cute bunny I saw you out with last night.
> **Doody:** Why Mr. Maynard, that was no bunny that was my arctic hare. (Forced laughter). (7)

Like *Newfoundland Night*, *Gros Mourn* generated a simple structure of oppositions between satire and lyrical realism. In contrast to the lampoons of notable figures (including a savage caricature of federal cabinet minister Jean Chrétien), the play included moments of emotional contact between audience and actors: at the end the actors set model houses afire in a powerful metaphor of the community's defiance of the legislated relocation.

Brookes' later work tended to be more complex in its dialectic of the theatricality and actuality, primarily because longer periods of research and rehearsal enabled him to explore narrative strategies in greater depth. In *Buchans: A Mining Town* Brookes clarified the techniques that would typify his subsequent shows. The obvious semiotic devices are still present, in the iconographic realism of the set made of mine shaft timbers, in the use of actual picket line signs and in the puppets and clowning, but they are integrated into a more developed, essentially gestic, narrative structure. This development of signs into theatrical gestures (equivalent to the scenes of conventional dramaturgy) replaces linear narrative in most of Brooke's shows; the exceptions are *The Bard of Prescott Street*, which tells the story of balladeer Johnny Burke in terms of character and plot, and *IWA*, in which Rick Salutin's contribution as writer appears to eclipse Brookes' typical structures.

Initially, the development of gestic elements by which narrative material is placed in the context of a defining theatrical idea was a matter of theatrical expedience; in a short rehearsal period the cast had to invent workable solutions to particular pieces of narrative or historical material. Typically in Canadian collective creations such gestic elements are introduced as transactions between scenes of documentary reportage. Brookes, like Paul Thompson at Passe Muraille, sought ways to present that material in terms of a physical metaphor that would express ideological context. At its crudest, this gestic tendency merely animates material as interesting performance: the gesture of the barber and client trading information (used in *East End Story*) is common in collective creations, as is the combat metaphor (such as the tractor pull in *The Farm Show* and the union-merchant engine pull in *Newfoundland Night*) in which historical divisions are personified as combatants in a ring. The minstrel show act in *Gros Mourn* is the simplest example of this process in Brookes' work.

This principle of a simple theatrical device developed into dramatic gesture can be seen in the evolution of the minstrel show idea from *Gros Mourn* to *What's That Got To Do With The Price of Fish?* Commissioned by Oxfam to explore economic underdevelopment, Brookes chose to bring the subject home by analysing the Newfoundland fishery as an example of Third World economy in Canada. In order to give that analysis concrete theatrical presence, he revived the minstrel show idea; now, however, the minstrel show functioned as the basic performance metaphor of the play. It begins by establishing a recurring motif and builds as a theatrical analogy of the play's political premise:

> **All sing:** Newfoundlanders sing this song
> Do da, do da.
> Boys there must be something wrong
> Oh da do da day.
> They hung us on a line in 1949

Confederation for the nation
Oh da do da day.

Ron: Newfoundlanders sing and shout
Do da, do da
Grand Bank's nearly all fished out
Oh da do da day. [...] (3)

The equation of the exploitation of Newfoundland with the oppression of American blacks points to another defining principle in Brookes' use of gestic theatricality: as much as possible the performance metaphors that framed the material bore an ideological or historical relation to the material expressed. Thus in *They Club Seals, Don't They?* the "media circus" that surrounded the seal hunt was transformed into a real circus on stage; *Irregular Entertainment*, about the place of bingo in the community, was structured as an interactive bingo game; the set of *IWA*, about the bitter loggers' strike in 1959, consisted of a large roll of newsprint used in various ways through the show. The relation of performance structure and context was not always as direct as these examples suggest: Brookes' final production, *Some Slick* (1979), about the possibly disastrous consequences of the anticipated offshore oil boom, was a bar show performed by the rock blues band Iceberg Alley. In that case the relation was not direct but oblique: the show expressed its analysis of Newfoundland's approaching economic crisis in terms of the *de facto* cultural vocabulary of today's working class.

In *Buchans: A Mining Town* Brookes emphasized the authenticity of documentary material more strongly than in his other plays because of his desire to create a genuine people's history of the community. The performance of the play was grounded solidly in carefully crafted characterizations within the context of which the semiotic theatricality reinforced the play's acceptance of the community's self-image: the effect was that of the townspeople themselves using puppets and clowning to tell their own story. The emphasis on documentary monologue in *Buchans* bore a superficial and misleading similarity to *The Farm Show*; it was this that led Urjo Kareda to complain in his review of the play's Toronto run in 1975 (under the title *Company Town*) that it was "built to a documentary drama formula and the exercise now seems tired and stiff."

In *Gros Mourn* the gestic theatricality foregrounded the actors' status as outsiders intervening in the community. In *Buchans* those same techniques, considerably muted, served the opposite function by strengthening the identification of actors and community. For the most part, *Buchans* advances through documentary monologues arranged in gestic sequences, frequently framed by improvised banter. The play depicts a community defined in terms of labour history, so that the union is presented as the authentic expression of the community. Those aspects of life outside of that community, such as management and government, are presented as puppets or near-puppets. This is not simply reductive satire but a theatrical argument that the organs of the society that profit from the dehumanization of the workers are themselves dehumanized. The "Les Forward Story" that closes the first act of the play is a graphic satire of this process of dehumanization as a strike leader co-opted by management as a foreman then fired is effectively transformed into a puppet on stage.

In each of his plays Brookes and his actors discovered new ways in which popular performance could express and comment on documentary material. From the lyric mime sequences in *Weather Permitting*, to the television-watching baby seal and the filmed slaughterhouse sequences of *They Club Seals, Don't They?*, to the raunchy rock & roll of *Some Slick*, Brookes' stage was a funhouse of clowns, jugglers, magicians, storytellers, balladeers and old-time mummers, all giving theatrical presence to the parade of ordinary Newfoundlanders with their stories of oppression, survival, and triumph. The apparent artlessness of Brookes' theatricality deceived most mainland critics who tended to acknowledge the passion of his shows, but dismissed the performances as "shrill hysteria" (Mallet) and "tatterdemalion" (Bryden). In Newfoundland, however, the Mummers received invariably enthusiastic reviews, a fact which supports Brookes' contention that artistic standards and perceptions are shaped by social context, and that his work can only be understood as a product of and response to a unique culture in a state of historical crisis. If the troupes' theatrical accomplishments have not been recognized by critics and scholars it is perhaps because the contexts that shaped the Mummers' aesthetic have been insufficiently understood.

Buchans: A Mining Town

While touring *Newfoundland Night* in 1973 the Mummers arrived in the mining town of Buchans near the end of a bitter six-month strike. After talking to the striking miners, Brookes decided to return to the town after the tour was completed to create a picket line agitprop. In the end, because of the Sally's Cove experience, he postponed the Buchans project until the following summer. Instead of an agitprop he would create a full-length community documentary.

Located in the geographic centre of Newfoundland, Buchans is an anomaly in the province in being one of the few communities removed from the sea. Founded in 1926, the town was completely owned by the American Smelting and Refining Company (ASARCO), since ceased operations. Most of the workers and their families lived in company housing, while a smaller number owned their own homes in an adjoining townsite. For most of its history Buchans had been free of serious labour strife but in 1971 the union, local 5457 of the United Steelworkers of America, called a strike over wages that lasted five months. Technically the strike was a success: the union won a modest increase, but two years later it rejected a further wage offer and called a strike that would endure for six months. By 1973 Buchans' deposits of zinc, copper and lead were close to depletion and the continued survival of the community was in question. That uncertainty added extra tension to an already tense labour situation.

Brookes returned to Buchans in July, 1974, with a cast of six actors that included Allen Booth, Donna Butt, Lee J. Campbell, Howard Cooper, Bembo Davies and

Connie Kaldor. Of the cast only Brookes and Butt were Newfoundlanders; Brookes had hired the rest in Toronto. They were paid sixty-five dollars a week, out of which they had to pay room and board in the ASARCO bunkhouse.

When the company arrived in Buchans they were without a clear sense of what the play would be. Prior to their arrival Brookes had defined four basic principles to guide them through the process. Firstly, the actors would rely wholly on tape-recorded interviews with townspeople:

> When invention was necessary, we would adopt a more obvious presen-
> tational style of performance so that the audience would know that we
> were inventing our terms, not theirs. (*Public Nuisance* 4)

Secondly, the play would be a people's history, "as much a history of union sensibili-
ties as of the community." Thirdly (and least defined) "we would be careful of our impact on the community." Finally, the actors would live in "total immersion." To this end Brookes arranged with ASARCO for the cast to live in the company bunkhouse. The mine management also agreed to allow the actors to accompany underground work shifts for research.

In order for the actors to create a "people's history" they had to become in short order experts on the history, sociology and industry of Buchans, and they had to find at the same time a theatrical form to express that expertise. They had to learn to perceive the life of Buchans from the point of view of the residents, and in the process abandon their own misconceptions about industrial labour. For those in the cast in Newfoundland for the first time, whose accents marked them as mainlanders, this was a particularly serious challenge.

As the actors began to make contacts in Buchans, as they began to isolate particular aspects of life in the community, their uncertainty about the structure of the play became an obvious problem. Throughout the process Brookes kept a diary; two weeks after arriving in Buchans [29 July 1974] he noted in it:

> Several good ideas this week for the pre-1914 period. 30's movie scene,
> square dance factory process.
>
> The group finds visual imagery—the handling of visual material—
> difficult. I think the group is lost as per dealing with the overall
> material—we're at the fuzzy point where we must (I must?) structure
> part of the stuff to give us a base, a see-how-it-can-be-done demonstra-
> tion, and get at least part of our material safely tucked away out of our
> overloaded minds. (*Buchans* 29)

If the play was to be a true "people's history" it could not be formed on first impressions, and a governing structure was necessary to focus the research. After the first two weeks the structure was apprehended only in vague chronological terms. The compression of research and rehearsal time meant that the shape would have to take form even as the actors were sorting out their initial responses to the town. The actors would spend the mornings and evenings researching and transcribing interviews, meeting in the afternoon to share what they found and try out scene ideas. If an idea seemed workable it would be put aside until there were enough scenes to suggest a solution to a particular segment of the play. To an extent, this process recapitulated the general process of collective creation developed by Canadian theatres, but in one major respect it differed from the prototype established by Theatre Passe Muraille in *The Farm Show* two summers earlier. *The Farm Show* is a compilation of the actors' impressions of the community they visited; it begins with an admission of subjectivity and a self-deprecating account of the actors' naivité. In *Buchans* the actors had to move beyond their subjectivity to discover how the community saw itself; they then had to transform their process of learning into a collective analysis that could be translated into theatrical form.

The idea of a chronological structure gave the actors a beginning point in rehearsal, but it presented a new problem. Some chapters in the town's history were either more colourful or better documented than others, and some of the major areas of attention (such as the experience of working underground) were ahistoric. It was apparent that the play would have to move both chronologically and thematically. The descriptions of various aspects of life in Buchans had to be integrated into an historical argument that would show the 1973 strike as the culmination of the community's entire development. The dramaturgical problem then was to find in each period the typifying factor that would advance the thesis. Certain periods suggested obvious choices, such as the harsh living conditions of the Depression years, or the first expressions of labour unrest in the 1940s. When the actors could not find an obvious story or incident to typify a period, they would use that segment of the play to describe an aspect of community life. Consequently, the play does not always adhere to logical progression. There is no logical dramaturgical reason, for example, why the sequence on women and domestic life should fall into the 1950s segment. Its inclusion there suggests in fact that the male-dominated cast had difficulty synthesizing women's experience in their understanding of the community; it can be argued that *Buchans* marginalizes women both thematically and historically.

At the end of the fourth week of the process, Brookes noted:

> By now we have accumulated masses of material and individual scenes but have not yet edited or structured long sequences. I sensed that we had a "handle" on the show but some of the cast were losing faith, unsure whether any structure is possible from the material. As we began piecing together segments, frustrations surfaced. There was a showdown over working methods, the question of improvisations. The sequences must be made "more realistic" some said, and more character invention would help. (*Public Nuisance* 10)

The compromise that emerged from this showdown was a modification of Brooke's initial idea of documentary juxtaposed with "expressionistic comment." The actors' comments on the material would be presented through "the staging (with puppets etc.) and simply by the editing process itself." These performance devices would be contained by strong realistic characterizations. These characterizations are not so much dramatic characters as typical personalities that emerge in the banter of the improvised narrative sequences such as the bunkhouse and underground scenes of act one, or the women's sequence of act two. In the end these characterizations strengthen the play by grounding it in a strong identifiable base for the audience; this allows the actors to integrate the semiotic performance devices, especially in the strike sequences, as forms of storytelling emerging out of the community.

Throughout the play we are reminded that we are witnessing popular history in the making. This is accomplished by means of two recurring devices. In the first case, the monologues that comprise most of the play retain a sense of the original inter-views with rhetorical questions and verbal indicators ("well now", "you know", "you see"). These deictic signs reinforce the actors' roles as typical townspeople telling their stories. At the same times, the play emphasizes popular traditions and performance forms. The tall tales that begin both acts, the traditional ballads and recitations, the mine-shaft banter and the solemn naming of names, especially of the dead, all serve to authenticate the performance as a "people's history."

The identification of the actors with the community is reinforced by the set, which consists of the Mummers' usual scaffold and a "square-set" of mineshaft shoring timbers borrowed from ASARCO. A sheet printed with mess-hall rules serves as a backdrop and a silent reminder of the constant presence of the company. The square-set is an open cube of massive timbers, used variously as a picture frame, a platform and, of course, a mine shaft; the scaffold serves as platform and mine elevator. In Buchans the performance took place in a school gymnasium, and although the room had a stage, the Mummers erected the set on floor level at the opposite end. There was no curtain, and as the audience took their seats their first impression was that of the square-set removed from its context and transformed into a sign of itself. The set, along with the presence of actual objects (most notably, picket line signs from the recent strike) and the actors' costumes of work shirts and jeans (the same clothes they wore when they met their audience as researchers), functioned as a declaration of documentary authenticity.

That authenticity is a necessary condition of *Buchans*. It gives the actors the right to speak in the name of the community by showing their performance as the result of an active working process. At the same time it enables them to justify the play's ideological analysis as a genuine reflection of the community's consciousness. *Buchans* is pro-union but it is not anti-capitalist; it recognizes that were it not for the mine company there would be no community to celebrate. At the same time, it accuses the company of irresponsible profiteering and criticizes it for depriving the townspeople of basic rights and dignity. Throughout the play the company is portrayed as the impersonal force that it was for the townspeople, but the union is the aggregate of all the subjective experiences that the audience has shared in the play.

Those experiences are transformed into a call for action by the remarkable piece that occupies the emotional centre of the play, based on an incident that occurred at the beginning of the second week of research. Brookes had the idea of including a scene in which the company's practice of presenting a gold watch to miners who had completed twenty-five years of service would become an ironic reflection of corporate exploitation. The improvisation took place in the union hall, observed by a group of retired miners. As Brookes describes the incident,

> We began our 25-year watch improv. One by one the actors of our group entered the presentation scene, refused to accept their watch and demanded to speak. The scene was not working. The improvised speeches sounded false, unlike what a real miner would say. Peter (a retired miner), sitting in the back of the bar, suddenly came forward, entered the scene, accepted the watch and politely asked the "company manager" for permission to speak. I switched on the tape recorder, and I suspect the remarkable speech which followed had been rehearsed for many years in Peter's mind. (Memoir)

This was a breakthrough for the actors, their first confrontation with the obvious superiority of documentary material. Brookes incorporated not just the speech but the whole incident in the play. The scene begins with a company official about to present a watch. He calls out a name, and Brookes, as director, intervenes by stepping into the play to describe the incident in the union hall. An actor then re-enacts the miner's intervention in the rehearsal. Brookes' interruption of the scene parallels the miner's intervention in the rehearsal hall: an outside element changes the substance and the context of an already established structure. The scene reminds the audience that the play itself is the product of a process of intervention.

The speech, which is the only one in the show attributed by name, lasts just under five minutes in performance, and is without question the most powerful moment in the play. With intense logic and scorn the miner refuses the watch not because of hatred of the company but because the watch is an insult, insufficient compensation for the sacrifices the miners have made, especially those who came out of the mines with silicosis. The speech ends with a moving tribute to his comrades:

> But to you, my fellow workers, I want to say this: we have worked hard together, we have worked underground, in dangerous places together, and I do not care where you go today—and you of the company will have to agree with this, that you will not find anywhere a harder working nor a more steady people than what you had working under-ground for you over the years. Thank you.

The scene is the play in miniature, transforming the raw material of actuality into an artistic reflection of itself in such a way that the process of transformation is made apparent in order to express historical meaning. Its inclusion in the play effectively validates the whole process of intervention in Buchans, a process it suggests that the community took seriously. By creating a context in which a retired miner could say what he had left unsaid for so long, and integrating it as the analytical pivot of the play, the Mummers created a popular history that depicts the community as more than passive subjects of historical forces.

The final strike sequence that follows the speech and brings the play up to date for the audience is shown as a necessary response to the sufferings the miner describes, and as an equally necessary pre-condition of the community's future. Without action, the play implies, there will be no future; the company will merely decamp and the town will wither away. This is, in fact, what came to pass when the company ceased operations a few years later; although the town hangs on, its economic base has disappeared. The text of *Buchans* survives not only as the record of a remarkable experiment in popular theatre in Newfoundland, but as the living record of a disappearing community.

(1987)

Notes

[1] For an analysis of the historical development of the Mummers Troupe and its relations to the funding agencies, see Filewod, "Life and Death." For a more detailed analysis of *Buchans: A Mining Town*, see Filewod, *Collective Encounters*.

[2] Brookes developed his analysis of the traditional mummers play as militant popular theatre in a paper presented to the Association for Canadian Theatre History in Halifax in 1981; it is included in his *A Public Nuisance*.

Works Cited

Brookes, Chris. *Buchans* rehearsal diary. 1974.

———. *Gros Mourn.* Typescript.

———. Memoir. "Company Town."

———. *A Public Nuisance: A History of the Mummers Troupe.* St. Johns: Institute of Social and Economic Research, Memorial University, 1988.

———. "Useful Theatre in Sally's Cove." *This Magazine* 8.2 (1974): 3–7. Rpt. *Canadian Theatre Review* 38 (1983): 38–50.

———. *What's That Got To Do With The Price of Fish?* Typescript.

Bryden, Ronald. "They Impale Bleeding Hearts, Don't They?" *Maclean's* 20 March 1978.

Filewod, Alan. "The Life and Death of the Mummers Troupe." *The Proceedings of the Theatre in Atlantic Canada Symposium.* Ed. Richard Paul Knowles. Sackville, NB: Centre for Canadian Studies, Mount Allison University, 1988.

———. *Collective Encounters: Documentary Theatre in English Canada.* Toronto: U of Toronto P, 1987.

Kareda, Urjo. "Mummers Troupe Shuns Risks." *Toronto Star* 9 June 1975.

Mallet, Gina. "Baby Seals Don't Club Baby People, Do They?" *Toronto Star* 2 March 1978.

Not Leaving Home:
Growing Up Artistically in Atlantic Canada

by Bryden MacDonald

After several years of feeling like I was going back to an abusive marriage every time I returned to Toronto from anywhere in Nova Scotia, I finally sought counselling. I realized that not only was I suffering from City Mouse/Country Mouse syndrome, but I had obviously—pregnant with hysteria—married far too young. A trial separation was recommended as the cure.

The healing process wasn't as painful as anticipated. I became involved with a project intimately connected with the East coast, a commission from Mulgrave Road Co-op Theatre to write a play about the demise of Via Rail passenger service on Cape Breton Island (which became *Eastbound on The Haunted 604: A Canadian Travesty*), followed by a very fulfilling summer season at The Stephenville Festival in Newfoundland, where I began the initial work on this article, the proposed topic being East coast artists taking more control of their own work. I went into overload upon realizing that tackling the East coast theatre scene in one article might be just a tad ambitious. The result is a mere scratch upon an ever-expanding surface; but one thing remains consistent throughout all of the conversations I had while researching the article:[1] artists either continue to hover or they land and gather. Above and beyond personal likes and dislikes, sex, hunger, gods, doing a budget while juggling fire, feeding the giant and mastering hockey on the side, in our search for things to inspire and employ, artists must eventually land, gather and work.

It's no secret that it is very difficult to survive as an artist in Eastern Canada. Frighteningly limited funding puts our artists in a state of flux that makes it hard to nurture an active community. This is not for lack of trying.

The doing it all and making it work even if you blow up theory is something of which former Halifax performance artist Ellen Pierce (now Theatre Awards Officer at the Canada Council) has firsthand knowledge. "Halifax always was a city where independent artists worked together," she told me. "We were cross disciplinary in 1971; in 1981 we had new dance and interaction between mediums. We used all available resources. However, Halifax—the Maritimes—doesn't see the value of its own potential reflected in the funding body. The funding body is not here for the individual artist. We have to get past funding only the business part of art—that's the easiest part to fund. There must be more concentration on the individual artist in order for anything to flourish. If someone gave me money and said 'make it work,' the administrator in me would develop everything that now exists and then wait for a while. As it stands now, you won't get it better anywhere else, being at one place with yourself and your work, than here; but somehow you have to get money for it or you die! I do expect a fruition of multi-talented people in the fields, but there's got to be resources. Maybe it's a place that will always have potential, but never be realized—that's the tragedy. We have to push. It's a long way, but we have to push."

Currently on the East coast, prodigal siblings are returning (landing and gathering after hovering) while others are coming out of hibernation. Mulgrave Road Co-op Theatre's new artistic director, Jenny Munday, who packed up and moved from Fredericton, New Brunswick, to Guysborough, Nova Scotia, to accept the position after too many years of "doing stand-up at lawyers' conventions," is one member of this landing party. "Given the current political climate in this part of the country," she believes, "it is getting harder and harder for artists to create their own work; as a result, the work we see is going to be more and more passionate—and more and more meaningful."

Mary Vingoe bounced back and forth between Ontario and Nova Scotia for the last six years before, what she calls, a "positive departure" from Toronto's Nightwood Theatre. She now resides outside of Halifax, much closer to her second home in Parrsboro, Nova Scotia, where she and Michael Weller are co-artistic directors of The Ship's Company Theatre. "The company grew out of a strong spirit of place and a deep sense of community," she describes. "In the beginning, necessity forced us to do all tasks ourselves and work very much for and about local community. Now the work is still for our community, but our definition of 'relevant' material has broadened and matured. Nevertheless, the early years created a strong sense of ownership and self-sufficiency which has carried over to the present. In a way, I think the progress of Ship's Company is analogous to the larger Maritime scene. We have survived against the odds and we are building a national reputation, but we are only as strong as the artists we can afford to attract and keep here. This part of the world has a personality that needs its artists to help it develop. We are, as artists, part of a much larger ecosystem which includes TV, film, and radio production, as well as university drama departments. We must work to make them all healthy and pull together. That's the challenge for Nova Scotia theatre in the '90s."

So here we are in the '90s beginning the decade with a very bold and positive move: the appointment of Linda Moore as artistic director of Neptune Theatre. Not only is Moore the first woman in Neptune's history to be appointed to this position, she is also the first artistic director "from" Nova Scotia. (She has lived and worked in Nova Scotia for the past 18 years.)

But will Moore be the messiah she is expected to be? "Obviously, Neptune can't provide it all," Moore argues, "but if what exists is healthy, then that opens doors. We have to be challenging on the main stage, but protect and nurture the main stage subscription audience in order to foster other activity—at this point we are still repairing. I want a good active second stage and a building also, but I can't fight for it without proving it's needed."

So how will she prove it is needed? Her first step appears to be by focussing more on writers than on stars and glitter. Her season includes plays by Canadians Wendy Lill and Antonine Maillet, as well as British playwrights Tom Stoppard and Timberlake Wertenbaker. (Moore's season also features Halifax's brilliant physical theatre troupe, Jest in Time, in the Christmas slot.) "Wertenbaker's *Our Country's Good* is a risk for me," Moore reveals. "It's pretty tough: brutality versus civilization; the power of language and the theatre changes the nature of the penal colony in 18th-century Australia. I'm gambling that the true eloquence of the play will carry it, that the audience will allow it to happen on their stage. It says everything I want to say about the theatre."

Then, smack in the middle of what has become a very positive and exhilarating chat, I mention the general nonavailability of money. Moore sighs, but immediately summons another burst of passion: "Ultimately it's more than money, isn't it? Culture has to be a food that people think is essential, that we think is essential—it won't survive if it's always the economic argument. It isn't the economic argument that makes the arts valid; it's the artists. Go away for a while if you have to, just get out there and work, establish yourself. We know who we are here. We're connected to this place and eventually we have to come back—we're driven back. But we also have to work."

Halifax actress Nicola Lipman, currently Canadian Actors Equity Association counsellor for the Maritimes and sitting on the boards of both The Neptune and The Ship's Company, is full of hope—but not so much that she doesn't realize the severity of some of the problems we face here. "Being 'somewhere else' isn't always Toronto anymore and that encourages me and supports what I've always believed in: do it where you are." Lipman continues, "Not just Maritimes artists are feeling it's important to do the work wherever they are—I find all regions take pride in their growth and don't feel they have to depend on the approval of Toronto anymore. The voices coming from the rest of the country are being heard from where they are. I don't feel we are isolating ourselves from each other as much. Regions of productivity are filling out in the country, the community is getting to know each other, the give-and-take is greater and that's what will give us our voice as Canadian theatre. There is a burgeoning of independent producers here—it's difficult, we have no money. For the eighth year in a row our money has been frozen. They're just keeping us quiet by giving us nothing extra and unfortunately the options are what they've always been: just keep asking for more. But people who have always considered themselves only one thing—an actress, for example—are initiating their own projects. I wouldn't have thought about doing that up until a few years ago, but we have to now—and we are. It all comes out of need. When you need food, you go out and grow some, right?"

"Need" is exactly what started Upstart Theatre, a Halifax-based company just beginning its second season and dedicated primarily to the production of locally-written plays, so far by such writers as George Boyd, Lynn Ostergaard and Catherine Banks. Deb Allen, former artistic director of The King's Playhouse in Georgetown, P.E.I., is one of its founding members. "Upstart was born out of a realization that there is talent here," she comments, "and we're breaking our necks to prove it. Fortunately, we received debt reduction money from the province, so we can begin our second season with a clean slate; but that doesn't mean we can stop fundraising for a minute. We can't survive without corporate support. It's impossible to do it all with just government money because the arts just aren't a priority."

Also on the new arrivals list is ACME Explosives, a new co-op initiated by playwright Glen Cairns to "allow artists to take control of production and produce independently without the constraints of a regional theatre mentality where, if you're lucky, you're an employee and, if you're not, you sit around and wait for the next set of general auditions." ACME Explosives' first project, Cairns' own play *Danceland*, has attracted artists from other mediums, including myself, lighting designer Brian Pincott and jazz musician Paul Cram.

As artistic director of The Stephenville Festival, Cliff Le Jeune, in his first season, managed to create what it takes most new artistic directors two or three years to make: a fresh and healthy environment. When the position became vacant after the untimely death of founder Maxim Mazumdar (and following the season of adjust-ment under Sean Mulcahy), Le Jeune went after the job of artistic director and got it. Apparently, the boards of both Neptune and Stephenville were of the same mind. Le Jeune, a native Cape Bretoner, has been pounding the boards of Maritime theatres for most of his thirtysomething years and he has spent nine summers at Stephenville. The audience knows him and he knows his audience. Directing and dancing in *West Side Story*, performing in both Edmund MacLean's production of *Observe the Sons of Ulster Marching Towards the Somme* and in my production of *Sincerely a Friend: The Music of Leonard Cohen*, while still managing to keep the company in sync, Le Jeune has blasted the Festival into a new decade.

And then there's Edmund MacLean, a wonderful madman and artistic director of Theatre Newfoundland/Labrador for the last 10 years; MacLean also recently terrorized Newfoundland audiences with his controversial production of *Miss Julie*. He is a founding member of The Artists Coalition. A report was recently handed down by the provincial government and these artists are not happy. "I've come to the point where I believe the government has no vision and sees no value in us as professional artists," MacLean rages. "They like to see us fight—it buys them more time. But with the formation of the Coalition we are gathering in a harmonious way to solve our differences. Why are the Arts and Culture centres here barren for most of the year and why do Newfoundland artists have so much trouble gaining access to them? I want answers to questions like these—WE want answers to questions like these—and we're going to get them."

So then I mention money. "What money?" MacLean snaps. "I don't see it. I only see it being abused: costumes that cost over $10,000 and are only seen on stage for one minute! Yes, the money should be spread out, but we have to get together and prove ourselves, do our work! Just because the government's priorities are fucked up doesn't mean ours have to be. Let's face it, the only time the government shows any interest in us is when the Queen comes to town, and then they parade us around in our tiaras for free!"

And so, even though being a professional artist in this part of the world can sometimes feel like being the understudy for the fourth dancer to the left in an endless tour of a bad American musical, the landing party is growing.

(1990/91)

Notes

[1] The places and dates of the interviews on which this essay is based are not recoverable—Ed.

The Subjects of *Salt-Water Moon*

by Robert Nunn

Contemporary critical theory has tended to strip the act of reading or receiving a text of its innocence. It is no longer the case that the text is thought of as an autonomous realm, nor is reading thought of simply as a matter of receiving the meaning inherent in the text. Rather, meaning is reconceived as an exchange between the text and the reader: its production is completed in the act of reading. Susan Bennett's recent *Theatre Audiences: A Theory of Production and Reception* (1990) applies reception and post-structuralist theory to the act of viewing the theatrical event. She adds the important consideration that the act of viewing is never ideologically innocent. The subject who views the play is always a subject constructed in ideology. One aspect of the subject's position, one which Bennett considers but not at great length, is gender. We do not approach any work of art without carrying our deeply-ingrained sense of sexual identity and sexual difference with us to colour the act of reception. When we consider that it is only on one side of the footlights that theatre has been for millennia dominated by men, while audiences have almost always been composed of men and women, the problem of *reception* of the theatrical text is foregrounded. What viewing position is elicited by texts predominantly produced by men, if the viewer is male, and again if the viewer is female? The idea that a specific gender position is *constructed* for the viewer was first explored in writings on film, first in the influential essay by Laura Mulvey, "Visual Pleasure and Narrative Cinema" (1975), and subsequently in work by among others Kaja Silverman, E. Ann Kaplan and Teresa de Lauretis. De Lauretis outlines the approach succinctly:

> The representation of woman as image (spectacle, object to be looked at, vision of beauty—and the concurrent representation of the female body as the *locus* of sexuality, site of visual pleasure, or lure of the gaze) is so pervasive in our culture, well before and beyond the institution of cinema, that it necessarily constitutes a starting point for any understanding of sexual difference and its ideological effects in the construction of social subjects, its presence in all forms of subjectivity... it is... the feminist critique of representation that has conclusively demonstrated how any image in our culture—let alone any image of woman—is placed within, and read from, the encompassing context of patriarchal ideologies, whose values and effects are social and subjective, aesthetic and affective, and obviously permeate the entire social fabric and hence all social subjects, women as well as men. (37–39)

More recently, feminist theatre critics have assimilated this work on film into the study of theatre: for example, Sue-Ellen Case and Jill Dolan.

David French's *Salt-Water Moon* is an interesting play to examine in the light of these theoretical explorations. A brief synopsis of *Salt-Water Moon* will suggest why. Jacob Mercer abruptly left Coley's Point, Newfoundland, a year before without even saying goodbye to his girl, Mary Snow. They are both in their late teens. He returns when he hears she is engaged to a young schoolteacher, Jerome McKenzie, whose father is a wealthy merchant and ship-owner. Jacob is a fisherman; he has spent the year in Toronto making concrete blocks. Mary is a domestic servant. He comes to her employer's house on a lovely night in August 1926, to find her waiting for her fiancé. He sets out to win her back. The play ends at the moment she casts her lot with him. Two vital pieces of exposition unfold through the play. We learn that Jacob left Newfoundland because he could not bear to see his father, who had fought so bravely in the Great War, being cruelly mistreated by his boss, Jerome's father. We also learn that Mary has become engaged to Jerome largely so that she can have her own home, and thus rescue her younger sister Dot from the orphanage (their mother is living, but has not been capable of caring for her children since her husband died in the Great War). At the crux of the play, Mary voices her suspicion that Jacob is trying to win her back only to settle the score with Jerome's father. Jacob, deeply offended, walks off. Mary cries out his name with all her might. He returns and the rest is Parts I, II and IV of the Mercer Tetralogy. The very fact that the play is about a young man wooing a young woman who does not want to be wooed indicates the position the audience is implicitly invited to assume. "We" are watching a man watching a woman for signs of weakness, "we" are invited to watch a woman's resistance weaken until she yields. The positioning of the audience as male is reinforced first of all by the gender of the playwright, second by the fact that the first production at Tarragon was directed by a man. Not surprisingly, given that positions of power in the theatre, such as playwriting and directing, have until recently been exclusively in men's hands, and still are predominantly so,[1] every one of the twelve subsequent productions of the play listed in *Canada On Stage 1982–1986* was directed by a man (266, 299, 353, 375, 387, 394, 445, 452, 493, 522, 569, 574). But every actor who played Mary Snow was a woman. This might seem too obvious to mention but for the fact that a woman *acting* (in several senses of the word) implicitly opens a gap in the closed circle of representation of women by men, and immensely complicates what seems at first glance a simple invitation to view the play from a masculine point of view. Thus it matters enormously that Mary too has a project, the rescue of her sister, which she pursues with something like heroism, and which she never loses sight of.

Some time ago I wrote a review of the published text of the play, in which I argued that it seeks to seduce its audience into accepting uncritically certain stereotypes about men and women: the entire action hinges on the old binary code, male=active, female=passive. Male pride, it is revealed, drove Jacob away from the place where his father was humiliated by his boss, the fiancé's father. Jacob models his behaviour on Tom Mix whom he saw in a movie gallop into a church and rescue the bride from being married against her will. The implication is that the bride's will has no bearing either on the wedding or the rescue. Jacob's behaviour throughout the play is calculated and manipulative; Mary's is *given off* like the scent of her hair—the stage directions call for her to tremble and swallow hard when he comes near her, take an involuntary step towards him, etc. At the climax, Jacob walks away, and he waits offstage, and the audience waits, for Mary to "let out a cry that splits apart the night." Even her one significant action is controlled by him and given off by her. (89)

I also argued that the play takes for granted its audience's complicity in the assumptions underlying the plot; that is, that the performance of the play *constructs* a position for the spectator, a position that is assumed either to be male, or to accept the male perspective as natural. [2] However, the simple position I outlined in the review has become complicated by the fact—more and more evident as I read and reread the play—that within the text itself are contradictions, resistances, to the dominant reading it tends to elicit, resistances that can be foregrounded in performance.

A distinction Pierre Bourdieu makes between the *doxa* and *orthodoxy* is relevant here. The doxa consists of those schemes of thought and perception which produce such a perfect fit between the natural and social order that the latter simply "goes without saying." It "goes without saying" because it "comes without saying." Orthodoxy is that system of cultural assumptions which have to be proclaimed and asserted *because they are contested* (164–70). In this play, orthodox assumptions about the positioning of male and female are asserted vigorously by Jacob *because* of the quiet but persistent questioning that Mary voices. The position of the spectator is hence equally complex. A persistent invitation to view the female character from the traditional male perspective is subject to interruptions and contestations.

I am going to base my argument on close readings of certain passages. The first scene we will examine occurs late in the play. In it, Jacob and Mary argue over the meaning of an earlier scene. In that earlier scene, Jacob claimed to disbelieve that there was such a thing as a blue star. He persuaded Mary that if she showed him one, he would leave (a promise he had no intention of keeping). The business of being shown the star allowed him to stand close to her and breathe in the fragrance of her hair and more importantly gauge her reaction to his nearness:

> **JACOB:** Look me in the eye and tell me you loves him, and I'll walk
> out of this yard and never come back.
> **MARY:** You made one promise tonight you never kept. You can't be
> trusted.
> **JACOB:** Try me once more. Tell me you loves Jerome McKenzie, and
> you'll never see the dust of my feet again.
> **MARY:** All right, and I'm holding you to it. *She turns and stares straight
> at him. Slight pause.*
> **JACOB:** You can't say it, can you? *then* Can you?
> **MARY:** I loves him. There. I said it.
> **JACOB:** *Beat.* No odds. I don't believe you. *He walks away.*
> **MARY:** No, you wouldn't believe the Devil if he snuck up behind and
> jabbed you with his fork.

JACOB: That I wouldn't.

MARY: No. All you believes is what you wants to believe.

JACOB: No, I believes in what's real. I believes in a young girl trembling at my breath on her neck. That's what I believes in.

MARY: What young girl?

JACOB: There's only one in the yard that I can see.

MARY: And just when was I trembling?

JACOB: When? I'll tell you when. When you pointed out the blue star of Vega tonight, and I stood behind you. I could feel you shaking under your dress like a young bride at the altar.

MARY: It's chilly out!

JACOB: Indeed it's not chilly out, or where's your shawl to?… Your heart was pounding, wasn't it? *then* Wasn't it?

MARY: Next you'll be telling me you could hear it.

JACOB: No, but I could see the pulse in your neck, Mary, beating like a tom-tom.

MARY: The Bible's got it all wrong. It's not the women who are the vain ones, it's the men.

Slight pause.

JACOB: You ought to wear yellow more often, maid. It really do become you. Suits your black hair and fair complexion. (58–61)

Mary is the object of a gaze that appropriates her and interprets her gestures and involuntary movements. Jacob has the key, he decodes. She resists this appropriation, with alternative explanations of her behaviour, which he dismisses, and a critical revision of the Bible, which he ignores. He reasserts the primacy of the male gaze, its power over her, with instructions on how she should look. When he speaks of her body trembling under her dress, "like a young bride at the altar," he is in effect telling her that her sexual desire is his property, not hers. The reference to the tom-tom connotes primitive, irrational "jungle" means of communication: the implied comparison is with his command of language and her exclusion from language. What Mary says, especially what she says she wants to do, is subject to appeal to the higher authority of the male gaze. *It* determines "what's real."

As I said a moment ago, this scene is a narrated and interpreted replay of the telescope scene early in the play. At that time Jacob himself does not interpret Mary's behaviour, or comment on it, unless to foreground her pauses and unfinished sentences; hence it is the spectator whose interpretative activity is called on and is presumed to be based on the same ideological premise as Jacob's interpretation in the scene we just examined. That is, inscribed in the text is the assumption that the audience already knows how to look at a woman.

One particular stage direction makes this very clear. This occurs at the moment Mary catches sight of the silk stockings Jacob has brought her from Toronto:

MARY says nothing. She takes an involuntary step and stops. From the look on her face you'd be hard-pressed to know whether she liked the stockings,

> *except for one thing: she can't keep her eyes off them. She stands several yards from JACOB, staring almost quizzically at his outstretched arm.* (50)

That is, the audience is assumed to interpret Mary's behaviour in exactly the way Jacob does. Quite consistently throughout the play, Jacob's objectives are shared with the audience, while Mary's objectives are subject to Jacob's and the audience's shared access to codes which permit "us" to read the primarily visual signs involuntarily given off by Mary. Jacob's objectives belong to him, while Mary's objectives seem to belong to the viewer. That is to say, the issue of the male gaze, which is central to the body of film criticism I referred to, is also central to this play.

It's significant that the play starts with Mary alone on the stage in a series of still poses that allow her to be looked at as an icon of feminine beauty. Then Jacob enters unnoticed, and for several seconds we watch Jacob watching Mary. It seems to me that this cues the audience as to who does the looking and who gets looked at. The same thing happens at the crux. After Jacob has left the stage, ostensibly never to return, we watch and wait, exactly as Jacob is watching and waiting offstage, for Mary to cry out his name. That is, the play is written in such a way as to conflate the two gazes, the one in the dramatic fiction, and the one in the auditorium. The latter is modelled on the former. After a pause, in which Mary is perfectly still, that is, composed as a picture to be looked at, Jacob returns and gazes at Mary for several seconds before she is aware of his presence. It is significant that this paradigm, consisting of the active male gaze and the passive female recipient of the gaze, begins the play and is repeated at the crux.

Twice Mary is alone on the stage. On both occasions she is silent for the most part. The stage directions call for her to assume poses that allow her simply to be looked at. At the beginning of the play "she sits on the front step. Once standing, she "peers at the sky through the telescope." Hearing Jacob's voice "she faces that direction, listening intently"; "she stands riveted to the spot"; "she resumes her study of the stars" (9–10). This last is the pose she holds as she is the object of Jacob's gaze. At the crux of the play, she is more active: after Jacob has left the stage, she tries to sing a verse of a song "defiantly"; then her feelings well up *against her will* (once again her real feelings are involuntary and are known by virtue of the spectator's interpretative activity); then she cries out Jacob's name; and then:

> *MARY stands looking down the road, her eyes straining to see, her eyes almost listening… but there is only the empty road, the moonlight, the silence…. She composes herself and returns to the porch step. She sits gazing at some middle distance, absently turning her engagement ring on her finger.*

> *At that moment JACOB walks quietly back onto the road, still carrying his suitcase, his fedora cocked at a jaunty angle. There is no grin on his face, however, as he stands staring at MARY for a long moment, waiting for her to notice him…. Finally, she does. She rises, but remains standing on the porch, looking at him.* (80)

The difference between the two poses is revealing. Mary's gaze is passive. Resigned, she gazes into the middle distance; her inaction permits her to be watched; her passivity allows her to be "looked at"—by the audience, and, the audience knows, by Jacob offstage. (Laura Mulvey refers to this characteristic form of representation of women as "to-be-looked-at-ness" [19].) Jacob, on the other hand, stands still and stares at Mary to *make her notice him.* It is a gesture implying an action, not a passive pose. Man does, woman is, as the saying goes. Finally, Mary returns the gaze; but here also, certain cultural codes determine how we "read" the two gazes. "She rises, but remains standing on the porch, looking at him," that is, waiting for something to be done, by him, not her. Jacob's silent gaze, on the other hand, again is a gesture indicating purposive action, which is to stretch out Mary's suspense. And it is up to him to break it with the line, "You had me worried there. I t'ought for a minute you wasn't going to call" (80).

Jacob is alone on the stage once, earlier in the play, after Mary has gone into the house and has slammed the door. But the difference between his behaviour when alone and hers is worth noting. There is a "slight pause," and then Jacob swings into action, taking one tack after another to get her to come back out. He knocks, he calls, he invites her to look at the moon, he tells a funny off-colour story, he invites her to consider the fact that he is making enough disturbance to wake up the village, and the corpse at the wake, he warns her that he is not going to budge until her employers and her fiancé arrive, and what are they going to think, he begins to sing one of those rowdy folksongs about a wedding celebration, more and more loudly, until "the door bursts open, and MARY comes striding out" (49). No "to-be-looked-at-ness" here. Unlike Mary when alone, he is engaged in constant purposive action, and the audience is not so much looking at him as they are watching him watch the door.

We should also take note of the fact that Mary is dressed to be looked at by a man. She is wearing a short-sleeved yellow satin dress and is lightly made up. Her bare arms are on display for her fiancé, whom she is expecting. The text several times calls attention to how she looks in the dress. For example Jacob says at one point that sarcasm doesn't become her whereas the yellow dress does (16). That is, her active resistance to Jacob's wooing is unbecoming, while her passive self-display in the yellow dress becomes her. To complete the ensemble, and to make her even more to-be-looked-at, Jacob has brought her two pairs of silk stockings from Eaton's in Toronto. Here too the audience is implicated: if Mary is on display for men to look at with pleasure, so is the actress playing Mary. Laura Mulvey relates this objectification of the woman to an unconscious struggle to neutralize the threat of castration always inherent in her sexual difference from the man (21). Here Jacob continually reassures himself with reminders that Mary herself has sought to transform herself into an object of a male viewer's visual pleasure.

The telescope figures prominently in the play, at one level simply as a stage metaphor for the activity of looking. At another level it is implicated in the politics of the gaze. For the first twenty-one pages of text, the telescope is in Mary's hands. Then Mary thrusts it in Jacob's hands and challenges him to find for himself the blue star they have been arguing about. When she tries to retrieve the telescope, Jacob will not give it back, and for the next thirty-six pages of text it is in his hands or at least not back in Mary's. (The text does not indicate at what point Jacob lays it down, although he still has it in his hands on page 45.) On page 69, Mary picks it up, and it is in her possession for the remaining fourteen pages of text. This small detail underscores the nature of the struggle between Jacob and Mary: he displays his possession of the telescope as a sign of his possession of the power of the gaze: she contests this appropriation. Or we might say that as long as Jacob has the telescope it signifies the phallus and Mary's empty hands signify the lack of the phallus and the threat of castration posed by woman. In Mary's hands it disrupts this identification of the phallus and hence of power with man. Whether it does so in the first few moments of the play, however, before Mary is aware of Jacob's presence, is questionable. On the one hand, she is actively seeking knowledge about the stars: in other words she could be seen as a strong active subject pursuing her own project of self-improvement. On the other hand, she is expecting Jerome McKenzie to turn up at any moment, and it is he who has been *teaching* her astronomy: in other words, once that piece of exposition has been accomplished, we could reinterpret her pose as a mark of submission to the power of a man. *To be seen* by Jerome in this pose would convey the old sexual double entendre: "teach me tonight." There is no question, however, that we will see her submit herself to Jacob as she has been intending to submit herself to Jerome. In the course of the play, the telescope comes to signify a struggle between Mary and Jacob over who has the power to gaze at whom, that is, a struggle over who is to be recognized as a subject, not an object.

In this light it makes perfect sense that the play ends in silence with the two figures staring intently at each other. Although Jacob assumes that as a man he is privileged to look at Mary and that her position is to be the receiver of his gaze, Mary's contradictory assertion of her subjectivity is never stronger than at the end of the play. Again, a close look at the text will prove rewarding. (The "Rose of Sharon" Mary will mention is the girl Jacob may or may not have gone out with in Toronto.)

> *JACOB kneels down in the yard and unties the rope on the suitcase. He looks over at MARY*
> **JACOB:** Don't be fooled by appearances, Mary. I've got more than songs up my sleeve. I've got your future and mine, all neatly folded on top of my plaid shirts and diamond socks. *He lifts the top of the suitcase and removes a pair of silk stockings, draping them over his arm.* All you have to do, Mary, is reach out, and old Bob can rest tonight with a grin on his face. *then* Well?
> **MARY:** *Beat.* What about my sister? Are you forgetting her?
> **JACOB:** I'm not forgetting.
> *MARY rises from the step. She crosses slowly into the road, but remains well away from JACOB. She stands looking out front as though her eyes are on a distant star. Finally, she speaks.*
> **MARY:** *Evenly, with great seriousness.* In the years to come, Jacob Mercer—and this is no idle t'reat, mind—in the years to come, if

you ever mentions Rose of Sharon, even in your sleep, I'll make
you regret the night you knelt in this yard with those stockings in
your hand and the moon for a witness. Do you understand me?
She turns and stares at JACOB. Do you?
JACOB smiles up at the serious face of this lovely young girl. His
smile becomes a grin until it is splitting his face from ear to ear. (83)

This is complex. Jacob stares at Mary, demanding that she receive his gaze and *their*
future which *he* is holding in *his* hands. She appears to comply, staring out front
at nothing, tacitly accepting both Jacob's gaze and the audience's. But what she says
contradicts the passiveness of the pose. Just before assuming the pose she has
demanded Jacob's assent to her project: "What about my sister? Are you forgetting
her?" And she has ignored the seductive silk stockings. Gazing as if at a distant star she
demands respect for herself, and follows up the verbal demand by turning and staring
at Jacob, demanding a response from him. The last moment of the play is equivocal.
Jacob responds with a smile that broadens into a grin—is it a grin of triumph? joy?
mischief?—while Mary continues to gaze intently and seriously at him. [3] The
resistance *in the text* to the orthodox positioning of male and female subjects is
evident in this passage, and even more so in the scene we are going to examine next.

In it, Jacob piques Mary's interest by hinting that he had a girl in Toronto whom
he took to the picture show. Mary has never been to a picture show. Jacob "takes" her
to one right there on the front step.

> **JACOB:** Look, will you sit down and watch the picture? This is one of
> the best Tom ever made. He rides right into a wedding chapel and
> snatches the bride from under the nose of the groom. *He grins.*
> **MARY:** I suppose you finds that funny?
> **JACOB:** It made me stand up, maid, and cheer.
> **MARY:** That's the most brazen t'ing I ever heard of. Why did he do it
> in the first place?
> **JACOB:** Why? Cause the girl was being married against her will, why
> else. Tom rode to the rescue.
> **MARY:** What if she *wasn't* marrying against her will? What then?
> **JACOB:** Then there would've been no picture. Besides, she had to be
> getting married against her will. If you saw the slouch of a bride
> groom, you wouldn't have to ask.
> **MARY:** No odds. He might be full of himself, this… this Mr. Tom Mix,
> but that don't give him the right to barge in and take what's not
> his.
> **JACOB:** Go on with you. Sure, even the horse looked pleased. He stood
> there on the carpet, Tony, all sleek and smug. Tom was sitting in
> the saddle, clutching the bride on his hip, the train of her gown
> brushing the floor. All eyes was on Tom. The Maids of Honour in
> their summer hats all gazed up at him, puzzled, and the minister
> looked on with his t'umb in the Bible, waiting to see what

> happened next.
>
> **MARY:** What did the groom do? I suppose he just stood by and never lifted a finger?
>
> **JACOB:** What could he do, the fool, against the likes of Tom Mix? He raised himself to his full height and gave Tom a dirty look, and Tom gazed right back down at him with that little smirk on his lips, as much as to say, "Too bad, buddy. Better luck next time." *Slight pause.*
>
> **MARY:** Well, Tom Mix had best climb back on his horse and ride off into the night. This is one bride he won't be stealing.
>
> **JACOB:** No?
>
> **MARY:** No. And he better ride off soon, too, before Mr. and Mrs. Dawe return from the wake.
>
> **JACOB:** Nobody puts the run on Tom Mix.
>
> **MARY:** Tom Mix is a fool. (67–69)

There are some interesting things going on in this scene. Within the fiction as Jacob describes it, it is very clear that certain powerful stereotypes about gender are at work. Tom Mix is active, the bride is passive. Although the bride is rescued from being married against her will, her will is not consulted: all the viewer has to do is to compare Tom Mix and the bridegroom to understand all *he* needs to know about the bride's will. "She had to be getting married against her will. If you saw the slouch of a bridegroom, you wouldn't have to ask." But Mary dissects the relation between the illusion of the film and the viewer. Even before the "film" starts, Jacob has formed a complete identification with Tom Mix. Tom Mix has become the imaginary ideal image in which the (male) spectator completes himself (Mulvey 20). Before Jacob describes Tom's gaze with the little smirk on his lips he describes practicing it on the fellow sitting in front of him at the picture show. And indeed he has modelled his behaviour throughout the play on "The King of the Cowboys." In fact we see the identification process taking place in this passage. Whereas the element of voyeurism is evident in the description of the look appropriating the bride's subjectivity, it is obvious that Jacob's subjectivity merges with that of Tom Mix... as Mary instantly recognizes: she understands perfectly that when Jacob says "all eyes was on Tom" he is imagining all eyes on himself. The position of the spectator of the play here, I venture, is quite contrary to what it is elsewhere. Here the spectator is not solicited to view Mary through Jacob's eyes, but exactly the reverse; here the orthodox viewing position is being deconstructed rather than constructed. Very odd. This scene is a perfect illustration of Laura Mulvey's argument that the viewer of the classic Hollywood film is constructed in such a way as to identify with the "male gaze" within the narrative: that is, that the form of representation in the fiction film codes the viewer as male. Mary's resistance to the assumption that the bride's "will" in the matter can be known entirely through the male gaze—a "resistant reading"[4] of the film text—runs into a brick wall.

> **MARY:** What if she wasn't marrying against her will? What then?
>
> **JACOB:** Then there would've been no picture.

The connotation here is that woman's will, woman's subjectivity, is unrepresentable within the conventions of narrative film.

This is oddly like the most far-reaching form of the argument I have just sketched in, which is that in Western culture, all forms of representation rest on the objectification of women: this is the argument Jeanie Forte makes in a study of women's performance art:

> As a deconstructive strategy, women's performance art is a discourse of the objectified other.... This deconstruction hinges on the awareness that "Woman," as object, as a culturally constructed category, is actually the basis of the Western system of representation. Woman constitutes the position of object, a position of other in relation to a socially-dominant male subject; it is that "otherness" which makes representation possible (the personification of male desire). Precisely because of the operation of representation, actual women are rendered an absence within the dominant culture, and in order to speak, must either take on a mask (masculinity, falsity, simulation, seduction), or take on the unmasking of the very opposition in which they are the opposed, the Other. (252)

Jacob's response also parallels the most provocative statement in Mulvey's essay, in which she states that the male desire to control castration anxiety by dominating and controlling the woman is the basis of narrative: "Sadism demands a story"[5] (Mulvey 22).

Curiouser and curiouser! This scene—a "found analysis" of the construction of the male gaze and the objectification of the woman—found inside the fictional world of the play—very accurately describes the mechanism by which this play constructs a viewing position for the audience in the theatre, a viewing position that "carries ideologically weighted gender markings" of maleness (Dolan 44). And, since this viewing position is contested, the potential for a powerful alienation-effect is there.

As I have implied throughout this essay, the process of constructing a male viewing position is most evident in the stage directions. Without going too far into the vexed question of the relative authority of dialogue and didascalia in the dramatic text, I can simply say that while the dialogue implicitly conveys a demand that this text be performed, the stage directions convey a demand that it be performed *in a certain manner.*[6] Throughout this text they call for the performer playing Mary to stand still to be looked at, to react involuntarily, or to act in such a way that the force of the act can be discounted. Thus, when Mary expresses exasperation at Jacob's flippant comment after she has called him back at the top of her voice, the stage directions read: "*She raises her elbow and clenches her fist in a parody of a threatening gesture. A gesture that is not coy but more the gesture of exasperation a woman might feel who is taken for granted*" (80). The gesture is to be played and interpreted as a womanly parody of a threatening gesture; that is, its force is reduced (but not too far, not to the point of being "coy"). It is further reduced in significance by Jacob's echo of the stage direction: "Now she makes a fist.... And such a little fist, too. Wouldn't bruise a hummingbird, let alone the King of the Cowboys" (81).

To return to the Tom Mix passage: it also alerts us to the fact that within the frame of the dramatic fiction, there is a resistance to the privileging of the dominant male subject: Mary's resistant reading of the Tom Mix film is but one of the subversive currents that run through the whole play, implicitly contradicting the conventional absence of female subjectivity within dramatic representation. This resistance, far more evident in the dialogue than in the stage directions, may well be reinforced by the fact that in any performance, the subjectivity of the actress playing Mary, *her* will and *her* desire, contradicts her presence on stage as simply an object of male desire. How this might work in performance is suggested indirectly by the comments of the black actress, Catherine Bruhier, who played Mary in the Theatre New Brunswick production of the play in 1989 (13–15). She says that while the production made no issue of the colour of one actor's skin, her own performance foregrounded lines in the text which "showed [Mary's] strength and desire to better herself," thus adding a subtext of struggle "to overcome not only poverty but oppression based on race." The actor's subjectivity thus can add a perspective that interrupts and contests an orthodox reading of the play, and can perhaps in Brechtian fashion produce a divided audience, one in which a woman and a man seated next to each other may have sharply different responses.

The contradiction we have been examining in the interaction between the characters is present thematically as well. The play is about wooing, but underneath that is the theme of courage and heroism. There are all sorts of variations on it, from the Newfoundland regiment charging over the top in terrible crossfire to the ridiculous warcry "Jennie Saunders or a wooden leg" to the bravado of a boy showing off to his date at the pictures by sticking his feet on the back of the seat in front and staring down the fellow who objects, just like The King of the Cowboys. All the models are male. When Mary seeks a model of courage to inspire her sister Dot, who is being bullied by the Matron of the orphanage, she takes her to look at Tommy Ricketts the druggist:

> I pointed out the drugstore where Tommy Ricketts was now the druggist, and we went inside and looked at him. He had the shyest smile and the kindest eyes, and him so brave in the War. The youngest soldier in the British Army to win a Victoria Cross.... Once outside, I told Dot who he was, and how she had to be like him. Brave like him and Father, only brave in a different way. I told her the matron was a coward, and like all cowards, I said, she was cruel, so the next time she puts her foot on you, Dot, I said, don't make a sound: don't even cry out, 'cause she'll only grind her heel into you all the harder. Just look into her eyes, I said, and let her know that no odds how often she knocks you down, no odds how hard she steps on you, the one t'ing she'll never destroy is your spirit. And maybe, just maybe she'd stop doing it, 'cause it's a funny t'ing, I said, about cruel people like the Matron, they only respects one

kind of person in the long run, and that's the ones they can't break....
(74–5)

Mary's advice to her sister depends on a male model of what it is to be courageous. Mary counsels Dot to exhibit a different kind of bravery. Endure, don't whimper, and look the tormentor in the eye. She advocates a passive version of the bravery of the war hero. That is to say, male courage is translated into a secondary, feminine copy.

Which is emphatically not acceptable for men or by men. Jacob's father is cruelly treated by Will McKenzie. But it does not seem to be an option for Jacob's father the war hero to look Mr. McKenzie in the eye and let him know that he cannot destroy his spirit. Destroy it he does, to the extent that Jacob's father cannot bear to look anybody in the eye, and Jacob cannot bear to live in the same country where such a thing could be done to a man, and abandons Mary without a word of farewell since he cannot bear to speak to her about it. Significantly, what Mr. McKenzie did to make Jacob's father fill out his contracted time as a hired-on fisherman when there were no fish to be caught was to make him rock an empty cradle on the front porch of the McKenzie house.

Is the play critical of the stereotypical male courage? Maybe.... Certainly Mary mocks the bravado Jacob displayed before another man when he had an excruciating toothache (21–22). But, more to the point: are we invited to draw a parallel between Jim Snow, Mary's father, marching off to war and leaving his wife behind, and Jacob Mercer leaving the island and Mary without looking back? In both cases it's the idea that "a man's gotta do what a man's gotta do" that drives them, while the women are helpless to stop them, and have no option but to suffer.

The important point here is that the shadow of the Great War looms over a play set in 1926. The raw memories of the war have contradictory connotations. On the one hand, the Newfoundlanders who died in the battle of Beaumont Hamel seem to be admired for their bravery, not wondered at for obeying insane orders. Jacob's description of the destruction of the Newfoundland Regiment on 1 July 1916 is deeply moving:

> Out of seven hundred and fifty men, only forty not dead or wounded... one regiment after another was wiped out—the Royal Dublin Fusiliers, the Border Regiment, the Essex. And then it came the Newfoundlanders' turn. Colonel Hadow walked twenty yards forward and gave the signal. The Captain blew the whistle, and the men went over the top, heading straight into the German cross-fire, knowing they was walking alone t'rough the long grass of No Man's Land into certain death. Not a single man flinched or looked back, just kept on walking in perfect drill formation, the sun glinting off their bayonets... all the observers noticed that day as the Newfoundland Regiment walked into the storm of machine-gun bullets and mortar shells: how all the soldiers to a man tucked their chins into their forward shoulders like sailors leaning into a gale of wind... (36–37)

On the other hand, the play contradicts its own celebration of male bravery in conveying the terrible cost of Jim Snow's useless sacrifice, multiplied seven hundred-fold. Mary's mother still sets a place for her husband at her table. Mary had to go into service and her sister Dot had to be placed in an orphanage because their widowed mother was too devastated by her loss to care for them: "When Father was killed, she'd slip into those queer moods that still haven't left her. Moods that last for weeks on end, staring at the floor, forgetting to comb her hair…" (25). In the Mercer family, Jacob began working at age ten because his father had gone off to war. Perhaps the scale of the devastation of the lives of women and children implies a critical perspective on male bravery.

In conclusion: I have argued that the form of representation in *Salt-Water Moon* is deeply complicit with orthodox codes which determine what it *means* to be male or female. These orthodox codes elicit an orthodox reading by an audience that is assumed either to be male or to accept a male viewing position as natural and universal. But, I have also argued, these solicitations are contested within the text, thus opening up the possibility of a resistant reading. Reviews offer the most accessible source of information on how spectators may respond to this contradictory weave of solicitations and disruptions. Robert Crew, for example, described Denise Naples' performance of Mary Snow thus: "[Naples' Mary was] feisty and iron-willed, a determined little chit of a thing." The diminution of "iron will" by the epithets "little," "chit" and "thing" (not to mention his description of the character as "steely little Mary") exactly echoes similar processes in the dialogue and the stage directions. Crew's outline of the plot similarly suggests what an unquestioning acceptance of the solicitation to view the play from a masculinist position might look like:

> [Mary] apparently wants nothing to do with Jacob. But we, the audience, know otherwise. The physical attraction is still there and Jacob will charm his way back into her heart and carry her off, just as Tom Mix does in the cowboy movie that Jacob tells her about. There is no tension here—her despairing cry of "Jacob!" will be answered.

In contrast, Marianne Ackerman's review of the Centaur Theatre production in Montreal suggests how a viewer (whether male or female) might produce a complex reading, responding both to the invitation to view the play from an orthodox male position, and to the resistance in text and especially in performance to that invitation. Thus, on the one hand she writes:

> For those who've not yet recognized language and wit as the most seductive weapons known to man, the 90 minutes that follow will be a thoroughly entertaining lesson in the art of successful talk.

It is "man" who knows how to use language and wit as a weapon to seduce the implied "woman." And the audience, women equally with men, will receive a lesson in how things are, a seductive lesson because "thoroughly entertaining." Yet later in the review, Ackerman writes:

> Lucy Peacock's Mary is a wonderful answer to Jacob's dancing wit. Innocence and strength combine to equal, sometimes surpass, the surprises rolling off Jacob's lightning tongue.

The mention of Mary's strength is not immediately qualified by epithets that discount it. The "lesson" seductively conveyed about man's ownership of language as a weapon is contradicted by an equally strong "lesson" about the strength of a woman. The reviews of the 1989 production at Theatre New Brunswick likewise suggest how a performance text may interrupt a simple identification of the viewer's position as masculine. We have seen that Catherine Bruhier wished to bring out Mary's strength and her struggle against oppression. We can assume that Sharon Pollock, who directed, shared and reinforced this concern. Anne Ingram, writing in the Fredericton *Daily Gleaner,* describes Mary as a "tough, feisty 17-year-old" and goes on to say "Miss Bruhier managed to reveal the streak of toughness and determination in the innocent servant girl." Jo Anne Claus, in the Moncton *Telegraph-Journal,* writes:

> Director Sharon Pollock maintained a strong tension at all times between the two young people. Catherine Bruhier, a New Brunswick actress from Saint John, played Mary as a passionate young girl with a steel core… Eric McCormack as Jacob has poetry and comedy to make him charming.

The extent to which this production may have disrupted a masculinist reading is suggested by the interesting switch in epithets conventionally assigned to men and women: it is Mary who is steely, Jacob who has charm.

As the reviews we have examined imply, the play, both as text and performance, is a tissue of contradictions, the site of a struggle between the construction of a privileged male spectator and a deconstructive analysis of "him." Equally it is a text which represents a woman as the object of a man's gaze and a man's desire, yet contradicts this with a representation of a woman as a subject in her own right, desiring, and in the last few moments of the play returning the gaze with interest. It is possible in performance to completely assimilate the resistant reading I have outlined into an old-fashioned love story, fashioned, that is, in the old narrative pattern: boy overcomes all resistance, especially girl's, to get her in the end. Otherwise, as Jacob might say, there would've been no play. Sheila Rabillard makes this point eloquently in a letter to me:

> I guess my only real worry about this paper is that it seems (at least as I understand it) almost too optimistic in its reading of the liberating function of the resistance to the masculine point of view you see in *Salt-Water Moon.* Can't the incorporation of an opposing voice within a larger structure still left standing serve to strengthen the encompassing structure that can contain it? (Like Mary's gesture with her clenched fist, which becomes read as a mark of her relative weakness, not her strength?) In terms of plot, the resistance of the heroine can serve not to inscribe her subjectivity but rather to add to the spice of pursuit and

conquest for the hero (and the male viewer who identifies with him). From this perspective, the bride whom Tom Mix snatches from the altar is not only an image of female passivity but also a metaphorical rape victim, her stimulating resistance indicated by the holy and virginal setting from which she is abducted. Of course, she is an unwilling bride who really wants to be carried off from her wedding by the hero; but that is another aspect of the masculine rape fantasy—that the woman underneath her resistance wants to be taken. In short, I am not disagreeing with your analysis of the several productions of the play that managed to read *Salt-Water Moon* against the grain of the stage direction…; I'm really just trying to say that woman's subjectivity perhaps enters this play *only* by such means, and that the "resistance" in the speeches the text gives Mary is one that in fact collaborates in the processes of the male gaze, in the narrative of masculine pursuit and conquest.[7]

The last word on this question does not belong in the pages of a scholarly journal but on the stage, in performances which, like that of Catherine Bruhier, might give the resistance in the text an autonomy, a story of its own to tell. The possibility exists, I believe, that a production of *Salt-Water Moon* might feature not one subject but two.

(1991)

Notes

[1] See the discussion of Rina Fraticelli's 1982 report on *The Status of Women in the Canadian Theatre* in Lushington.

[2] Mulvey refers to "the 'masculinisation' of the spectator position" (29).

[3] A very different reading of this passage is possible. One of the readers of this essay in his or her report writes: "Of crucial importance is the fact that she says explicitly her primary concern is her rivalry with Rose of Sharon. What greater homage to pay to a man in a patriarchal world than for a woman to say that her greatest concern is her rivalry with another woman? As long as this is the case, he is in complete control."

[4] The term is borrowed from Fetterley.

[5] See also de Lauretis, "Desire in Narrative," in *Alice Doesn't* 134–57.

[6] See Ubersfeld: "le théâtre dit moins une parole que comment on peut ou l'on ne peut pas parler. Toutes les couches textuelles (didascalies + éléments didascaliques

dans le dialogue) qui définissent une situation de communication des personnages, déterminant les conditions d'énonciation de leurs discours, ont pour fonction non pas seulement de *modifier le sens* des messages—dialogues mais de *constituer des messages autonomes,* exprimant le rapport entre les discours, et les possibilités ou impossibilités des rapports interhumains" (230–31).

[7]   I am grateful to Sheila Rabillard for permitting me to quote from her letter.

Works Cited

Ackerman, Marianne. "*Salt-Water Moon* Shines Bright at Centaur." *Montreal Gazette* 9 November 1984: Fl.

Bennett, Susan. *Theatre Audiences: A Theory of Production and Reception.* London: Routledge, 1990.

Bourdieu, Pierre. *Outline of a Theory of Practice.* Trans. Richard Nice. Cambridge UP, 1977.

Bruhier, Catherine. "Darkness Visible: A Multiracial *Salt-Water Moon.*" *Theatrum* 20 (1990): 13–15.

Canada on Stage 1982–1986. Toronto: PACT Communications Centre, 1989.

Case, Sue-Ellen. *Feminism and Theatre.* London: Macmillan, 1988.

_____, ed. *Performing Feminisms: Feminist Critical Theory and Theatre.* Baltimore: Johns Hopkins UP, 1990.

Claus, Jo Anne. "Newest TNB Hit Charms Audience." Moncton *Telegraph-Journal* 1 December 1989.

Crew, Robert. "Charming *Salt-Water Moon* Crafted to Win People's Hearts." *Toronto Star* 3 October 1984.

de Lauretis, Teresa. *Alice Doesn't: Feminism, Semiotics, Cinema.* Bloomington: Indiana UP, 1984.

Dolan, Jill. *The Feminist Spectator as Critic.* Ann Arbor: UMI Research, 1988.

Fetterley, Judith. *The Resisting Reader: A Feminist Approach to American Fiction.* Bloomington: Indiana UP, 1978.

Forte, Jeanie. "Women's Performance Art: Feminism and Postmodernism." *Performing Feminisms: Feminist Critical Theory and Theatre.* Baltimore: Johns Hopkins UP, 1990. 251–67.

French, David. *Salt-Water Moon.* Vancouver: Talonbooks, 1988.

Ingram, Anne. "*Saltwater Moon*—Great Play, Well-Acted, Don't Miss It." Fredericton *Daily Gleaner* 16 December 1989.

Kaplan, E. Ann. *Women and Film*. London: Methuen, 1983.

Lushington, Kate. "Fear of Feminism." *Canadian Theatre Review* 43 (1985): 5–11.

Mulvey, Laura. "Visual Pleasure and Narrative Cinema." *Screen* 16.3 (1975): 6–18. Rpt. *Visual and Other Pleasures*. Bloomington: Indiana UP, 1989. 14–26.

Nunn, Robert. "*Salt-Water Moon, Jennie's Story* and *Under the Skin*." *Canadian Theatre Review* 60 (1989): 89–90.

Rabillard, Sheila. Letter to the author. 1 July 1991.

Silverman, Kaja. *The Subject of Semiotics*. New York: Oxford UP, 1983.

Ubersfeld, Anne. *Lire le Théâtre*. 4e ed. Paris: Éditions Sociales, 1982.

AnOther Story: Women's Dramaturgy and the Circulation of Cultural Values at Mulgrave Road

by Ric Knowles

In an essay first published in 1978 Teresa de Lauretis called for "a feminist theory of textual production" that was neither a "theory of women's writing nor just a theory of textuality," but was instead a theory of "women as subjects—not commodities but social beings producing and reproducing cultural products, transmitting and trans- forming cultural values" (92–93). It is neither my purpose nor my place to propose such a theory, but it may be useful to examine some of the ways in which women as subjects and social beings—theatre workers, community members, and audiences— have engaged in the production, transmission, and transformation of cultural values in the limited context of a small rural theatre company, the Mulgrave Road Co-op Theatre in Guysborough, Nova Scotia, since its founding in 1977. In doing so, I want to suggest that these women, both individually and as a group, have constructed what de Lauretis calls "a new practice and vision of the relation between subject and modes of textual production" (92). They have developed one model through which Maritime women, as theatre workers and as audiences, can take possession of their cultural (re)production, including the construction of gender.

Mulgrave Road is not a women's theatre company. It was founded as a collective in 1977 by three men—Michael Fahey, Robbie O'Neill, and Wendell Smith—and only one woman—Gay Hauser. Rather, it is a touring company dedicated to producing new work by Nova Scotians about the Maritimes, primarily north-eastern Nova Scotia. Nevertheless, and although its organizational structure has varied over the years, the co-op is dedicated to operating collectively and by consensus, and as Cindy Cowan, one of its best-known playwrights, has suggested, this has made the company congenial to many women theatre workers in a way that theatres in the region with more traditional administrative structures have not been ("Messages" 105).[1]

Women's dramaturgy began at Mulgrave Road in 1977 with a monologue and song created and performed by Gay Hauser in the company's first production, a collective creation called *The Mulgrave Road Show*. In the middle of a show she created with Fahey, O'Neill, and Smith, in which Hauser herself and the women of the community's past and present that she represented played primarily supporting roles, the actor used the now familiar image of the quilt in a song that was woven into the narrative form of a woman's monologue about loneliness and isolation. Alone on stage and the centre of focus for the only time in the show, Hauser sat with an old quilt in her lap, and as she told her story she punctuated it with verses of a song about a quilt "of a thousand pieces," of "moments sewn in heartache/Cuttings joined in joy and pain." The song, the speech, and the image of quilting created, according to Cindy Cowan, "a powerful moment of recognition for any woman watching in the audience" ("Messages" 106).

This moment worked more or less as an intervention in *The Mulgrave Road Show* itself and the community history it presented, first to deconstruct the conventional and condescending distinction between arts (including theatre) and crafts (including quilting), a division which privileges the former term and relegates to secondary status much of the cultural production of women. Secondly, Hauser's intervention modeled further interventions by herself and other Co-op women in the operations of the theatre company itself, together with interventions by the women of the company and the town in the life of the community. Finally, as the quilting metaphor has done for other communities of rural women (notably as represented in Donna Smyth's 1982 novel, *Quilt*[2]), its use in this scene may be seen to figure forth for Mulgrave Road the communal creativity of women in rural Nova Scotia.

With this monologue, in fact, Gay Hauser initiated a pattern of cultural intervention and cultural production that served to shape the creation and structure of a broad range of women's plays that have emerged at Mulgrave Road in subsequent years.[3] Included in that pattern is an informal but interdependent kind of networking over the course of many productions, in which women who took part in one women's collective creation, scripted play, workshop, or other project,[4] eventually produce or initiate the production of their own play, often involving the company women from the earlier shows, workshops or working groups. Cowan suggests, moreover, that "what gives strength to the women in the Mulgrave Road Co-op is the attempt they have made to build upon each other's work from year to year. Picking up where the last woman left off, they have incorporated the last "message" or experience and attempted to go one step further in developing plays for women" ("Messages" 105).

In any case, all of the women who have eventually emerged from the Co-op as playwrights, including Mary Vingoe, Cindy Cowan, Carol Sinclair, Jenny Munday, and Mary Colin Chisholm, had previously been involved with other Co-op women in collective creations and/or scripted plays by women, and this pattern is often reflected in diachronic series of intertexts among the shows, as well as structural reflections and parallels in what seems to be an evolving women's dramaturgy at Mulgrave Road.

Because of the unique material conditions shaping the production of theatre in Guysborough County, moreover, there is also a kind of parallel synchronic process involved in any one production. There's not much else to do in Guysborough when a show is in rehearsal. The population is just over 500, there is only one real restaurant (closed much of the time during the off-season—that is, the theatre season), and the Legion Hall houses the town's only bar. The result is that the rehearsal hall itself, which, together with the usual collection of musical instruments assembled for a show, contains a small kitchen, tape decks, and other comforts, usually becomes a focal unit and social centre outside of scheduled rehearsal hours, where parties and informal get-togethers frequently include both resident and visiting theatre professionals and members of the community. Not surprisingly, conversations tend to revolve around the current project. Individual shows, then, evolve through an intensely focused creation-and-rehearsal process in which a group of theatre workers engage in concentrated interaction with one-another and with the community through an extended period of creative isolation and immersion. As Jan Kudelka said in an interview about her production of *Another Story* (from which this essay takes its title), "the positive thing about collective drama is that when it works in a community, you end up getting a bonding sense with that community."

Theatre workers in Guysborough are either part of the community in and about which they write—Gay Hauser and Cindy Cowan lived and raised their families there, and Jenny Munday remained in the town for a time when after her stint as artistic director ended—or, more often, are billeted with local residents throughout the workshop and rehearsal processes, often with the same people over several shows. This has resulted in a number of close and long-standing friendships among women of the Co-op and the town, friendships which, finally, are a part of the production and reproduction of theatre, and of cultural values, at Mulgrave Road and in Guysborough County. In its most immediate form, this results in the representation of women from the community as characters in the plays, representations such as Mary Colin Chisholm's portrait of a prominent Guysborough citizen, Co-op Society member, and friend, in her play *Safe Haven*, a character actually performed by the playwright in the revival at the Blyth Festival, Ontario, in 1993. More significantly, however, as Gay Hauser suggests, the ways in which women's plays are produced at the Co-op repro-duce the social interaction of the women that are the plays' subjects and audience. Portraying these women theatrically, she claims, reinforces "bonding" *within* the company. "Rural women aren't aggressive," she continues "What gives them strength is their friendships, their open dependence on each other, and their community. The result is if they need to mobilize to help each other they can do so quickly" (qtd. in Cowan, "Messages" 106–107). [5]

I have suggested that "women's plays" at Mulgrave Road incorporate an inter-connected and associative range of intertexts among the plays themselves, to a degree that other plays that have been produced at Mulgrave Road do not. The pattern for this was set by the 1980 collective creation, *One on the Way*, the Co-op's first play created explicitly by and for women (with musicians Michael Fahey and Stephen Osler), which developed out of the original quilting monologue in *The Mulgrave Road Show*, and out of a workshop held by Gay Hauser at Guysborough Municipal High School. "Conceived," as the program says, by Gay Hauser, and created by director Svetlana Zylin and actors Mary Vingoe, Nicola Lipman, and Hauser herself (who was five months pregnant at the time), the play used an evocative associative structure to deal with social issues having to do with pregnancy and motherhood that were of direct concern to rural women in 1980; it contained echoes of and references to material from the earlier collective creations, *The Mulgrave Road Show* (1977), *Let's Play Fish* (1978), and *The Coady Co-op Show* (1979); and it also anticipated characters and situations that were later developed by, for example, Cindy Cowan in *Spooks* (1984), and Jan Kudelka and the company (including Cowan and Vingoe) in *Another Story* (1982), a collective creation about the daytime "soaps" and the women who watch them. These shows, in turn, inspired and were reflected in others, in an expanding intertextual (and intertextural) pattern that, among other things, insists on the *recognition* of work of all kinds performed by women, including creative work, and refuses to let it be lost (see Cowan, "Messages" 108).

The intertextuality of these productions derives directly from their *modes* of production, and it is typical of women's theatre at Mulgrave Road. It also combines with the productions' immediate and recognizable references to and reflections of their specific social and cultural contexts in Guysborough County to open the shows outward to the audience as community. It attempts, that is, to create an interactive dramaturgy in which the subject is at once writer, performer, and audience, and in which participation in the theatrical event functions as a constitutive act of the participant *as* subject. [6] Achieving their sense of authenticity from a structural grounding in shared experience, rather than from authenticating documents or objects, as in the documentary collective creations of companies such as Theatre Passe Muraille, or from shared prior political commitments as in the work of explicitly constructed Marxist or feminist collectives, these plays root themselves more fully than do most Canadian collective creations in the community that they share with their audiences. Moreover, they tend to function more fully as collectives, even on those occasions when one playwright officially fulfills what Foucault calls "the author function" (101–20).

I have been concerned to this point primarily with the social production and reproduction of cultural values in women's plays at Mulgrave Road, but, of course, what is in question is not simply the *transmission* of cultural values based on territorial (as opposed to relational) notions of community rooted in landscape and history, but their *transformation*, including the (re)construction of gender. [7] These plays are, of course, socially *produced*, performed *in* the world, but they are also socially *productive*. "Performed *upon* the world," as Louis Montrose has put it in reference to Renaissance theatre, "by gendered individual and collective human agents." Versions of society, of history, and of gender are instantiated, but they are also contested and, potentially, transformed (Montrose 23).

Transformation has been seen by feminist theatre critic Helene Keyssar not only as a theme, but as a frequently-employed structural principle in women's dramaturgy. In this formulation, transformation replaces the essentialist, universalist, and "affirmative," in Marcuse's sense (88–133), Aristotelian principles of reversal and recognition (of a pre-existing normative subject), with an activist encoding of the possibility of social change. It is possible to see a development in women's dramaturgy at Mulgrave Road of transformative modes of theatrical representation that not only reject traditionally self-contained patriarchal structures of linear narrative—reversal, recognition, and closure—but that also reproduce structurally and represent dramatically their own modes of production. Play after woman's play at

Mulgrave Road [8] experiments "interstructurally" with and around forms in which community, and the circulation of community values, serve as both subject matter and organizing principle. These plays are different from one another, and they employ different strategies for cultural intervention, but they also seem *structurally* to "quote" one another much in the same way as they contain networks of situational and linguistic intertexts.

A brief look at a few representative plays by Co-op women will show more clearly how they function. Each of these plays eschews mystification or mythologizing in favour of directly and explicitly addressing concrete historical and social situations;[9] each replaces focus on a single central character with a structure in which the community itself functions as hero(ine); each employs, in its own way, interwoven strands of story and lyrical expression rather than traditional linear narrative; and each explicitly or implicitly explores issues that are constructed as having to do with women's cultural production, or the production of women's culture.

Mary Vingoe's *Holy Ghosters, 1776* focuses on three strong women of three different cultures and generations at the precise historical moment of the Eddy rebellion and the battle that kept New Brunswick and Nova Scotia from becoming the fourteenth American colony. *Holy Ghosters* is typical of women's plays at the Co-op in that it is structured around an ensemble of actors playing a community of characters rather than around the story of its best-known (male) historical figure, Richard John Uniacke. In its first production the play was criticized for this by reviewers.[10] As Cindy Cowan remarks, "I suppose when you put a famous man on stage and then upstage him with three women you are inviting trouble" (Messages" 108). But, in fact, the replacement of a unified central story line with an overlapping narrative structure, built around four stories at various stages of development over the course of the action, can more usefully be seen as the production's characteristic strength than as a weakness. This innovative structure functions in *Holy Ghosters* to create, for the audience as well as the characters, a diachronic sense of community over time that reflects the play's own relationship to its dramatic predecessors at Mulgrave Road.[11] In spite of the almost overwhelming sense of displacement that is the experience of all the play's *characters*, Vingoe employs three basic devices to create for the *audience* an oddly reassuring sense of *constant* change: 1) the vagaries of a problematized historiography (the question of who controls the historical record is implicit throughout); 2) an evolving, ever-changing tidal marshland setting, a landscape swept by "the ever-wind"; and 3) a shifting sense of both territorial and relational community in a dramatic action in which allegiances are unstable and interests divided, as family and other units dissolve, fracture, and re-assemble throughout the play. The contemporary Nova Scotian audience discovers, then, in the experience of displacement that they share with the characters and with one another, an ironic but unsentimental sense of *continuity* over time. The play ends, moreover, with the promise of renewed community among the women, as its two central women share a baked potato dug from earth scorched by the victorious British troops. The conclusion leaves the audience with recognition of fragmentation and isolation as experiences that are or can be *shared*, a sense of dislocation that is also, ironically, *located*, as a "site" of potential change. [12]

Jenny Munday's *Battle Fatigue*, even more clearly than *Holy Ghosters*, sets out to recover women's history, and is based on extensive personal research on the experiences of women in World War II. Munday structures the play around envelopes of flashbacks to three time periods, and, like Vingoe, around an ensemble of actors doubling roles and acting out different but parallel stories. Both playwrights, moreover, portray the coming together of women of different backgrounds and sensibilities to frame the possibility—not always realized—of new or different kinds of community among women who have made different and apparently incompatible choices. Both plays, then, echo the experience of the groups of women from different backgrounds in the communities, theatrical and other, through which they were produced. *Battle Fatigue*, moreover, makes its potential for intervention in the contemporary culture of its audiences explicit by framing its historical action within a series of present-tense scenes in which a feminist daughter stands in for the audience, as she and we learn from her mother about the older woman's wartime past. As the play ends, mother, daughter, and audience become aware that "the point is… what do we do now?" (74).

Both *Holy Ghosters* and *Battle Fatigue* also move towards a characteristic of the "new textural form" called for by de Lauretis, in which "rational historical inquiry is continually intersected by the lyrical and the personal." Not only do both plays inter-cut the documented, historically verifiable "facts" with explorations of their subjective impact, [13] but they introduce lyrical passages, personal "arias" that problematize the historical and document what de Lauretis calls "the resonance of the (documented) historical event in the subject" (92). *Holy Ghosters*, for example, features a choric character, an ageless Acadian woman, Old Aboideaux, who wanders homeless on the marshes and whose Lear-like odes to wind and weather provide historical and poetic resonances even as the character embodies the direct and personal impact of abstract historical events such as the expulsion of the Acadians prior to the play's action. *Battle Fatigue* less clearly and less frequently employs the lyric mode—though scene-change songs are used effectively—but the play is full of subjective expression in personal narratives about the historical past that function as personal histories, or what might usefully be called "documentaries of subjectivity," recording, like *Holy Ghosters*, the material impact on people's lives of the abstractions of history.

Carol Sinclair's musical play *Idyll Gossip* moves still further away from the formal realm of historical documentary and further towards both lyrical expression, through song, and the explicit exploration of rural maritime women as producers and transformers of culture. This play also employs an ensemble of actors to portray a community as its central character, but more clearly than in any of the other plays under discussion, this one both partakes of and is *about* women's circulation of cultural values through the arts, and women's reclaiming of agency in the construc-tion of gender in the Maritimes. A metatheatrical musical created by Maritime women about Maritime women creating music, *Idyll Gossip* was inspired by stories of women such as Rita MacNeil, or the women of Mulgrave Road, who struggle against the overwhelming and functionally hegemonic resistance to women's participation in the performing arts within the conservative patriarchal culture of the rural Maritimes. The play's external action concerns itself with a group of rural women who form a band, gradually overcoming first their own and then their society's reluctance to take their musical aspirations and abilities seriously. However, the real life and energy of the play derive less from this narrative than from the songs that are performed by the women throughout, songs that demonstrate and assume the subjectivity of women as cultural workers and audience members. Ranging from satirical ("Shackwacky Blues") or parodic ("Girls Are Just Guys Played on 45") to deeply expressive in tone ("If You Think It Was Easy"), these songs cumulatively create a powerful sense of women's subjectivity. In fact, there is a sense in which the subjective—traditionally regarded as inappropriate to the supposed "objectivity" "natural" to the dramatic mode—takes over from and transforms the play's "real" external narrative, which by traditional wisdom is the *essence* of drama, but which in this play is often improbably, farcical, or absurd when compared to the expressive (and subjective) sensibilities, interpretations, and viewpoints of the women themselves, both actors and characters. A medley which ends the play by reprising several of its songs moves from "Hormones/Can this be real?/Hormones? It's the way I feel!" to "We're getting into the action/And we do it just like you/But we move a little faster/And we see it through and through." It concludes, literally and figuratively, with "self respect" (64–65).

These plays, then, like all of the women's plays so far produced at Mulgrave Road, function both as products of the cultural conditions, theatrical and otherwise, through which they have emerged, and as agents of transformation within those cultures. But it is important not to romanticize the involvement of Mulgrave Road in the community. Although the engagements that I have described above are central and essential, the degree to which the co-op is capable of effecting meaningful cultural intervention derives in part from its existence at a point of intersection between cultures, including its bringing to Guysborough theatre works of different, and occasionally locally disruptive backgrounds, interests, and lifestyles. Mulgrave Road's efficacy rests in its being at once part of, mimetic of, and external to the community in and through which it works, a positioning which allows it both to celebrate and criticize that community, but one which is also fraught with potential and occasionally very real tensions and conflicts within the company and between the company and the community. In practice, and even in part as a result of these tensions, the company at its best functions as a transformative "fissure" in an often rigidly closed culture by introducing elements new to it, and by providing focal points for women and others who are members of the community, but are constructed by it as "other" or ex-centric. In part, then, the Co-op functions as a continually shifting and liminal community that is both transformed by and transformative of the culture and society of Guysborough County, but within parameters that, though fluid, are defined at any one time by the degree to which the company's shows *are* products of the culture which they represent. It may not be incidental to note, for example, that Mulgrave Road has so far been able to intervene only in very limited and almost imperceptible ways in the gendered construction of class, race, ethnicity, or sexual orientation in Guysborough County, except perhaps insofar as its work has helped to make possible future interventions in these areas *as* the products of what is now a shifting cultural ground. [14] Neither is it incidental, however, given the cultural interventions effected by women within and through "women's plays" produced at Mulgrave Road, that change has been effected within the structure of the company itself, which can be seen, importantly, to serve as an exemplary employer in the town of Guysborough: Mulgrave Road's last three Artistic Directors, Jenny Munday, Allena MacDonald, and Emmy Alcorn, have been women. All of their predecessor's in the position were men. [15]

• • •

I want to end this essay, not with a conclusion or an invocation of closure, but with what I think of as "*dis*closure." The essay itself, of course, is both a product of and an intervention external to the workings of Mulgrave Road and the larger communities of Guysborough and the Maritimes. As a man, from urban Ontario, I have an outsider's tendency to romanticize my own discursively constructed pastoral understandings of both "the maritime sense of community," and "the community of women," and thereby potentially to gloss over practical problems, personal frictions, and less than ideal (or even adequate) material circumstances surrounding and shaping the production of theatre in an impoverished and isolated area. [16] As a theatre worker and member of the Mulgrave Road Co-op who has lived and worked in the Maritimes, moreover, and as an academic critic who has written about Mulgrave Road, I have a stake in celebrating and perpetuating the work of the company. I hope, nevertheless, that there is a limited liminal role for a paper such as this one in reproducing, with inevitable and perhaps constructive shifts, the work of Co-op women in the frame of another discourse; in supporting (and publicizing) the production and reproduction of cultural work by the women of Mulgrave Road; and in the transmission and transformation of cultural values in the Maritimes. [17]

(1995)

Notes

[1] For a history of the early years of the company, see Knowles, "Guysborough." For a discussion of one representative version of the company's administrative structure, see Knowles, "Voices" 108–09.

[2] Smyth's description of quilting provides a remarkable parallel to the process of play production at Mulgrave Road that I am outlining: "It was their quilt now, a thing they were doing together.... As the design became clear, so did all the stories....

They'd told each other these stories, all the time working and stitching. Watching how it fit together, becoming something other than the pieces they held in their hands" (49). The breakdown between male "art" and female "craft" has been actively pursued, of course, by visual artists such as Joyce Weiland, whose famous "reason over Passion" quilt provides a particularly apt example.

3   "Women's plays" at Mulgrave Road, with dates of first production, include: *One on the Way* (collective, 1980, unpub.); *Another Story* (collective, 1982, unpub.); *Holy Ghosters, 1776* (Mary Vingoe, 1983, unpub.; *Spooks: The Mystery of Caledonia Mills* (Cindy Cowan, 1984, unpub.); *A Child is Crying on the Stairs* (collective with writer Nanette Cormier and based on her book of the same name [Windsor, Ontario: Black Moss P, 1983], 1985, unpub.); *A Woman from the Sea* (Cindy Cowan, 1986); *Beinn Bhreagh* (Cindy Cowan, 1986, unpub.); *Idyll Gossip* (Carol Sinclair, 1987); *Battle Fatigue* (Jenny Munday, 1989); and *Safe Haven* (Mary Colin Chisholm, 1992). This list is somewhat arbitrary, in that there have been other plays by women, collective creations that were predominantly the work of women, and productions that were directed by women and/or cast women in central roles. Moreover, the plays that I have listed all involved men, in some capacity, as actors, musicians, designers, directors or technicians. I have, however, selected productions of plays that were identified by their creators as plays by, for, or about women.

4   Mulgrave Road has hosted or initiated many community-based projects within their theatre building around which theatrical activities revolve. These include such things as hosting meetings of GLOW (Guysborough Learning Opportunities for Women); initiating and hosting the meetings of a weekly creative writing workshop open to anyone in the community; producing interventionist plays and workshops on such things as child abuse (such as *Feeling Yes, Feeling No*) in local schools; school tours of Christmas shows, "Roadies," a theatre camp for children offered each summer; and so on. Interestingly, writing about the co-op, including my own, here and elsewhere, has tended to focus on the so-called "major productions," and to marginalize these other, equally important projects, many of which have to do with areas traditionally seen as "women's issues."

5   It is true that many of the women in the community who have forged friendships with theatre workers have been those of sufficient economic standing to be able to afford homes with extra room to billet actors. This has often (but not always) meant that the theatre's connections have been with women in leadership positions within the community—doctors, school teachers, and so on. There have been fewer direct associations with working-class women, and fewer still with the relatively large Black community on the edge of town.

For a less sanguine account of the material conditions for the production of theatre in Guysborough than the one I have provided, told from the perspective of an Artistic Director of the company, see Munday.

6   Insofar as the mandate of the company is the production of new work in and for Northeastern Nova Scotia, particularly Guysborough County, virtually all theatrical

productions at Mulgrave Road serve this function, not just those that I have called "women's plays." The latter, however, although they are performed before a general audience, are distinctive insofar as they are pro-actively constitutive of an explicitly gendered regional subjectivity.

[7] The distinctions between territorial and relational notions of community are derived from Phillips. Phillips defines territorial communities as those determined primarily by geo-political boundaries, and relational communities as those determined primarily by the nature and quality of inter-relationships among membership with shared interests. What I am describing as being forged in Guysborough by the work of the women of Mulgrave Road is perhaps usefully seen as a relational community, or community of interest, existing within the boundaries of an isolated rural territorial community, in which the memberships of both territorial and relational communities have traditionally been marginalized.

[8] A group of plays that include the collective collaboration with Nanette Cormier, *A Child is Crying on the Stairs*, and Cindy Cowan's three plays, *Spooks*, *A Woman from the Sea*, and *Beinn Bhreagh*, are partial exceptions to the patterns I am examining here, and require separate treatment. Cowan's plays, moreover, especially *A Woman from the Sea*, seem to take and to invite a radical feminist approach which I don't feel is appropriate for or available to me as a male critic, unlike the materialist feminist theory on which I am drawing (but which I hope I am not appropriating) here. For a radical feminist approach to *A Woman from the Sea*, see Hodkinson 133–58.

[9] See de Lauretis 92. Interestingly, again, Cindy Cowan's *Spooks* and *A Woman from the Sea* would seem to be the only exceptions to the general rule that plays by women at Mulgrave Road have avoided mysticism and mythologizing. In the former, Cowan attempts to deconstruct media manipulations of the story of a young girl accused of setting fires in her parents' home in 1921; and in the latter she tries to construct a radical feminist and socially conscious myth of origins and other things.

[10] See, for example, Senchuck.

[11] Cowan notes that *Another Story* was instrumental in leading Vingoe "to initiate her own production, *Holy Ghosters*" (108).

[12] For a more detailed discussion of *Holy Ghosters* on which this discussion draws, see Knowles, "A Sense."

[13] The primary source for *Holy Ghosters* is Thomas Raddall's novel, *His Majesty's Yankees*, but Raddall is famous for his original and detailed historical research. Moreover Vingoe also drew extensively on primary sources, notably John Robinson and Thomas Rispin's (1774) *Journey Through Nova Scotia*. *Battle Fatigue* is based on an extensive series of interviews with Maritime women of Munday's parents' generation who lived through the Second World War.

[14] The Co-op has addressed some of these issues, in productions such as *Victory! The Saga of William Hall, V.C.* in 1981, which told the story of the first Nova Scotian, and the first black man to win the Victoria Cross, in the Battle of Lucknow; Mary Colin Chisholm's *Safe Haven* (1992), which treated the intrusion of AIDS into the community; and *Another Story*, in which class is at least implicitly at the heart of the play. These interventions have been important, and if vestigial are in no way insignificant. Rarely, however, has the Co-op faced racism, classism, or homophobia in the community itself head on, at least to the time of this writing.

[15] MacDonald's stint in the position, in fact, began as a co-Artistic Directorship with Lorne Pardy, but Pardy resigned before they had completed their first season and MacDonald remained in the role for a three-year term.

[16] For examples of these various difficulties, see Munday, "The View."

[17] Since this paper was written Mulgrave Road, sadly, has abandoned its co-operative structure. It now operates under the auspices of a Board of Directors made up of artists and members of the community. The Board appoints the Artistic Director and the company's administrative staff.

Works Cited

Chisholm, Mary Colin. *Safe Haven. Theatrum* 38 (1994): S1–S15.

Cowan, Cindy. "Messages in the Wilderness." *Canadian Theatre Review* 43 (1985): 100–10.

———. *A Woman from the Sea. Canadian Theatre Review* 48 (1986): 62–110; rpt. in *The CTR Anthology*. Ed. Alan Filewod. U. of Toronto P, 1993. 339–88.

de Lauretis, Teresa. "Gramsci Notwithstanding, or, The Left Hand of History." *Technologies of Gender: Essays on Theory, Film, and Fiction*. Bloomington: Indiana UP, 1987. 84–94. Rpt. of "The Left Hand of History." *Heresies: A Feminist Publication on Art and Politics* 4 (1978): 23–26.

Foucault, Michel. *The Foucault Reader*. Ed. Paul Rabinow, New York: Pantheon, 1984.

Hodkinson, Yvonne. *Female Parts: The Art and Politics of Female Playwrights*. Montreal: Black Rose Books, 1991.

Keyssar, Helene. *Feminist Theatre*. New York: Grove P, 1985.

Knowles, Ric[hard Paul]. "Guysborough, Mulgrave, and the Mulgrave Road Co-op Theatre Company." *People and Place: Studies of Small Town Life in the Maritimes*. Ed. Larry McCann. Fredericton: Acadiensis P, 1987. 227–46. Rpt. as "The

Mulgrave Road Co-op: Theatre and the Community in Guysborough County, N.S." *Canadian Drama/L'Art dramatique canadien* 12.1 (1986): 18–32.

———. "'A Sense of History Here': Mary Vingoe's *Holy Ghosters, 1776.*" *The Red Jeep and Other Landscapes: A Collection in Honour of Douglas Lochhead.* Ed. Peter Thomas. Sackville & Fredericton, NB: Mount Allison U & Goose Lane, 1987. 20–27.

———. "Voices (off): Deconstructing the Modern English-Canadian Dramatic Canon." *Canadian Canons: Essays in Literary Value.* Ed. Robert Lecker. Toronto: U of Toronto P, 1991. 91–111.

Kudelka, Jan. Interview with Basil Deakin. "Collective Creation: *Another Story* Wowed Audiences in Guysborough." *The Chronicle-Herald/The Mail Star* [Halifax] 6 April 1982.

Marcuse, Herbert. *Negotiations: Essays in Critical Theory.* Boston: Beacon, 1969.

Montrose, Louis A. "Professing the Renaissance: The Poetics and Politics of Culture." *The New Historicism.* Ed. H. Aram Veeser. London & New York: Routledge, 1989.

Munday, Jenny. *Battle Fatigue. Canadian Theatre Review* 62 (1990): 50–74.

———. "The View From Inside the Electrolux." *Canadian Theatre Review* 71 (1992): 88–91.

Phillips, Derek L. *Looking Backward: A Critical Appraisal of Communitarian Thought.* Princeton: Princeton UP, 1993.

Senchuck, Barbara. Review of Mary Vingoe's *Holy Ghosters, 1776. The Chronicle Herald/The Mail Star* [Halifax] 3 November 1983.

Sinclair, Carol. *Idyll Gossip.* Compuscript. Toronto: Playwrights Union of Canada, 1987.

Smyth, Donna E. *Quilt.* Toronto: Women's Educational P, 1982.

On the Margins:
Eastern Canadian Theatre
as Post-Colonialist Discourse

by Mary Elizabeth Smith

Canada became a country in 1867 through the Confederation of the two small eastern (Maritime) colonies of Nova Scotia and New Brunswick with the larger, more inland colonies of Upper and Lower Canada (Ontario and Quebec). Yet the flag remained the British Union Jack and the constitution resided in London. Canada's own flag was raised only in 1965, and the constitution repatriated only in 1982, both events accompanied by considerable controversy within the nation. The political controversy then (and now) reflects a constantly ambivalent attitude of Canadians towards the relationship between identity and nationalism, an ambivalence that encompasses protean forms of nationalism, including essentialist nationalism and a more elastic concept which recognizes the legitimacy of emotional and cultural ties beyond the national borders.

Alan Filewod points out that the term post-colonial is problematic, "in part because it implies a state of emergence from colonialism, whereas in fact post-colonial societies find themselves defined and often confused by numerous intersecting and very present colonialisms" (4). [1] The theatre (including unperformed drama) of eastern Canada exhibits the presence of such intersecting colonialisms (English, Scottish, Irish, and American), and reaches towards "exploring, questioning, and… celebrating the discovery of *place*" (Saddlemeyer 210). Our primary focus will be on the germinative theatrical culture in the years preceding and following the defining moment of Confederation in 1867—from 1860 to the end of the nineteenth century—but we shall begin with a more recent context, the beginning of the twentieth century when the imperialism of the American theatre had become intolerable to Canadian nationalists.

Bernard K. Sandwell, addressing the Canadian Club of Montreal in 1913, called for theatre in Canada to shake off cultural dependence on the United States through the establishment of a series of regional repertory theatres after the English model, and performance of Canadian plays. The call was prompted by years of control by powerful American syndicates over playing houses and performance repertoire. Sandwell's not unreasonable assumption that a recognizably Canadian drama could only develop in Canadian owned and run theatres was, paradoxically, linked with his advocacy of close co-operation with the British theatre as a means of encouraging development of the Canadian one. According to Sandwell, "The British drama is the drama of our own people, of our brothers and fellow subjects. The American drama is an alien drama (102).[2]

As if to illustrate the paradox inherent in Sandwell's call, the Imperial Theatre opened in Saint John, New Brunswick, in 1913. It was designed and constructed by Americans, owned by the Keith-Albee circuit based in New York and Boston, and named patriotically in keeping with the sentiments of Empire.[3] But the initiative was local: William Golding—a life-long friend of the movie magnate Louis B. Mayer, a fellow Saint Johner, who kept in constant touch with theatre people in New York and Boston—created the opportunity to direct external capital towards a fine theatre for amateur as well as touring productions through persuasion. Golding's entrepreneurship in relation to the neighbouring power had already been directly responsible for the introduction of orchestras throughout the entire Keith-Albee circuit.[4]

Fifty years followed before the first regional theatre was established in the Maritimes. In 1963 the Neptune Theatre opened in Halifax, Nova Scotia; the Fredericton Playhouse (home of Theatre New Brunswick) opened in 1964; and lastly the Charlottetown Festival began in 1965, one year after construction of Prince Edward Island's Confederation Centre. In its first two years the Neptune theatre produced some Canadian material, including several scripts by the Haligonian Dr. Arthur Murphy (a strong moving force behind the Neptune's conception). The tenth season in 1973 (something of an anomaly) contained many plays by Canadians: James Reaney, Michel Tremblay, Michael Cook, David French, and David Freeman.[5] The Fredericton Playhouse followed with scripts by its first artistic director Walter Learning and the poet Aldon Nowlan and with an all-Canadian season in 1985–86. At the insistence of summer theatre-goers, the Charlottetown Festival has been dominated by the perennial musical favourite *Anne of Green Gables*, based on the popular children's novels by the Island's own Lucy Maud Montgomery.

Development of Indigenous Theatre

In 1980 Diane Bessai analysed regionalism in Canadian theatre as a mark of a post-colonial era, arguing that "localism in its contemporary theatrical forms is a demonstrably important phase in the establishment of a mature, decentralized culture" (11). In the context of a Canada with a multivalent voice, where the sense of being a Maritimer or an Albertan can easily precede the sense of being Canadian, Bessai was probably right (assertions that Canadian literature is monolithic generally represent an upper-Canadian voice that claims to speak for all).[6] At the same time, to be conscious of region does not preclude a sense of national identity, as an adaptation of a passage from the historian Gertrude Himmelfarb suggests: "To think of oneself as a Haligonian or a Nova Scotian does not preclude thinking of oneself as Canadian. Indeed, the first may reinforce the second: one may believe that Halifax (or Nova Scotia, as the case may be) is the "true" Canada: National identity does not imply national homogeneity" (126).[7]

Bessai's definition of regionalism is broad; she finds it "rooted, indigenous, shaped by a specific social, cultural physical milieu," but also owns that it "reflects the past as well as the present and at its best absorbs innumerable influences from beyond its borders" that illuminate the regional perspective (7). Some contemporary plays from the Maritimes resist regionalism, however, by seeking recognition through an internationalist stance, for instance, Nowlan and Learning's *Frankenstein* (1975), Dan Ross's gothic spoof *Murder Game* (1982), and Norm Foster's fast-paced light comedies (1982–), all of which have enjoyed considerable success across Canada and beyond. On the other hand, Nowlan and Learning's *The Dollar Woman* (1977) and Marshall Button's *Lucien: A Labour of Love* (1986) with its sequel, *Lucien's Labours Lost* (1993), are scripts in which place is constituted in terms of particular historical experience: their first appeal is to the shared experience of a community. *Dollar Woman* makes a nineteenth-century pauper auction in Sussex, New Brunswick, the site of its exploration of social issues of poverty and justice; *Lucien* is a satiric view of the determination, doubts and uncertainties of a present-day Acadian worker at a pulp mill in northern New Brunswick. While identity is putatively rooted in Acadian culture in *Lucien*, it has degenerated into cultural stereotyping through satire that reinforces attitudes about the indolence of a certain class of worker. One looks outside the regional theatre environment to the town of Guysborough, Nova Scotia, for the particularly local collective creations of the Mulgrave Road Co-op Theatre whose goal is to "develop innovative forms and produce work of a kind and quality which respond to the history, tradition, and culture of Northeastern Nova Scotia" (Knowles 109).

The tension between the poles of internationalism and regionalism (or localism) is evident also in plays emerging out of the amateur movement that filled the breach in the 1930s after the American touring companies stopped coming to the Maritimes, halted, as elsewhere, by the harsh economic realities of the Great Depression and by the advent of movies. As it happens, both poles are represented in an award shared between two New Brunswickers for the best Canadian play performed at the Dominion Drama Festival in 1938. Jean Sweet's *Small Potatoes*,[8] an Orwellian depiction of the State of Technomania, argues the cause of individual freedom with the beguiling simplicity of a children's fable (at a time when the spectre of totalitarianism was much on the minds of a generation), while Jack Thurrot's *La Tour*, located historically and geographically, explores the mid-seventeenth-century struggle of the Frenchman in what is now southern New Brunswick. However Thurrot's *La Tour* and Francis Parkhill's 1967 recovery of the same historical moment, *The Fair Country*, are retrospectives of the French drawn from Scottish or British-Canadian perspectives for persons living in English-speaking Canada; they present the regional perspective as in complicity with imperialism. In the moving story of the final struggle between the La Tours and the Charnisays for control of the fur trade at the mouth of the Saint John River in April 1645, Parkhill found fertile soil for romance, witty dialogue and engaging characterization. But the new world setting of her historical recollection is incidental to the tale of rivalry among Europeans in that it does not engage with the indigenous culture at all; rather its foregrounding of the colonizers relegates the native culture to the silence of non-existence.

Similarly imperialistic in outlook and effect is the earlier *De Roberval* (1888), a heavily allusive, blank-verse closet-drama[9] about an obscure sixteenth-century French colonizer by John Hunter Duvar, a Scots resident of Prince Edward Island. Duvar makes no pretension to historical accuracy; rather, he romanticizes and embellishes as he creates a mythology whose archetypal hero is the brave, resolute, and fair-minded explorer with a strong love of and loyalty to his new land.[10] The mythology passively incorporates an European hegemonic ideal, as Duvar's French invaders relegate the Indian people to the status of "savage" otherness: "Cartier says they have a fund of cunning,/and are ferocious and most barbarous" (40).[11] The modern reader will find the objectifying of the female by the soldiers as "meat for our master" horrific: "If this should be a woman, now, and she/An average sample of the belle sauvage,/Twould be no task to populate the land" (58). Moreover, since the love that grows between De Roberval and the Indian woman Ohnawa is idealized, and she is given Elizabethan-style diction to speak and is depicted as Diana, she never emerges from the objectified position of the stereotype into personhood. Duvar only possibly gestures towards dialectic (and thus towards questioning the historical narrative of the colonizer) in Ohnawa's keeping of her native religion and in the Aged Chief's assertion of sovereignty over the land; yet Ohnawa does not choose as a free subject but as someone under the patriarchal protection of De Roberval, and the words available to the Chief are so profoundly patronizing that they *de facto* deny status and identity:

> Chieftain! when the Great Spirit made the earth
> And gave it to all men to dwell theron
> He placed the Paleface by the rising sun,
> And set great seas to keep him in his place.
> To His Red Sons he gave these forest worlds
> And meted out to each his hunting bound. (83)[12]

The dominant cultural influences on the theatre in the Maritimes in playwriting, theatre criticism, and audience are English, Scottish, and Irish. In Halifax, Nova Scotia, founded in 1749, theatre was first the preserve of British troupes garrisoned there, whose involvement and support through patronage continued to the end of the nineteenth century. There was the patronage of General Sir Patrick MacDougall, Commander-in-Chief of the Forces in North America from 1878 to 1883. From the earliest years, many regiments had their own dramatic associations, and military personnel were also frequently associated with civilian amateur societies. Over time, many of the thespians in the British army had been born in the colonies. For example, F.H.D. Veith, a Haligonian born in 1838, was at eighteen a garrison-amateur with E.A. Sothern's company at the Halifax Lyceum. He delivered the prologue on the opening night of the Halifax Academy of Music in 1877, and was in charge of theatricals at Government House during the tenure of the Marquis of Lorne.

Appeal to British cultural assumptions was the refuge against opponents of the theatre who argued that it was undermining the moral fabric of society through importation of undesirable American values along with actors from New York and Boston. For instance Robert Murray, the twenty-four-year-old editor of the Halifax *Presbyterian Witness* and bitterly hostile to the stage, harangued against E.A. Sothern's company: "Surely we can find enough to import from the States without importing their fourth-rate mountebanks, play-actors, and actresses, to corrupt the morals of those whose morals are already sufficiently corrupt" (16 August 1856). [13] Sothern's rebuttal in the Halifax *Morning Chronicle* touted his royalist alignment; he noted that all but two of his actors were British subjects and that, moreover, to abuse the theatre as "a hot-bed of vice" was to revile "with unchristian malignity" Shakespeare and others whose names "find a home in the heart of every Englishman," as well as to belittle the example of Queen Victoria who visited the theatre regularly with her children (16 June 1856). While it is plain from this altercation that the Maritimes were the site of competing dominating discourses of Britain and the United States, the failure of Maritimers to recognize their relationship with England as a dominated one (though they verbally resisted American influence) derives from choices made by the United Empire Loyalist settlers at the time of the American Revolution.

Significant impetus for the establishment of a culture imitative of England had come with the great influx of Loyalists fleeing the fledgling American Republic to the south in the late 1770s. A search of any record of early Loyalist settlement reveals that the new arrivals represented every segment of society, the majority being people of position and influence (civil and military officers, clergy, lawyers and merchants), the Loyalist elite. These were a people of strong political conviction who had chosen the challenge of a mainly undeveloped land at the expense of position and wealth so that they might defend the monarchist principle and, particularly, their allegiance to George III. Their earliest dramatic pieces are impassioned defences of toryism and the Loyalist cause (e.g. Bailey, Winslow). Like later waves of immigrant Scots and Irish, they came with a sense of culture and identity that was clearly dependent on ties with some place other than the new homeland. [14] The new colonists were mostly epigones; if culture flourished in any form in Britain, the colonists could claim whatever was produced there as their own. As the poet and critic Fred Cogswell has pointed out, this allegiance to and imitation of antecedent forms prevented Maritime writers from committing "the barbarisms perpetrated by many frontiersmen elsewhere," but often at the cost of "unique expression" (118–19). While America was defined by its revolution, the Maritimes were defined by their opposition to the Revolution and their loyalty to the pre-Revolutionary situation. Because America was founded in opposition to a prevailing political/cultural situation it was ripe for writers and artists who would seek to provide some definition of a new land. The cultural imperative in the Maritimes, on the other hand, was first of all about preservation of past rather than creation of present. Even as late as 1876, for instance, the sentimental *A Fireside Drama* by William Murdoch, drama critic for the *Saint John Daily News*, presented the Scots' strong love of home through Scottish humour and verse imitative of the dialect of Robert Burns.

Looking towards Britain was willing cultural and political alliance with imperialism, and a kind of anti-colonialist or anti-imperialist attitude in that it regarded the real threat of political domination as lying to the south, whereas Britain was across the ocean and thus less of a threat to daily life. Residents of the Maritimes would have considered themselves a fiercely independent people who used whatever resources lay at hand for their own betterment. Thus the same characteristics of independence that led to resistance of the goals of the American Revolution led, a century later, to intense debate over the issue of Confederation.

Confederation and Theatre

Stephen Johnson, in "'Getting to' Canadian Theatre History: On the Tension Between the New History and the Nation State," discusses the difficulty of discovering any relationship between Confederation and the local cultural character of Wellington County, Ontario. His conclusion, based on reading of local newspapers and the American trade journal, *The New York Clipper*, is that the founding national event had no more than a minor effect on daily life, and none at all on the theatre:

> Regular and frequent amateur fund-raising concerts, occasional amateur readings and dramatic events, touring lectures, professional singers, minstrel troupes, an occasional circus and theatrical troupe—all continued without a noticeable change in character or venue or audience, from any evidence in these documents. (68)

So, in the Maritimes, these kinds of entertainments continued as before, as did the sporadic professional seasons in the Temperance Hall in Halifax and the regular summer seasons offered by J.W. Lanergan's company in the Saint John Dramatic Lyceum. Yet, that the relationship was more politically engaged in the Maritimes than that in Wellington County can be seen briefly in performance and especially in the spate of serialized and anonymous political dramas that appeared in the years just before and just after Confederation.

On Confederation Day itself, 1 July 1867, Halifax was draped in black as it was on many anniversaries following. Citizens with nothing to celebrate (for the city believed it had much to lose through the union) went about their lives as normally as possible. Moses Fiske's company at the Temperance Hall took note of the event only by supplementing the regular evening performance with a matinee, as was the custom on any non-working day.[15] The programme at the Saint John Dramatic Lyceum was more in keeping with a mood of apprehension. Ironically, the bill for the Saturday evening preceding the Monday 1 July event was *Chamber of Death!* or, *La Tour de Nesle!*, a melodramatic tale of adventuring, ambition, lust, and murder that includes the murder of the Prime Minister of France, while that on 1 July was *The Merchant of Venice*. A scheduled outdoors concert by the anti-Confederationists of Saint John failed to materialize, however, thus allowing the pro-Confederation *New Dominion and True Humorist* to comment sarcastically:

> It was a great disappointment to very many that the Concert advertised in our last did not come off. The sudden illness of the leaders… was the

cause of the disappointment, for the "tame followers" of the shattered and discomfited Antis had no confidence in *their own* ability to carry the thing through successfully. (6 July 1867)

Reminiscences of Saint John in the 1850s by J.W. Millidge, a prominent local businessman, reveal apprehension about possible alienation as a result of the proposed union:

> Canada was a foreign land to us. We knew there were two cities, Montreal and Quebec, and that was about all we did know... Liverpool was our great headquarters; all our ships went there for sale, most of our deals were shipped there. (135)

Millidge makes no mention of Ontario's cities at all. In speaking to the conference of delegates that met in Quebec in October 1864 to discuss possible union, the Hon. S.L. Tilley of New Brunswick felt the need to reject a subservient position:

> The delegates from the Maritime Provinces are not here seeking this union... I consider it right to make this remark, inasmuch as it has been asserted in certain quarters that the Maritime Provinces, weak and impoverished, are endeavouring to reap the benefits resulting from such a union. This is not the case. Look at the immense amount of shipping we own. I am in a position to state that, for the year 1864, after paying the interest on all our debts, and after providing liberally for roads, bridges, and other public works, we shall have a surplus of half a million. Therefore, we are not coming in as paupers, but are coming to put something in worth having. (Lawson 193–94)

When the Quebec Conference decided to proceed with union, the New Brunswick electorate expressed its opposition by defeating the government; yet confusion among the electorate is evident in that it next returned to power a government in favour of Confederation, thus allowing the union to proceed. There was strong opposition in Nova Scotia also, and Prince Edward Island rejected the plan; all were concerned about domination by the larger provinces to the west, which is, in fact, a present-day Canadian reality.

The political play, *The Government in Session*, serialized in *The New Dominion and True Humorist* between 13 December 1865 and 7 April 1866, is that paper's attack on the anti-Confederate government of Albert James Smith. Smith, a politician outspoken against privilege and in support of the rights of the ordinary citizen, believed that Confederation would bring "direct taxation, loss of trade, an assumption of the immense public debt the Canadas owed for railways, and domination by Upper Canada" (Smith, "Three" 146). The play, set mainly in Saint John, where the premier had moved the seat of government at the behest of his Irish Catholic ally, the editor T.W. Anglin, [16] is a series of mock conversations among members of the government "in session" through which the *Humorist* attempts to expose alleged corruption and inefficiency. That some of those engaged in the Confederation debate viewed politics as theatre anyway is apparent, for instance, in a biting prose essay in the *Saint John Morning News* headed "The New Political Drama":

> The signs of the times indicate that when the curtain next rises our old friends the Antis will appear in an entirely fresh character in the new and amusing farce of *The Protestants...* but a few months ago they drew a crowded house in Fredericton by their renderings of the high tragedy, "*Anti Confederation, or the Empire Dismembered.*" What an unprecedented run of success they had is well remembered. Then came the low comedy, "*Constitutionalism*; or, *How to throw dust, etc.*"... Truly they are possessed of infinite tact in rendering themselves ridiculous. (13 June 1866)[17]

A dozen years after Confederation had become a *fait accompli*, the same former Premier Smith was again the object of derision in another, more lively, more dramatically sophisticated satire, the four act *Done in Darkness: A Comedy of Today*. Serialized in the conservative *Moncton Daily Times* between 14 and 24 November 1879, a year after that paper had bitterly derided Smith's knighthood and launched an unsuccessful campaign to unseat him in the House of Commons, it uses a parochial election in his home riding as an excuse to draw together federal and regional concerns. In elevated iambic pentameters, fractured French, prose interspersed with songs, and mock heroic prophecies of doom, it lambastes Smith mercilessly for his supposed villainous deeds, while the appeal to a reading audience rooted in British cultural identifications allows humour to be derived from lyrics that comfortably fit tunes from Gilbert and Sullivan's *Pinafore* and model themselves on the rhythm of the British national anthem "God Save the Queen."

Other political plays of the period have some of the same cast of characters and employ similar principles of appropriation, while confining themselves principally to local issues. For instance *Northumbria* (1869) is advertised in *The New Dominion and True Humorist* as "A new play in five acts, one of the most celebrated dramas since the days of Shakespeare" (6 March 1869), and concerns machinations surrounding a local by-election, while *Measure by Measure, or the Government in Secret Session* (25 February–8 April 1871), is equally laden with Shakespearian allusion and attacks the government that introduced free non-sectarian schools into New Brunswick. These political plays share with the propaganda plays written by members of both sides in the American revolutionary period[18] the characteristics of immediacy, passion, and caricature, and trace their lineage back to the English political play of the eighteenth century. They target as audience an intellectual elite educated in the canon of British literature, and are written from the politically engaged position of toryism.

Maritime Theatre

Far from being mere vehicles of appropriation, however, the political plays from New Brunswick employ subversive strategies of playful parody. They appropriate from the centre to create their own centredness in the margins, thus demonstrating awareness of the illusion of the centre. They manipulate inherited forms and ideologies for their own aesthetic and political purposes rather than evoking nostalgic longing for an irrecoverable past. Thus they are part of an equalizing process between the "former" centre and the "becoming" centre. Relentlessly they plunder Shakespeare, Milton, Dryden, and the Bible for allusions to distort in order to further their own agenda of lampooning those in positions of political power and the public (and private) issues with which they were associated. So the attack in *Measure by Measure* on George Hathaway, representative in the "House" of the Legislative Assembly from "York" County, and on George E. King, Attorney General from Saint John, begins with a parody of the opening lines of *Richard III*:

> Now is the winter of our discontent
> Made glorious Summer by this son of *York*.
> And all the clouds that lower'd upon our *House*
> Scattered forever by this Coalition.

Much more eclectic is the plethora of bastardized quotations put into the mouths of sundry members of the "House" in the brief sketch *The Fall of the King-lie Die-nasty! containing the dying confessions of "the United Wisdom."* [19]

A different audience (though again a politically astute one) is assumed for the plays of the Irish Catholic lawyer, John Carleton, beginning with *More Sinned Against Than Sinning* published in New York in 1883. Set in Killarney at the height of the Land War, the melodrama's chief dramatis personae represent elements of the conflict—the villainous English land agent Belhaven; the Irish landowner Squire Hilton, neglectful of his tenants and an easy dupe of Belhaven; and Hilton's son Marmaduke who, in embracing the peasants' cause, is estranged from his father. In Carleton's Saint John the 54.1 per cent of the population of Irish origin could follow news of the actual dispute in the *Sun* and could demonstrate concern through establishment of a local branch of the Land League, by fund-raising for the Irish relief effort, and by providing actors and audience for the Father Mathieu Society productions of *More Sinned* on St. Patrick's Day. While this play, and also the thematically related *Coom-na-Goppel* (1906), both demonstrate a non-elitist solidarity with suffering in the ancestral land, Mark Blagrave thinks that the solutions for political and social reform proposed show a peculiarly Canadian as well as an international perspective:

> Had they been written by Englishmen, the plays, might have ended with the simple victory of the paternal forces over the forces of dissent. Had they been written by Americans, the plays might have ended with bloody murders of the paternal figures and the establishment of a wholly new order. As it is, the moderate political stance suggested by the outcomes... is reflective of a prevailing temper in Canada, a temper dictated by a belief that the relationship with the mother country worked out in Canada in 1867 might be applied equally successfully elsewhere. That the heroes of these Canadian plays set in Ireland do not usurp the crown or kill their fathers is an affirmation of the virtue of the relationship between the young dominion and its mother country. ("Ireland" 144)

Canada remains loyal to the maternal; imperialism is domesticated, tamed, and adjusted to the Maritime ethos.

Carleton's plays through performance (mostly amateur), especially *More Sinned Against Than Sinning*, reached out to audiences in several Canadian provinces and in the United States. In this way, then, the Maritimes contributed to the wealth of enormously popular performance literature associated with Ireland and the Irish, a literature in which the politics of dominance and subservience still prevails.

The larger centres of the Maritimes (at least Saint John and Halifax) thought of themselves as belonging to a larger environment. As I have noted elsewhere, "Whatever the vicissitudes of the theatre, there remained a general attitude of superiority in Saint John—a feeling that Saint John was at least equal to any other city whether in Canada, Britain, or the United States" (*Too Soon* xi). That the values and taste of that larger environment informed much theatre criticism is made explicit in George Stewart's essay, "The Decline of the Legitimate Drama," published in his own *Stewart's Quarterly* in October 1869. [20] Stewart, drama critic for two Saint John newspapers, describes himself as "a disciple of the classics" who insists on morality and who reads the London critics. The tone of reviews reflects the education and taste of "gentlemen who gave to the learned professions grace and dignity, and who emerged... from the busy haunts of trade and commerce, from the lawyers office, the abodes of Esculapius, from the highest social circles" (*Progress*, 19 March 1892)—those whose money and influence chiefly supported the theatre. Persons with money and leisure to do so (or for business reasons) frequently travelled to Boston and New York (seldom to Montreal or Toronto) and also crossed the ocean to London, visiting theatre on those occasions. Thus a reviewer could call on the authority of "a gentleman who has seen a great deal of theatrical life on both sides of the Atlantic" to support a claim that Boucicault's *London Assurance* had never been played better in England or America, (*Halifax Morning Herald*, 31 October 1884), or could feel qualified himself to say that the manner in which W.H. Lytell presented *Youth* and *Michael Strogoff* "would do credit to any of the large cities of the United States" (*Halifax Morning Herald*, 22 July 1882).

Despite these obvious attempts to resist peripheral status and to assert connections to the metropolitan centre, the making of comparisons itself suggests a defensive self-consciousness about place and hints at an underlying feeling of being marginalized from centres of value. So the anticipatory preamble to the Boston Museum Company's production of *London Assurance* acknowledges that it was "hardly to be expected" that "the best Boston has to offer in the dramatic line" would visit Halifax (*Halifax Morning Herald*, 29 October 1884), while the commendation of Lytell's spectacular presentations owns that without his enterprise "we would have small opportunity of witnessing any of the great plays which meet with such success on the American boards" (*Halifax Morning Herald*, 22 July 1882). There are references to a rumour in the States that "it does not pay great stars to visit Halifax" (*Halifax Morning Herald*, 4 July 1887). Indeed, the long and tiresome journey, the difficulty of inducing stars of Grace Kellogg's stature "to come so far from the great musical centres" (*Halifax Morning Herald*, 6 May 1887), the limited size of the theatre-going public in Halifax and its small support for Arthur Rehan's Company of Comedians lend substance to such rumour (*Halifax Morning Herald*, 3 June 1888).

Attention has been drawn frequently to the notion of theatre in the touring era (from about 1880) as a North American enterprise in which Canadians participated, in contrast to the activity of the amateur theatre movement that took hold early this century. Not enough attention has been paid to the contributions of the little theatre movements that coexisted alongside the imported professional theatre through much of the nineteenth century. The 1860s, 1870s, and 1880s were a beehive of amateur theatrical activity in Saint John; numerous civilian and military dramatic and minstrel groups performed regularly and sometimes toured in the region. Though amateurs had been responsible for initiating the dramatic tradition in the region and had been active inconsistently in both lean and prosperous economic conditions, the impetus for the burgeoning activity came from the solid encouragement of J.W. Lanergan's regularly returning company from 1856 to 1875. Lanergan used amateurs as support for his professionals and participated himself in amateur productions; he legitimated the playwriting of a local woman, Beatrice Jones, by giving her plays professional productions; he encouraged local people to embrace a theatrical career and, significantly for the development of theatre in the region, he helped to raise up William Nannary and H. Price Webber to professional directorial and managerial roles. The tours of Webber (an immigrant to Saint John from England) were favourites in the Maritimes until the end of the century, while Nannary (born in Saint John of Irish stock) actively encouraged the building of theatres and briefly succeeded in establishing and operating the first and only theatrical circuit in the region that included all three Maritime provinces and Newfoundland. Nannary, a dry goods clerk, was at once proof that one who was not from the highest social echelons could significantly affect the development of theatre and proof that success was ultimately dependent on the backing of a social/cultural elite, for George Stewart's vicious reviews in the *Watchman* in 1875 taught him this. To be sure, Nannary's efforts were carried on within the North American context in that he too recruited in New York and produced (as his means allowed) those pieces that America (and his Maritime audiences) wanted to see, and eventually he failed because of this inability financially (and perhaps artistically) to imitate the main centres adequately. Nevertheless, local consciousness of and participation in all aspects of theatre was strong.

The various serialized political dramas (1865–79) speak strongly of particular situations, of the struggle to create something of significance in a chosen land, though they do so in the language of a translated culture, and the very wrestling itself is intensified by the tears and expectations rising out of the translation. While the focus of the struggle in its practical applications is geographically located in Canada, a place understood as home, the plays do not separate themselves from the cultural authority of the European centre but rather draw from it to further their own ends. In the process, they resist a new feared centre of imperialism in Ontario and Quebec, their partners in Confederation.

The voice of Duvar in *De Roberval* (1888) is that of a European seeking to form a grand and sweeping Canadian mythology for a land and a people he has not managed to separate from his European perspective, and the Scottish sounds of Murdoch's *A Fireside Drama* (1876) reveal a soul in exile. Carleton (1883, 1906) writes back, as it were, from the perspective of a specifically Irish Canadian, to the injustice in Ireland; while Sweet (1938), living in New Brunswick and also in a world under the Fascist-Nazi threat, breathes a breath of encouragement that crosses geographical and ethnic boundaries.

In recent times Nowlan and Learning's *The Dollar Woman* challenged New Brunswickers to care for the poor through reference to a nineteenth-century poor-auction that happened there; its lukewarm reception may suggest that audiences did not recognize themselves. Although some Acadians reportedly claimed to recognize themselves in *Lucien* on its first production, approval came mostly from the largely anglophone audiences of Theatre New Brunswick who failed to distance themselves from the cultural stereotyping and thus were complicit in it (see Button). The collective creations of the Mulgrave Road Co-op Theatre seem to express the frustrations and hopes of a part of Nova Scotia economically devastated by change (local people have participated in making the dramas, have housed the company, and have claimed to recognize themselves and their problems). These last three examples, from 1977 to 1994, resonate with different tones, having in common only that they all present hardship and frustration, a note that has been sounded with increasing frequency in eastern Canada since Confederation.

Confederation has made some difference, though cultural imperialism still persists. Recruiting of theatrical personnel is now done in Toronto instead of New York. Some people would say that the new cultural, economic and political imperialists are Ontario and Quebec, as the opponents of Confederation feared they would be. The "second stages" of the region, which have most determinedly attempted to speak into local realities, have not been heard by large numbers of people. The main stages engage in a perpetual struggle to stay alive, attempting both to educate and to entertain, but still reaching largely a middle and upper-class elite. Television and videos, the popular theatre of today, import much American culture (and some British) through consent. The Maritimes realize their identity through their difference from Ontario, New York, and London, not through their essence.[21] Yet there is indeed an acute awareness in the Maritimes and in all of Canada that Canada is not America and is not Britain, and indeed that a Maritimer is a Maritimer and simultaneously a Canadian. Perhaps that awareness is found as much in the reading of cultural symbols as in the producing of them.[22]

(1996)

Notes

1   I am using the term "post-colonial" in the sense in which it is used in *The Empire Writes Back,* "to cover all the culture affected by the imperial process from the moment of colonization to the present day. This is because there is a continuity of preoccupation throughout the historical process initiated by European imperial aggression" (Ashcroft, Griffiths and Tiffin, 2).

2   Sandwell's was one of many voices that took up the cry for cultural independence from the United States in the early years of this century. For a helpfully documented overview of the move towards cultural nationalism at this time see Salter.

3   See Armstrong. In 1994 the title "Imperial" has been reinstated to an excellent restoration of Golding's fine, but long unused theatre, thus indicating, however nominally, current acceptance of a traditionalist heritage stance. The theatre had been renamed the Capitol upon lease to Famous Players in 1929 and was the Full Gospel Assembly church (Pentecostal), from 1957 until its purchase by a citizens' group in 1983 with a view to restoration.

    In the narrative of Maritime theatre, the only facility other than the Imperial to have been owned by Americans was James West Lanergan's immensely popular Saint John Dramatic Lyceum (1856–77), also built in response to local initiative. Other significant structures, such as the Academies of Music in Saint John (opened 1872) and Halifax (1877), and the Opera Houses in Moncton (1885) and Saint John (1891), were financed and operated by local merchants, doctors, and lawyers.

4   Golding was manager of the Nickel cinema, leased by the Keith-Albee company. Despite opposition from the company he introduced an orchestra which was so successful that the entire circuit copied his idea. Five other cinemas in Saint John were owned locally (two of them by Golding).

5   There has been an ongoing controversy about what constitutes a Canadian writer.

6   Cf., for example, "Canadian literature… remains generally monolithic in its assertion of Canadian difference from the canonical British of the more recently threatening neo-colonialism of American culture" (Ashcroft, Griffiths, and Tiffin 36). Contrast with this: "The Maritimes, because of their longer history of European settlement, have maintained a cohesive traditionalist stance approximating a Canadian equivalent to the ethos of New England" (Keith, 14). The Maritimes have been as often eager to assert difference from Ontario as from the United States and Britain.

7   Himmelfarb refers to Paris, the provinces, and France, where I have substituted Halifax, Nova Scotia, and Canada.

8   Jean Sweet was one of the founders of the Saint John Theatre Guild whose constitution, in line with Sandwell and Massey's objectives, included a preference for Canadian and British plays. See Sweet.

⁹ However, see Mark Blagrave, "Playwriting," who argues that there is nothing in *De Roberval* that could not be put (indeed, was not put) upon the nineteenth-century stage. See Blagrave, "Playwriting" 154–79.

¹⁰ In attempting to give to pseudo-historical incident a variety of nationalistic/mythological significance, Duvar was following in the tradition of writers like Sangster, Roberts, or Richardson who, in poetry and prose fiction, were attempting the same thing.

¹¹ The Earliest scripted drama from the Maritimes, the marine masque *Théâtre de Neptune* by Marc Lescarbot (1606), is clearly colonial, a celebration of European expansionist ideology. Performed off Port-Royal, Nova Scotia, on ships decorated to imitate chariots belonging to Neptune and his Tritons, in canoes manoeuvred by Frenchmen costumed as Indians, and for an audience that included both Frenchmen and Indians, the mythological spectacle honoured Sieur de Poutrincourt on his return from a voyage of discovery, and was obviously designed to express the supremacy of the King's representative in New France, to inspire French patriotism, and in all likelihood to awe a subject people. Its purpose is political as well as ceremonial, blatantly civilizing and polemical, employing hegemonic cultural values as ideal, presuming to portray and to speak for (an in front of) the "Other."

¹² It is helpful to place *De Roberval* alongside Bentley's discussion of the ways in which four poets of Georgian Canada treat the Indians stereotypically, thus denying them status and individual identity.

¹³ Where full citational information (titles, page numbers) are unrecoverable, newspaper names and dates will be inserted parenthetically in the text—Ed.

¹⁴ Davies (30–47) provides a useful discussion of Loyalist writing in the Maritimes.

¹⁵ The matinee at the Temperance Hall was *Ten Nights in a Bar Room* and the evening performance a combination of *Actress by Daylight*, *Toodles*, and *The Lady's Maid*. Professor Horton's Elocution class presented *Cinderella* and *Old Peabody's Visit to the City* elsewhere.

¹⁶ Anglin was anti-Confederate editor of the Catholic organ, *The Saint John Morning Freeman*. Following Confederation he became a member of Parliament and Speaker of the House of Commons. He was father to the well-known Canadian actress, Margaret Anglin.

¹⁷ For another example of this kind of writing see the description of the opening of Willis and Hatheway's Dramatic Company (the Provincial Legislature) at Fredericton under "Provincial Entertainment" in *The New Dominion and True Humorist*, 18 March 1871.

¹⁸ See Philbrick. In his Introduction Philbrick states that "at least thirteen propaganda plays and dialogues, exclusive of nontheatrical tracts, were printed in the colonies" (1–2).

[19] *New Dominion and True Humorist,* 3 March 1870. Elsewhere I have discussed in some detail how *Measure by Measure* turns "Shakespearian tragedy into mock-heroic verse drama for the purpose of influencing public opinion on contentious issues of the day" (*"Measure by Measure"* 172). Some non-political plays from New Brunswick mock inherited form and substance, as well. For instance, *The Lost Half-Penny! or the Pea-nut Boy's Revenge!* is a very short, five-act piece that mocks the conventions of melodrama.

[20] Fullerton discusses Stewart's theatre criticism and his various literary activities.

[21] Realization of identity through difference rather than essence is characteristic of post-colonial societies. Cf., for instance, Ashcroft, Griffiths, and Tiffin: "Just as the two geographical entities, the Occident and the Orient, in Said's terms, "support and to an extent reflect each other," so all post-colonial societies realize their identity in difference rather than in essence. They are constituted by their difference from the metropolitan and it is in this relationship that identity both as a distancing from the centre and as a means of self-assertion comes into being" (167).

[22] I am grateful to my colleagues, Mary Brodkorb and Robert Moore, and to my graduate students, Susan Flagel and Carl Killen, for stimulating discussions about the material for this paper.

Works Cited

Armstrong, Christopher. "The History of the Imperial Capital Theatre." Unpub. report for Bi-Capitol Project Inc. Saint John, 1987.

Ashcroft, Bill, Gareth Griffiths, and Helen Tiffin. *The Empire Writes Back: Theory and Practice in Post-Colonial Literatures.* London: Routledge, 1989.

Bailey, Jacob. *Humours of the Committee, or the Majesty of the Mob.* Ed. Patrick B. O'Neill. *Canadian Drama* 15.2 (1989): 231–54.

Bentley, David. "Savage, Degenerate, and Dispossessed: Some Sociological, Anthropological, and Legal Backgrounds to the Depiction of Native Peoples in Early Long Poems on Canada." *Canadian Literature: Native Writers and Canadian Writing.* Ed. W. H. New. Vancouver: U of British Columbia P, 1968.

Bessai, Diane. "The Regionalism of Canadian Drama," *Canadian Literature* 85 (1980): 7–20.

Blagrave, Mark "Ireland and the Irish in Three Canadian Plays (1882–1906)," *Canadian Drama* 16.2 (1990): 133-46.

———. "Playwriting in the Maritime Provinces: 1845–1903." Dissertation, U of Toronto, 1983.

———. "Ireland and the Irish in Three Canadian Plays (1882–1906)," *Canadian Drama* 16.2 (1990)

Button, Marshall. *"Lucien." The Proceedings of the Theatre in Atlantic Canada Symposium.* Ed. Ric[hard Paul Knowles]. Sackville, NB: Centre for Canadian Studies, Mount Allison University, 1988. 169–92.

Carleton, John. *Coom-na-Goppel.* Chicago & New York: Dramatic Publishing, 1906.

———. *More Sinned Against Than Sinning.* New York: Dewitt, 1883.

Cogswell, Fred. "Literary Activity in the Maritime Provinces, 1815–1880." *Literary History of Canada.* Ed. Carl Klinck. Toronto: U of Toronto P, 1976. 102–24.

Davies, Gwendolyn. *Studies in Maritime Literary History.* Fredericton: Acadiensis, 1991.

Duvar, John Hunter. *DeRoberval, A Drama: also the Emigration of the Fairies, and the Triumph of Constancy, a Romaunt.* Saint John: McMillan, 1888.

Filewod, Alan. "Between Empires: Post-Imperialism and Canadian Theatre." *Essays in Theatre* 11.1 (1992): 3–15.

Fullerton, Carole. "The Theatre Criticism of George Stewart." *Theatre History in Canada* 9.2 (1988): 147–56.

Himmelfarb, Gertrude. *The Old History and the New: Critical Essays and Reappraisals.* Cambridge, MS: Harvard UP, 1987.

Johnson, Stephen. "'Getting to' Canadian Theatre History: On the Tension Between the New History and the Nation State." *Theatre Research in Canada* 13.1/2 (1992): 63–80.

Keith, W.J. "Third World America: Some Preliminary Considerations." *Studies on Canadian Literature: Introductory and Critical Essays.* Ed. Arnold E. Davidson. New York: Modern Languages Association, 1990.

Knowles, Ric[hard Paul]. "Voices Off." *Canadian Canons: Essays in Literary Value.* Ed. Robert Lecker. Toronto: U of Toronto P, 1991. 91–111.

Lawson, Jessie I. and Jean MacCallum Sweet. *Our New Brunswick Story.* Toronto: Canada Publishing, n.d.

Millidge, J. W. "Reminiscences of St. John from 1849–1860." *Collections of the New Brunswick Historical Society* 10 (1919).

Murdoch, William. *Discursory Ruminations, A Fireside Drama.* Saint John: H. Chubb, 1876.

Parkhill, Frances. *The Fair Country.* Transcript, private collection. St. Stephen, NB.

Philbrick, Norman, ed. *Trumpets Sounding: Propaganda Plays of the American Revolution.* Salem: Ayer, 1977.

Saddlemyer, Ann. "Thoughts on National Drama and the Founding of Theatres." *Theatrical Touring and Founding in North America.* Ed. L.W. Conolly. Westport, CT: Greenwood Press, 1982. 193–211.

Salter, Denis. "The Idea of a National Theatre." *Canadian Canons: Essays in Literary Value.* Ed. Robert Lecker. Toronto: U of Toronto P, 1991. 71–90.

Sandwell, Bernard K. "Our Adjunct Theatre." *Addresses Delivered Before the Canadian Club of Montreal: Season 1913–1914.* Montreal: n.p., 1914.

Smith, Mary Elizabeth. "*Measure by Measure* and Other Nineteenth-Century Satires from New Brunswick." *Theatre History in Canada,* 5.2 (1994): 172–84.

———. "Three Political Dramas from New Brunswick." *Canadian Drama* 12.1 (1986): 144–48.

———. *Too Soon the Curtain Fell: A History of Theatre in Saint John 1789–1900.* Fredericton: Brunswick, 1981.

Sweet, Jean MacCallum. "Small Potatoes." *The Curtain Call.* 1938: 11–13.

Winslow, Edward. *Substance of the Debates of the Young Robin Hood Society.* MS accession 113. Saint John: Saint John Regional Library, 1795.

Too Distant Voices: The Publishing
of Dramatic Texts in the Maritimes

by Bruce Barton [1]

I

Writing about the publishing of drama in the Maritimes (Nova Scotia, New Brunswick and Prince Edward Island) is a little like composing a treatise on woodland sprites, in that printed texts written by local playwrights and published by Maritimes imprints are similarly rare, equally unfamiliar to the average citizen and just as likely to be surrounded with a sense of the miraculous. The conditions responsible for the scarcity of local publishing opportunities for Maritimes playwrights are neither simple nor obvious in nature, although, to be sure, straight-forward financial considerations play a central role. But numerous other factors are involved: some are the consequences of physical geography, others of cultural priorities and practice, and still others of attitudes and idiosyncrasies of the discipline. Yet while opportunities for publication may be scarce, there is no shortage or perspectives regarding the sources of—and potential solutions to—what is seen by many as a fundamental obstacle facing Maritimes playwrights aspiring to recognition beyond their native region.

This article presents a gallery of these perspectives—the thoughts of Maritimes playwrights (resident and departed), publishers, artistic directors and educators—on the topic of the regional publication of dramatic texts. Of course this is, as such, a study both incomplete and inconclusive—more a collection of snapshots of this diverse region, and an identification of issues and concerns worthy of more focused inquiry. The first part of this article considers the conditions and constraints within which Maritimes publishers work; the second part explores the concerns and issues of playwrights and theatrical producers. Of necessity, significant aspects of publishing are excluded here. Discussion of journal publication and the complicated potential of electronic publishing have not been explored within this present consideration of the more traditional book form. Within these limited parameters, there emerges a picture of relative agreement in terms of the status quo. On the topic of the next-step or steps to be taken, however, there is a considerable range of response.

Clearly it is an understatement to say that there is little dramatic publishing done by Maritimes publishers. Modest by national standards in terms of the number of titles produced, as well as in sales, publishers in the region survive by defining relatively clear, circumscribed and frequently non-fiction niche markets. In the words of Laurel Boone of Fredericton's Goose Lane Editions, "If you run a dress store, you can't sell a cake." And there is a strong sense among most Maritimes publishers that there are already quite enough cake sellers (i.e., publishers of drama) on the national scene. For even those that move beyond non-fiction focus almost exclusively on prose and poetry.

Louise Fleming of Charlottetown's Ragweed Press notes that there are only two or three specialty drama publishers in the country (i.e., Talonbooks in Vancouver, Blizzard in Winnipeg, Playwrights Canada in Toronto). A small press like Ragweed, Fleming suggest, simply cannot compete with these houses—nor has it any interest in trying. The investment of time, energy and focus required to research possible titles and cultivate potential markets is beyond the means of a small house that has no intention of making drama a central aspect of its offerings.

Ragweed's sole foray into dramatic publishing in the last decade is, in fact, not a Maritimes play. *Miss Auto Body* (1993), by the Québécois theatre troupe Folles allies, was published under Ragweed's feminist imprint, Gynergy Press. Intended to appeal to Gynergy's established feminist readership, the play was thus less a departure than it initially seems. Yet, although the publishers reportedly found working on the text rewarding, and the volume sold reasonably well (approximately 600 copies), Fleming does not see Ragwood pursuing future drama opportunities. A case in point: Ragwood's recent volume *At the Edge* (1997), an anthology of experimental works, includes only a single, short dramatic entry. Even so, the decision to include "Jack meets the Cat" (an excerpt from *Jaxxmas* by the Newfoundland troupe Sheila's Brush) was a difficult one for the publishers who were uncertain as to its potential audience. Ultimately, it was the piece's largely narrative, storytelling theatre format that secured its inclusion.

Drama maintains a similarly peripheral positioning in the offerings of those Maritimes houses that have, in fact, published plays. Breton books (home of Sheldon Currie's multiple manifestations of *The Glace Bay Miners' Museum*) has published a single play—Beatrice MacNeil's *The Dream*—as part of a book of her works called *The Moonlight Skater: 9 Cape Breton Stories & The Dream* (1993). Notably, UCCB (University College of Cape Breton) Press recently released a collection of Cape Breton playwright Michael Melski's plays entitled *Blood on Steel* (1996), and has plans for a volume to include a play and four monologues by fellow Cape Breton writer Wayne Mackay in 1999. Certainly the activities of these houses (and particularly those of UCCB Press) provide encouragement. But the publication of drama remains a small aspect of both publishers' production—one to which neither is necessarily committed. Breton Books has no future plans for drama at this time (Caplan), and at UCCB Press (which has a mandate to publish material about the history and culture of Cape Breton), hopes for a children's book may preclude the appearance of another drama selection in 2000 (Marshall).

Often, not surprisingly, the deciding factor for publishers in the Maritimes considering dramatic texts is the necessity of breaking even—and the hope of turning a profit—on all publishing ventures. Unfamiliarity with a small, specialized, and highly competitive national market effectively discourages exploration of regional possibilities. According to several publishers, this situation is further exacerbated by the current climate of publishing subsidization through grant funding. The Canada Council provided Block Funding to the Maritimes region in the amount of 422,900 dollars in 1997–98 (185,400 dollars to New Brunswick, 176,700 dollars to Nova Scotia and 60,800 dollars to Prince Edward Island) and 40,900 dollars for Emerging Publishers (29,500 dollars to Nova Scotia and 11,400 dollars to New Brunswick) (Arts Services Unit). The province of New Brunswick provided an additional 50,000 dollars for publishing, while Nova Scotia contributed (approximately) 10,000 dollars for Block Funding and 8,000 dollars for Project Funding (Department of Education and Culture). (Provincial support through the Prince Edward Island Council of the Arts does not provide dedicated funding for publishing. Of the grants awarded in the writing category in the last two competitions, none were intended for publication expenses) (PEI Council). Goose Lane's Boone asserts that these levels of funding represent a serious decrease in government support for publishing over the last twenty years, given rates of inflation and rising expenses. (By comparison, the 1994–95 Canada Council contribution to the Maritimes totaled 411,951 dollars). Referring to a 1982 financial statement (prior to the publisher's conversion from Fiddlehead to Goose Lane), Boone notes that the ratio of grant subsidization to revenues from sales was approximately four to one. In 1997, that ratio was almost exactly reversed (Boone).

Despite these formidable obstacles, two small publishers in Nova Scotia have recently released dramatic texts. Stage Hands Press is located in La Have, Nova Scotia. Run by Ronnie Denil—a publisher, graphic artist and designer—the company evolved out of a puppetry business of the same name. (Despite the retained name, Stage Hands does not specialize in dramatic tests; originally announced plans include a range of genres.) In the last twenty-four months Stage Hands has published works by two well-known Maritimes authors: George Boyd's *Two, by George!* (1996), which includes *Consecrated Ground*, a production of which opens in January 1999 at the Neptune Theatre in Halifax; and Lance Woolaver's *World Without Shadows* (1996), which has also had several successful productions in Nova Scotia. Also on Nova Scotia's South Shore is Roseway Publishing, which Kathleen Tudor runs out of Rockport, Nova Scotia. Previously a publisher of both poetry and prose, Roseway released its first dramatic offering last year with *Growing Up Salty, and Other Plays* (1997) by Natalie Meisner (founder of Halifax's Chestnut Tree Theatre.)

A recounting of the experiences of the principal figures in these three publishing events demonstrates the range of obstacles and opportunities facing regional writers and the small presses who attempt to present their works. In particular, the Stage Hands situation offers clear evidence that getting a book to print is only the first of the ongoing challenges associated with a successful venture. Despite the quality of both the works selected and the presentation of the texts themselves, a lack of clarity regarding responsibilities associated with the promotion and marketing has resulted in disappointing sales (even in terms of dramatic publishing) (Denil; Woolaver). At this date, Stage Hands has suspended publishing drama for the foreseeable future, and Boyd and Woolaver have both decided to pursue centrally located publishers with national status and proven marketing expertise (Boyd, Woolaver).

Conversely, Meisner's relationship with Roseway has been entirely rewarding. It was Tudor, in fact, who requested that Meisner contribute a selection of her plays after the author had submitted prose and poetry for the publisher's consideration. Sales of *Growing Up Salty* have been, in Tudor's word, healthy, particularly during the period immediately following its publication. This is no doubt due in part to the fact that Meisner vigorously marketed the collection through readings and other forms of self-promotion. With the author presently on the West Coast, completing an M.A. in Creative Writing at the University of British Columbia, sales have slowed—evidence of the necessity of ongoing promotion and author visibility. That the investment of time, energy and money such active marketing requires is often beyond the resources of both individual playwrights and independent, small-scale publishers remains a serious constraint on the success of Maritimes dramatic publishing.

Intriguingly, the French language Acadian publisher Les Éditions d'Acadie (located in Moncton, New Brunswick) has had considerable success with dramatic texts. The publisher has offered two drama titles in each of the past two years and remains committed to the genre. Significantly, however, only one of this year's releases is a contemporary play—Herménégilde Chiasson's *Aliénor*. The second title published in 1998 is in fact a printing of a text written in 1875—Pascal Poirier's *Les Acadiens à Philadelphie*. Equally significant, as Les Éditions d'Acadie's Marcel Ouellette explains, is that, within the publisher's mandate to present Acadian work, the approach to dramatic writing is distinctly reader-centred (as opposed to perform-ance-oriented). Plays that read well as literature, and which are not dependent on the reader having a familiarity with theatrical production, are favoured (Ouellette). Ultimately, it is perhaps not surprising that one of the most well-known of Acadian authors—Antonine Maillet—is published by Leméac in Montreal.

II

Two of Canada's most successful playwrights have direct connections to the Maritimes. Daniel MacIvor (*House*, 1996; *Here Lies Henry*, 1997) was born in Cape Breton, although he now makes his home in Toronto. Wendy Lill (*All Fall Down*, 1994); *The Glace Bay Miners' Museum*, 1996), while born in Vancouver, now makes her home in Nova Scotia. (She is also the Federal NDP Member of Parliament for Dartmouth.) Yet, although both writers have numerous publications, neither is represented by a Maritimes publisher (MacIvor is currently published by Playwrights Canada; while Lill currently, by Talonbooks). Many other Maritimes-born writers have followed a path similar to MacIvor's and sought greater recognition—and, possibly, a living—west of the New Brunswick/Quebec border. A few, born outside of the Maritimes, have, like Lill, chosen to make their homes in the region—without compromising their national reputation or surrendering their Toronto or Vancouver publishers. For the most part, however Maritimes' playwrights who remain in their native region find it extremely challenging to achieve recognition beyond its territory. Despite successful productions in Nova Scotia, New Brunswick and/or Prince Edward Island, many writers resident in the Maritimes have great difficulty securing productions outside of the region. Plays are born here, says George Boyd, and they die here.

"Sometimes I feel that I'm only doing it for myself, and a few select friends," says Bryden MacDonald (*Whale Riding Weather*, 1994; *The Weekend Healer*, 1995). Published twice by Vancouver's Talonbooks, MacDonald has the uncommon status of a Maritimes' writer with a national profile who still lives in the Maritimes. Yet his sense of place is at odds with an experience of isolation, and a frustration with the lack of opportunities for both production and publishing in the region. Having just directed a staging of—ironically—Lill's *The Glace Bay Miners' Museum* in Antigonish, MacDonald uses terms of reference to describe the publishing situation in the Maritimes that have been encountered repeatedly throughout the researching of this article. Noting that production is always his first priority, MacDonald speaks about publishing with a degree of detached fascination that he shares with many of his fellow playwrights in the region. "I really don't know much about it," is a phrase that punctuates his comments. Publication is, he speculates, an important vehicle for the creation of production opportunities. But he has little confidence in the printing of his plays as a means to generate a readership. While Macdonald remains committed to the theatre, and is first and foremost a playwright, he feels, the only way to get written words read is to work also in another form. Accordingly, while awaiting the publication by Talonbooks this spring of his latest play, *Divinity Bash*, he also hopes to soon be finished his first novel. [2]

That there is value in reading plays for anyone other than those interested in production is not, in fact, a common assumption among Maritimes playwrights. Certainly for PEI writer Nils Ling, the conditions of production have largely precluded questions of publication. Both of Ling's recent full-length works have been contractually bound to a specific theatre (The Jubilee, in Summerside), and publication has simply not been part of the equation. (Although, he notes, should it become one, he will no doubt seek a Toronto publisher in order to secure the widest possible distribution).

It is, in fact, intriguing to discover that many of the playwrights consulted not only do not consider publishing a priority but actually see little or no relationship between publication and production opportunities. Specifically, emigrant Maritimes writers such as Ken Garnhum and Paul Ledoux and Don Hannah assert that there is little to no direct causal link between the page and the stage. Canada is still the very small vast country it has always been, explains Garnhum, people hear things—because they listen. The theatre community in Canada has a very efficient grapevine, concurs Norm Foster (*The Melville Boys*, 1986; *Office Hours*, 1997, who, born in Newmarket, Ontario, now resides in New Brunswick. A writer's play will get known quickly if it is successful at one or two theatres.

The notable exception, however is the case with foreign sales. A published play, apparently, can be "heard" beyond Canadian boundaries. Foster credits a production of one of his plays in San Francisco in 1996 to the fact that the director discovered it on a New York bookshelf. Similarly, the presence of a copy of Ledoux's *Cheatin' Hearts*

(1995) in the Playwrights Union of Canada Reading Room in Helsinki led to a production in that city (Ledoux). Clearly, these writers—each of whom, with the exception of Foster, attained considerable success only after leaving the Maritimes region—consider as exceptional these incidences of a published text serving as long-distance advertising. But is it not legitimate to discover a parallel within the aspirations of resident Maritimes writers seeking national distribution of their printed plays?

For Halifax playwright Carol Sinclair and many of her Maritimes colleagues, publishing provides transportable evidence of a writer's credibility. Sinclair shares the conviction that a playwright's first priority is production—indeed, she attributes, in part, recent productions of her play *Sabina's Splendid Brain* in Canada, South Africa and Australia to the fact that the work was included in the anthology *Going it Alone* (1997), published by Winnipeg's NuAge. Similarly, Scott Burke, playwright and Artistic Director of the Ship's Company Theatre in Parrsboro, Nova Scotia, suggests that publication provides a degree of status and puts a stamp of approval on a work. Inevitably, he suggests, this serves to popularize and market the work beyond a local or regional audience.

In addition to issues of advertising and promotion, however, a concern that frequently arose in discussion with writers, Artistic Directors and educators through-out the Maritimes is the role of publication in the fostering of a healthy, more integrated theatrical community and culture. While the allure of having one's work represented through a printed text on the other side of the country or even the world is undeniable, there emerged a common perception that printed playtexts—in bookstores, in libraries and, most particularly, in schools—can also effectively serve to foster a sense of theatrical awareness and appreciation in the lives of individuals and communities *within* the Maritimes.

Repeatedly put forward is the argument that inexpensive copies of the texts of plays in production should be made available for sale "on site." Most of the successful precedents come from outside Canada: Prince Edward Island's Ron Irving (*The Chapel Diary*, 1970, with Harry Baglole) noted Britain's Royal Court Theatre, while fellow Islander Michael Hennessey referred to Ireland's Abbey Theatre. But, as Scott Burke points out, Canadian Stage in Toronto is providing a similar service for its current production of Brian Drader's new play *The Norbals* (1998). Burke's own Ship's Company sold copies of Herb Curtis's novel *The Americans Are Coming* in the lobby during the run of its theatrical adaptation by Curtis and Jenny Munday. Had a printed text of the play (turned down by the publisher of Curtis's novels, Goose Lane [Munday]) been available, it would have been greeted by a captive audience for the duration of the production (Burke).

Mary Vingoe, playwright and Artistic Director of Eastern Front Theatre in Dartmouth, Nova Scotia, is particularly intrigued by the possibilities of cooperation between Theatre companies, publishers and the education system. In this, she joins a chorus of voices calling for such joint initiatives. Vingoe cites the impressive advances in Australia—where four contemporary Australian plays are produced, published and placed by region on the high school curricula yearly, in a successfully orchestrated program—as evidence of the potential in collaboration. Implemented within the Maritimes, Vingoe suggests, a similar program could result in heightened appreciation (and increased remuneration) for local playwriting talent. Realized on a national level, it holds the potential to alleviate the sense of distance and isolation experienced by as-yet-undiscovered Maritimes writers.

Such a proposal may, in fact, be timely. A Dramatic Arts initiative is currently being implemented in PEI high schools (although its "Maritimes content" level is, at this point, disappointingly low) (PEI Education); the Provincial High School Drama Festival held in Fredericton each year continues to grow and draw increasing participation from schools and students throughout the province (NB Education); and the Nova Scotia Writers Federation is reportedly being told by that province's educators that the newly established Arts Elective has resulted in an immediate need for Maritimes plays suitable for high school students, as, apparently, there currently is a shortage (NS Education).

Christopher Heide (*I Ain't Dead Yet!*, 1988) is well acquainted with the benefits of participation in the school system. Heide is one of the founding members of the Dramatists' Co-op of Nova Scotia and the editor of the sole anthology specifically dedicated to Maritimes plays. The book's publisher, Nimbus, approached Heide in 1988 when it perceived a void in the school curriculum. *Maritime Lines*, the resulting text, was thus an anthology of plays meant not so much for performance as study. Heide's current roles include Artistic Director of the Chester Playhouse in Nova Scotia and Associate Director of the Mermaid Theatre School program, where he is in charge of youth theatre. As well, Heide is a regular participant in the Nova Scotia Writers Federation Writer-in-the-Schools program. Deeply invested in the study of community in general and, specifically, the community in which he lives, Heide is conscious of the value of the study of printed texts, and of the important role of dramatic publishing in an education system that values, and sees as integral, theatrical performance.

As noted at the outset of this article, much of significance concerning the publication of dramatic texts in the Maritimes cannot be considered here. Of note, the possibilities inherent in electronic publication emerged as central in numerous conversations—in particular with Theatre Prince Edward Island Artistic Director Rob MacLean, who has made the development of local playwrights the first priority of that organization. Discussion with Edward Mullaly, a professor at the University of New Brunswick and one of the authors of the ACTS (Atlantic Canada Theatre Site) web site, only began to identify some of the publishing potential of the World Wide Web. These and other innovations—both technological and conceptual—may in fact mediate some of the challenges associated with more traditional forms of publication in the Maritimes. These same innovations will, of course, involve new challenges and complications of their own. It is not clear just what the next step is for dramatic publishing in the Maritimes. What is evident, however, is that publication—allowing for multiple interpretations of that term—will be an important aspect of theatre's presence, both within and outside of this region, as Maritimes' playwrights continue to seek means to communicate their talent, energy and determination to their immediate neighbours, to the rest of the country and beyond.

(1999)

Notes

[1] Questions and points of clarification can be directed to the authority at bruce. barton@utoronto.ca

[2] Should this article give any unintentional impression to the contrary, the author would like to emphasize that playwright Bryden MacDonald remains fully committed to the theatre, and is first and foremost a writer for the stage.

Works Cited

Arts Services Unit, The Canada Council for the Arts. Fax. 1 December 1998.

Boone, Laurel. Telephone interview. 18 November 1998.

Boyd, George. Telephone interview. 30 November 1998.

Burke, Scott. Telephone interview. 20 November 1998.

Caplan, Ronald. "Publishing Drama." Email to author, 4 November 1998.

Denil, Ronnie, Telephone interview. 24 November 1998.

Department of Education and Culture, Nova Scotia. Telephone consultation. 1 December 1998.

Fleming, Louise. Telephone interview. 27 November 1998.

Foster, Norm. "Canadian Theatre Review." Email to author. 18 November 1998.

Garnhum, Ken. "CTR Article: response." Email to author. 20 November 1998.

Hannah, Don. Telephone interview. 16 November 1998.

Heide, Christopher, ed. *Maritime Lines: An Anthology of Contemporary Plays.* Nimbus: Halifax, 1988.

———. Telephone interview. 23 November 1998.

Hennessey, Michael. Telephone interview. 23 November 1998.

Irving, Ron. Telephone interview. 26 November 1998.

Ledoux, Paul. "Canadian Theatre Review." Email to author. 17 November 1998.

Ling, Nils. "Canadian Theatre Review." Email to author. 24 November 1998.

MacDonald, Bryden. Telephone interview. 19 November 1998.

MacLean, Rob. "Thoughts?" Email to author. 27 November 1998.

Marshall, Penny. "Publishing Drama." Email to author. 24 November 1998.

Munday, Jenny. Telephone interview. 14 November 1998.

New Brunswick Department of Education. Telephone consultation. 1 December 1998.

Nova Scotia Department of Education and Culture. Telephone consultation. 1 December 1998.

Ouellette, Marcel. Telephone interview. 1 December 1998.

Prince Edward Island Council of the Arts. Telephone consultation. 1 December 1998.

Sinclair, Carol. Telephone interview. 12 November 1998.

Tudor, Kathleen. Telephone interview. 19 November 1998.

Vingoe, Mary. Telephone interview. 27 November 1998.

Woolaver, Lance. Telephone interview. 27 November 1998.

Icycle: New Languages: Newfoundland's Artistic Fraud Creates New Languages for Theatre, New Languages for Icebergs

by Denyse Lynde

Artistic Fraud's latest production, *Icycle,* continues this Newfoundland Theatre company's mandate to develop new and innovative processes of production and performance. Since it was formed in 1994, Artistic Fraud of Newfoundland has produced, presented and/or toured several strikingly original productions, earning Artistic Director, Jillian Keiley, the John Hirsch Prize for emerging directors in 1998. *Icycle* clearly builds on Artistic Fraud's earlier productions, *Under Wraps, Cheats* and *Signals,* but it also pushes the company in new directions with the use of a giant puppet and suspended xylophone bars. What has not changed, however, is the meticulous and inspired work of director Keiley and her special and complex approach to productions, self-termed, kaleidography.

In 1994, Keiley burst onto the Newfoundland stage with *In Your Dreams, Freud.* Termed an adult musical comedy, *Freud,* written by Keiley and Chris Tolley, was a fanciful romp peopled by characters such as Sigmund Freud and his daughter Anna, and a tipsy Zeus, along with Jocasta, Oedipus and Teiresias, backed by a game show host, and a jury that doubled as a chorus. The plot is like an onion, layer upon layer, until finally the appropriate execution happens off stage, thanks to the last-minute intervention of Aristotle, as the facilitator, long since forgotten, announces that all has gone as planned and the entire cast rallies for one last song celebrating masturbation.

By 1996, Artistic Fraud began to be known for its daring and spectacular productions as Keiley began to explore in earnest kaleidography. Playing with the word kaleidoscope, kaleidography demands transformation.

Specifically this approach to theatre forces an entire cast to move and flow into images, one after another, creating the effect of a giant kaleidoscope. *The Cheat,* with an eighty-four member cast, was Keiley's first production using kaleidography and, appropriately, it was staged during the St. John's Sound Symposium, always a heady forum of new and experimental productions. In 1997, Artistic Fraud unveiled *Under Wraps: A Spoken Opera,* and it is perhaps with this production that kaleidography can best be illustrated. *Under Wraps,* written by Robert Chafe with a musical score by Petrina Bromley, tells the familiar and sad, but comic, tale of unrequited love, or in this instance the story of Mark, a self-deprecatory gay man who falls in love with the straight David. David, of course, is young and cheerful, if slightly obtuse. What caused standing ovations in St. John's and in selected cities across Canada was less the story than the manner in which it is told This spoken opera features two actors who perform the roles of the young men. However, supporting this duo is a cast of sixteen invisible performers who move, sing and chant throughout the production under a huge, semi-opaque white sheet which covers the entire playing space.

This invisible group works as a conventional chorus, framing and commenting on the action. At times, it also takes on the role of the gay protagonist's conscience, arguing with him through various courses of action, or perhaps more accurately, inaction. This moving tarp, however, also functions as the ever-changing setting, instantly becoming a swimming pool, a discotheque, a sofa and so on. The physical effects, coupled with strong dialogue and a brilliant musical score combine to create truly stunning theatre.

Never taking the easy road, Artistic Fraud's next plan was to tour *Under Wraps* to the mainland. In order to take such a large production on the road, they had to raise funds. Their fundraiser was a kaleidographic version of *Jesus Christ Superstar*. For this production, Keiley again turned to the large chorus approach as the underpinning of the entire production. Staged at the St. John's Arts and Culture, this version of the popular musical was once again strikingly original. Once more, she used a clear stage, but this time, instead of a tarp, she added a series of platforms arranged at the back of the theatre with a wide central staircase. What is crucial to understanding the nature of this production was the grid carefully marked out on the floor. Once again cast became chorus, who in turn functioned as setting and as individual characters. Using the grid and the music to choreograph movement, this version of *Jesus Christ Superstar* was visually stunning, as Christ moved through a human labyrinth, or lay on a human cross. With a turn of a cape, this set-*cum*-chorus was uniformly brown, or a patchwork of individual colours. Not surprising this production, with the local rock band Drive in the orchestra pit, quickly sold out over an Easter weekend. This spectacular fundraiser reached its target and Artistic Fraud took *Under Wraps* to the mainland.

Keiley, like all directors in Newfoundland, works with other companies in a variety of capacities. Either as director-for-hire or as artistic collaborator, her work is always distinctive. In 1995 she worked with Dick's Kids on a cross-dressed multi-media version *Julius Caesar*, which actually worked. The text was not cut or altered except for the obvious simple word transformations of he's and she's. In summer 1998, Keiley joined forces with Place of First Light Festival to produce *A Midsummer Night's Dream* in a mineshaft. The Place of First Light Festival took place in and around the abandoned mineshafts on Bell Island, a tiny island off the Avalon Peninsula. Taking advantage of the natural inky blackness of the shaft, Keiley used black light and fluorescent patterned costumes and masks to create the magic of this fairy world.

Throughout this period, Keiley continued to develop her distinctive style of production with a kaleidographic version of Barbara Nickel's *SchumannBrahmsShumann* in 2000. Once again Keiley was back at the L.S.P.U. Hall where *Under Wraps* and *Freud* had been unveiled. And once again, this production was visually arresting, the tightly choreographed approach further heightening the already carefully nuanced text. Also in 2000, Keiley and her company opened the Sound Symposium with Signals, another collaboration with *Under Wraps* playwright Robert Chafe.

Keiley, whether as director-for-hire, as collaborator with playwright Robert Chafe or as Artistic Director of Artistic Fraud, always seems to be pushing all the boundaries, and Artistic Fraud's latest show, *Icycle*, continues this exciting exploration. Originally created by Keiley when she was participating in a millennium project hosted by the Yukon Arts Centre, *Icycle* is about the life and death of icebergs. As she developed the script, Keiley brought in her team from *Under Wraps*, namely Petrina Bromley as co-writer and director and Robert Chafe as dramaturge. This new production is all about, according to Keiley, "new theatre" rather than experimental theatre. While inspired by the Yukon workshop, this play is set in Newfoundland in a place such as Twilingate, where icebergs are frequent. At the heart of the piece is Keirnan, who can communicate with icebergs, and hence it is about the creation of a new language, the language of iceberg spirits. The entire play has a text sung in English interspersed with this new language. Like so much of the work of Artistic Fraud, timing and precision are crucial to the production, in which Keiley relies on "call-and-move" sheets, and the actors must remember their parts in terms of beats, as the production involves the integration of a new language, the innovative use of the xylophone, and the centrality of a huge puppet handled by three puppeteers. The xylophone bars are suspended individually across the centre of the stage and the performers strike it as choreographed. The ensuing sound and movement effectively capture the qualities and atmosphere of a northern land where icebergs control the everyday life of a community. The huge puppet, Toorhenya, is manipulated by three actors, one of whom is Robert Chafe, who is always present, interchanging with the rest of the cast.

Using the call sheets to co-ordinate music and movement, Keiley takes her brand of kaleidography even further than the constantly moving tarp in *Under Wraps* and the chorus-*cum*-setting in *Jesus Christ Superstar*. In *Icycle*, Keiley uses a physical, almost conventional setting, but, as in all her work, the stage area is transformed. Over the floor is laid a blue and white sea-floor cover. From stage right projects the giant iceberg, which is balanced stage left by a dock. Within this space, three performers handle the puppet's majestic movements as the tale of the isolated community is told, accompanied by the sound of the xylophone bars and the stylized movements.

The plot of *Icycle* is deeply rooted in Newfoundland culture. At the play's beginning, a huge iceberg is sitting outside a small community and the youth of the community want to go pan jumping. If you remember the terrible tragedy that occurred two years ago just outside St. John's you will know what jumping pans means. You jump from ice pan to ice pan. Evan asks his father, Keirnan and his mother, Emma, if the ice will hold. Keirnan and Emma have an almost supernatural ability to talk to icebergs and Emma says the pans have told her they aren't moving until the next morning. Unfortunately, Evan's friend, Jack, drowns, and Emma denies the power she shared with her husband, terming it a "a criminal act of foolishness."

Keiley uses this terrible accident to create an iceberg mythology. In *Icycle*, icebergs are spirits of the sea that come to rest at their final destination, waiting to die. At the moment they implode into a thousand pieces, their spirit leaps out of the ice and flies straight up and joins the northern lights in the winter sky. The reason why Keirnan and Emma talk to icebergs is clarified by Emma's explanation to Jack, the boy who subsequently drowns: "They are like real old people. Now they know all about the northern lights. All the same, it's a scary thing to go. And sometimes they need a little nudge. That's why Keirnan and I talk to them." As she makes clear, it is the most natural thing. People gazing at these stunning ice structures do tend unconsciously to will them to implode. However, the drowning forces Emma to take her son and leave the small community, leaving Keirnan alone to encourage and care for the aged iceberg, Toorhenya. Toorhenya, who is nearly 20,000 years old, is afraid, but Keirnan offers to accompany him, despite the incredible personal danger. In fact it becomes clear that Keirnan doesn't care if he lives or dies, and as he readies his boat the tension mounts. However, his son returns home and it is the son who calls out to Toorhenya in the magical mystical language of the icebergs and urges the giant to go.

It is how Keiley stages this story that is striking and it is pure Artistic Fraud. Throughout the play, a voice-over offers insight into the life of icebergs and their bird companions. In the second act, when the giant puppet appears, it is clear that what is represented is Toorhenya's thoughts. From the opening moments, music and sound ground this production. The cast of eight is constantly moving to and from the suspended xylophone bars, striking them with soft mallets or sticks, striking the sticks rhythmically to the ground, stamping their feet to ever-changing beats, or clapping their hands in various patterns. Kiernan, the father, alone by the dock, creates a duet by singing with his wife as she prepares to leave with her son. The birds, who always follow the path of icebergs, fly in and out on suspended sticks as the actors run on and off. In rehearsal and watching from the rehearsal room, one could see the actors count beats not unlike the ways musicians do. If they are "off" for a moment, it is only a moment, merely time to tuck their mallet away and go and work with the puppet, or get a bird, or switch a stick.

In rehearsal, if Keiley stops to adjust something, the company must start at the beginning of a "Schedule," a word that Keiley uses to describe the many sections in the performance text. In "Schedule 8, Column One" of the script, for example, there is a character list. The middle column is dedicated to form, and the final or right hand column, to content. Characters one to seven designate actors. The actors in Schedule 8 who play Emma and Jack also manipulate the puppet, fly the birds, and become townspeople. Only one actor plays a single role, namely Bryan Hennessy, playing Kiernan. Robert Chafe, who is the chief puppeteer in the second half, performs a multitude of roles in the first act. In Schedule 8 Keirnan watches Emma try to teach her son the iceberg language while four actors with mallets at the suspended xylophone bars play their assigned parts. In this Schedule, they are just playing, but at other times they also move and sing. In one section, five of them perform a panning dance as they mime jumping from ice floe to ice floe in time with their scene. The scene is simply arresting.

In production, Keiley's Kaliedography approach gently supports and deepens the iceberg tale. The audience never loses sight of the family's pain, or Kiernan's devotion to this gentle giant. It is a Newfoundland tale, it is a family show, it is fine theatre. Perhaps what is different about Artistic Fraud's approach to theatre is finally generational. When Keiley teams up with Bromley and Chafe truly magical things happen. Disliking the word "experimental" and preferring "New Theatre," Artistic Fraud does genuinely create new theatre, and in *Icycle* they present a new language of icebergs. They also present a new language of production, in which grids, music, sound and movement are orchestrated by a company of actors who closely resemble highly trained members of a fine orchestra.

(2003)

Cultural Evolution in Newfoundland Theatre: The Rise of the Gros Morne Theatre Festival [1]

by Michael Devine

The theatre culture of Newfoundland, in both its history and modern practices, is distinct in many respects from that of the rest of Canada and even the Maritime provinces. Newfoundland's complex history prior to its relatively recent conjoining with the Canadian federation played a crucial part in the development of both urban and non-urban cultural expression. The region's tortured legacy as a resource-rich commodity, colony of the British Empire, and short-lived nation are elements which have conspired to create performance modes and an approach to the making of theatre which from its earliest manifestations demonstrated a transgressive approach to traditional colonial conventions with respect to the boundaries between spectator and performer. Rooted in traditional folk practices and attitudes influenced by the isolated nature of outport communities, the development of non-urban theatrical expression in Newfoundland is an area of study rich in potential for theatre scholars.

The history of professional theatre in Newfoundland is short and tumultuous and has its roots in the establishment of small, scattered settlements across the coastline of the island. The colonization of Newfoundland has been described by commentators such as G.M. Story as "deliberately retarded"("Mummers"12). The forces arrayed against its development were numerous: competing commercial interests centred in Bristol and London (Cell 101); a series of anti-colonizing policies of the British government enacted in 1634, 1661, and 1671 (O'Flaherty 30–42); French army raids on the English in 1696–97 and 1709 (Major 109–17); and a sequence of disasters that included tidal waves, shipwrecks, destructive storms, and three catastrophic fires in the city of St. John's. Beginning with the arrival of Cabot on the *Matthew* in 1497, colonization in Newfoundland pursued a course as rocky as the island's coastline. The active advocacy of entrenched mercantile interests in England mitigated against anything more than a trickle of settlement for over two hundred years. Between 1637 and 1677 various measures were enacted by the Crown to discourage settlement, abetted by the fishing industry. Although the policies were inconsistent—the "six mile" rule was suspended in 1677, for instance—the effect was to threaten settlers already established on parts of the coastline and to diminish to a trickle the number of new settlers. Outports thus took shape as small, isolated communities, existing at the whim of a far-off government and left largely to their own devices for most of the year. [2] Settlers were careful to build their "tilts"—small, ramshackle shelters used primarily by hunters—well into the woods and away from the prying eyes of His Majesty's ships. Seasonal fishermen brought over from Bristol who wished to stay could not keep up permanent drying and salting facilities under the law, nor the appearance of a settlement. Nevertheless, a small trickle of immigrants defied the laws and began to congregate along the eastern and northern coastline throughout the late 1600s.

As settlement gradually picked up pace in the eighteenth century, this evolving pattern of avoidance—mirrored, ironically, by the island's aboriginal peoples, the Beothuk, who avoided contact with white settlers whenever possible—produced cultural manifestations. As outport communities slowly took shape, a culture of wariness towards outsiders took shape along with them. Although there was intermittent contact between communities, a lack of visible institutions or support from colonial authorities meant that these settlements largely fended for themselves.

One of the off-shoots of this requisite self-sufficiency was the community concert. Originally organized as a fundraising activity to aid local services, the concert (and its larger social cousin, the "Time") combined songs, sketches, dialogues, and recitations. Originally sponsored by a church or local benevolent organization, the show was moderated, and therefore mediated, by an insider—i.e., a locally-born individual—performing the role of "chairman," interacting directly with the audience and offering commentary on each sequence (Skinner 117). The community concert was indisputably local in orientation, although it could include material acquired from abroad. Popular song lyrics were changed to include local references, scene dialogues inserted these references wherever possible, and the oral history of the community took centre stage through recitations and the highlighting of status relationships, often inverted or subverted, in the parceling out of roles to community members.

Many elements of what may be called professional indigenous theatre [3] in Newfoundland find their roots in the community concert. Aspects of its preparation remain a hallmark of the theatre culture today, although multiple reasons may be found for the maintenance of such practices. A truncated rehearsal period, the use of multipurpose spaces, the arbitrary changing of canonical or "established" text (localizing it through the addition of topical references or one of the island's many dialects), the technique of direct address, the use of song as both a narrative and non-narrative device, and an intense level of spectator-performer interaction all stem from the practices of the concert.

A second basis of Newfoundland theatre culture arrived with folk traditions brought by emigrants from the English West Country, probably with Sir Humphrey Gilbert (Story, "Mummers" 167). Mumming dates back in some cultures as far as perhaps the eleventh century and has a long and well-documented history in Devon, Dorset, Somerset, and Cornwall. Though there are many forms of mumming, as typologized by Herbert Halpert, "the form most closely bound to Newfoundland texts [...]"—and therefore its theatre is the "[...] Hero-combat Play" (57). The text of this performance is usually known as *The Play of St. George*, and it continued to take place in various disparate outport communities across the island even after the practice of mumming was banned in 1861 by the Newfoundland Legislative Assembly (Story, "Mummers" 179–81).

In *The Play of St. George* a group of mummers knocks at the door of a local resident. The knock alone is indicative of the visit of strangers.[4] A mummer speaks out in an ingressive voice: "Mummers allowed in?" If the occupants of the house agree to allow the Mummers in, they then enter. The play is performed in any space deemed big enough to allow for its rough-and-tumble physicality. Again, a large degree of spectator-performer interaction is assumed, and spectators in the Hero-combat play are often co-opted as performers. There is also much use of direct address and bolder spectators may engage in repartee with the performers. Indeed, perhaps most notable about this particular type of mumming is that the border between spectator and performer is almost erased. The performers *invade* the protected spectator space (the home). There is no stage, no proscenium. While there may be a space between spectators and the performers, the performers are as likely to transgress that border as not, and to drag spectators across it as well.

Both the community concert and mumming are popular folk traditions. The activities of mumming, so closely linked to the status-reversal of the medieval Feast of Fools, and the community concert, with its inversion of status roles and its inclusion of popular performance modes, demonstrate a nascent theatre tradition derived from working class origins. These elements of folk culture, as well as such later traditions as music hall and vaudeville, have the objective of mocking gentrified attitudes and airs. As such they find a natural opposition in the entrenched mercantile and political interests of a community: that is, in Newfoundland, the emerging bourgeois and landed gentry of the island (Story, "Newfoundland" 12). As Newfoundland developed a proto-national identity in the late nineteenth century, two streams of cultural expression vied for dominance. On the one hand was the powerful influence of imported "high culture" in the form of visiting theatre troupes and the production of established plays; on the other was the developing community concert model which relied for its appeal on direct local references, song and sketch material, and participation. This competition would intensify in the latter part of the twentieth century. The arrival of a colonial theatre troupe in the 1950s, aptly-named the London Theatre Company and headed by Leslie Yeo, did nothing to aid the development of local writers and performers. Between 1951 and 1957 Yeo's troupe performed 107 plays. They employed one Newfoundland-born performer, who was recruited in England (Yeo 124) and, with the exception of their annual *Screech* revues, produced no Newfoundland plays.

The high culture model was perpetuated by the development of an active amateur theatre scene in St. John's, starting with the founding of the St. John's Players by playwright Grace Butt in 1937.[5] The Players were the first and most influential of the island's amateur theatre companies, dominating local and regional competitions for nearly forty years. Although they produced three works by local writers between 1940 and 1947, and strove to educate their performers through play readings and visits by instructors in aspects of performance (Soper 29–34), the Players can at best be credited with increasing the expectations of the local theatre audience and the capacities of its amateur actors. A truly indigenous theatre scene in St. John's would have to wait until the 1970s. The vast majority of productions of the St. John's Players were of British and Irish plays and the performance style was conventional when compared to contemporaneous theatre practice in Europe and the United States. Nevertheless, the production of F.R. Emerson's one-act play *Proud Kate Sullivan* in 1940, and particularly Butt's full-length *The Road To Melton* in 1945—the first three-act local play produced in Newfoundland—and the same author's *New Lands* in 1947 (Soper 48, 45), may be considered landmark events in the history of Newfoundland theatre.

With the advent of Confederation, Newfoundland became eligible to enter the Dominion Drama Festival. None of the competing amateur companies produced the work of a local playwright until 1952, when the Northcliffe Drama Club of Grand Falls revived an out-of-competition production of Fred Emerson's *Proud Kate Sullivan*. In 1956 Northcliffe presented an adaptation of Ted Russell's radio play *The Holdin' Ground*. However, these two offerings were exceptions to the rule. The Emerson play had been produced, as previously noted, by the St. John's Players in 1940, and Russell's *Holdin' Ground* had been produced on radio in 1954 and was written by the province's most famous radio humourist (Rose 4).

Nineteen sixty-seven marked the arrival of British emigré Michael Cook, a teacher and aspiring playwright of considerable charisma and erudition. Through the Extension programme at Memorial University, where he was employed, Cook began to influence a younger generation of students who had been touched, like other students across Canada, with a new nationalism. He began to write articles in the local press and the fledgling *Canadian Theatre Review* advocating for a local theatre scene stocked with local artists and producing local plays. Taking the matter into his own hands, he formed the Open Group with Clyde Rose and Richard Buehler in 1970 and began to produce his own plays. Three have become seminal examples of the emergent Newfoundland drama: *Colour the Flesh the Colour of Dust* (1973), *The Head, Guts and Sound Bone Dance* (1973), and *Jacob's Wake* (1975).

As has been thoroughly documented elsewhere (see especially Brookes), Cook's efforts to establish a local professional theatre scene were joined by the work of Lynn Lunde and Chris Brookes. In 1972 Brookes and Lunde formed the Mummers Troupe, whose agit-prop, politicized theatre won no friends amongst the mandarins of the Culture Ministry. In 1973 the Mummers and Cook were boosted in their efforts by the explosive success of CODCO, a group of Newfoundland-born performers who returned from a successful show of collectively-created material in Toronto to general acclaim in their home province (Peters, *Plays* xi). The commercial success of CODCO, along with the counter-culture work of the Mummers, the playwright-centred work of Cook and the Open Group, and the experience given young performers by Dudley Cox's Newfoundland Travelling Theatre Company (Brookes 43), effectively created an alternative theatre scene in St. John's—even without the existence of a regional theatre to which it could pose an alternative.

The preceding forms the backdrop to the development of theatre on the west coast of Newfoundland. If, given the social and political history of the island, it is no surprise that a professional indigenous theatre arose as a response to neo-colonialist theatre practice which marginalized those outside the urban bourgeoisie, it is in some manner ironic that on the west coast of the island, where so many of the policies of the British and Canadian governments have proven detrimental to the population, colonialist traditions proved even more enduring.

While community concerts continued and vestigial evidence of mumming survived, theatre in the urban centres of Corner Brook and Stephenville had become resolutely colonial with the advent of amateur theatre groups like the Playmakers of Corner Brook. The arrival of British-born Maxim Mazumdar led to an explosion of professional theatre activity on the west coast (in 1976 he served as an adjudicator for the Provincial Drama Festival; he moved to Newfoundland in 1978). Within three years Mazumdar had established both the Stephenville Festival (in Stephenville) and Theatre Newfoundland Labrador (TNL) in Corner Brook (Brunner). These theatrical ventures were based on different elements of the model borrowed from Britain. Stephenville emulated the festival model used in establishing the Stratford and Shaw Festivals (in Ontario) and the Lennoxville Festival (in Quebec), while TNL was created along the lines of regional theatres established across Canada in the 1960s.

Mazumdar's arrival changed the course of west coast Newfoundland theatre. In this he was aided by the decline of the Dominion Drama Festival, which had disappeared by the time he arrived on the scene. Its demise left a large number of people in Corner Brook who had developed strong skills in such elements of theatre as set building, props construction, publicity, administration, and costume design, as well as a host of backstage technical skills. Furthermore, the Playmakers had established a local audience for theatre, particularly through their popular *Home Brew* revue, a refinement of the outport community concert. While he was a conventional theatre practitioner of the British stripe, Mazumdar's accomplishment was to recognize that Newfoundland's cultural history had always involved an intense participation by the community in the making of a "show." They did not want simply to see the foreign and mainland performers who passed through Corner Brook and Stephenville, performing at the newly erected Arts and Culture Centres. Audiences were accustomed, through events like community concerts and mumming, to being part of the show.

With this in mind Mazumdar set up TNL, as noted, partly on the Canadian regional theatre model of the 1960s, but with its true function as a community-based organization. It remains so to this day. The company veers back and forth between professional and non-professional status: its community play and Youtheatre initiatives, which were the company's most popular programmes until the late 1990s, feature non-professionals. However, its Fall/Winter mainstage season in Corner Brook, now discontinued, featured performers in a mix of plays which followed the Canadian regional theatre formula—a formula well known in the 1970s for its dearth of Canadian (or Newfoundland) offerings. Mazumdar's particular innovation was the establishment of youth training programmes at both TNL, in the fall and winter, and Stephenville, during its summer season. This was a first step in the establishment of a base of professional local professional performers.

The two companies managed to survive past their founder's death in 1991—a considerable achievement in the challenging economic climate—fuelled initially by Mazumdar's entrepreneurial zeal and then by considerable volunteerism on the parts of the communities of Corner Brook and Stephenville. However, both remained anomalies in the increasingly indigenous Newfoundland theatre scene due to their concentration on non-Newfoundland work and their steady importation of actors from the mainland. Unlike St. John's, ten hours away by car, the small towns of the west coast could not support a local population of professional actors.

On the East Coast the professional theatre had become sufficiently established by the mid-1970s that it could survive the demise of one company, the Newfoundland Travelling Theatre Company of Dudley Cox, and the fracturing of the Mummers into two entities, including the newly established Community Stage, later known as Rising Tide Theatre (Brookes 180). Rising Tide took local theatre in a different direction. From its inception, it blended a populist outlook with festival theatre programming and the use of local artists and plays. The company's founder and Artistic Director, Donna Butt, borrowed from both the urban and outport aspects of Newfoundland theatre culture in creating a successful hybrid form.

In 1992 Rising Tide decided to shift its base of operations from St. John's—where its previous seasons had featured collectives and text-based plays at conventional theatre venues like the Arts and Culture Centre—to Trinity, a small community in Trinity Bay, where it established its highly successful "Summer in the Bight" Festival. While not the first of Newfoundland's summer theatre festivals, this initiative was far more ambitious in scope than Stephenville. Further, with its proximity to St. John's, it made use of—and helped develop—a wider base of professional theatre artists.

The Summer in the Bight Festival features a diverse array of performances: a "New Founde Land Pageant," a form pioneered by Grace Butt in tandem with the Newfoundland Travelling Theatre Company; songs and sketch comedy evenings, like the popular *Revue*, which take the form of the community concert and the *Screech* shows created by the London Players in the 1950s; collective plays modeled after the work of CODCO and the Mummers; and commissioned plays written by local and Canadian playwrights. As well Donna Butt's company featured new play development workshops that were focused on pieces being prepared for production. From this description of activities it is hard not to conclude that Rising Tide's success heralded the arrival of the first truly mainstream, home-grown regional theatre company in Newfoundland.

The rise of a successful theatre festival on the east coast occurred at a fortuitous time for TNL. Declining audience numbers for its fall and winter seasons forced the board of directors to look for ways in which the company could remain viable in a small community. The answer lay across the island in Trinity Bay, where, with a local population even smaller than that of Corner Brook's Bay of Islands region, the Summer in the Bight Festival was increasing its audiences dramatically every year. Donna Butt had expanded her target audience to include mainlanders and other visitors "from away."

Of course, the festival model could not be said to guarantee success; while Stephenville was surviving, it was hardly prospering. However, in contrast to Stephenville's stagnant mix of Broadway revues and mainland actors, Rising Tide was using primarily young performers and featuring more and more local material. The establishment in Corner Brook of a theatre training programme at Memorial University's Sir Wilfred Grenville College in 1988 offered similar promise of a pool of young, trained actors. South of Corner Brook lay Stephenville, with its well-established festival. The route, then, would lie north.

The Great Northern Peninsula possesses its own rich history, one which includes the initial landing of the Vikings in North America at what is now L'Anse aux Meadows, early Paleo-Indian settlement in the area around Port Au Choix, the medical voyages of Wilfred Grenfell, and the inspirational stories of outport nurses like Myra Bennett. In August 1973 the Peninsula had even, inadvertently, become part of the island's theatre activity: the Mummers Troupe descended on Sally's Cove as that community faced expropriation at the hands of the federal government, which had embarked on the process of creating a new national park and with it the forced movement of some communities, and the elimination of others, within its boundaries (Brookes 78–96). As Alan Filewod has noted, the resulting protest production, *Gros Mourn*, changed nothing in the course of the establishment of Gros Morne National Park, but it proved to be a watershed in the work of the Mummers (122).

It fell to Varrick Grimes, the Artistic Associate at TNL in 1995, to conceive of a theatre festival devoted to local works on the Great Northern Peninsula. In an interview conducted for this article, Grimes noted that at the time he felt that Theatre Newfoundland Labrador, while possessed of a all-encompassing title, had never adequately represented the entire region of Newfoundland, much less Labrador. A graduate of the theatre programme at Sir Wilfred Grenfell College, Grimes felt he could draw on a pool of talented young actors eager to find fulfilling work close to home. The startling success of the Summer in the Bight Festival was setting a new template for theatrical work in the province. All these factors, added to Grimes's restless ambition and strongly-held belief in the importance of Newfoundland culture, created a set of conditions which enabled him to ignite the interest of TNL's board of directors. Arguing his position with enthusiasm, and volunteering to take on the initial responsibilities involved, Grimes was given the go-ahead by TNL's board to scout out the cultural terrain of Gros Morne Park in 1995.

By this point Newfoundland had the beginnings of a written theatre history, not only with the publication of Chris Brookes's *A Public Nuisance* (1988) but as a result of a series of articles published in *Canadian Theatre Review*, *This Magazine*, and the *Atlantic Advocate*, amongst others, between 1970 and 1995. An anthology of CODCO plays had been published (Peters, *Plays*), two more anthologies were in the final stages of preparation (Peters, *Stars;* Lynde, and a conference on Newfoundland drama in 1992 had created a groundswell of interest in documenting the development of theatre in the region. Donna Butt's festival in Trinity Bay had created a model which could be borrowed from, if not copied. It was an auspicious time to explore the possibilities of a theatre festival dedicated to homegrown work.

Grimes had read Chris Brookes's history of the Mummers Troupe and took particular interest in the section on the creation of *Gros Mourn*. He was also influenced through having read Augusto Boal's *Theatre of the Oppressed*, which deals with Boal's work with disenfranchised communities in Brazil. Travelling from community to community on the Great Northern Peninsula, interviewing older citizens and committing their stories to tape, Grimes shared Brookes's perspective on preserving Newfoundland's cultural legacy (if not his training in political theatre). In addition, it could be said that by 1995 there was now what could fairly be considered a modern indigenous performance style based on an amalgam of traditional cultural sources, oriented towards collective creation and audience-performer interaction, with a particular emphasis on giving new life to local history. However, Grimes was constrained to some extent in his ambitions. He was, after all, an employee of a much more conservative organization than the Mummers had been. If theatre was going to flourish amidst the razor-sharp rocks of the Long Range Mountains under the auspices of TNL, he would have to tread carefully.

Grimes had already successfully integrated traditional Newfoundland material into TNL's programming. As TNL's Youtheatre coordinator, he had successfully produced two of the "Jack" plays based on traditional Newfoundland folktales rediscovered and reworked by Andy Jones in collaboration with the company Sheila's Brush (Peters, *Stars* xxiv–xxvi). However, Grimes had bigger plans. Each summer, TNL's Artistic Director Jerry Etienne joined the acting company of the Atlantic Theatre Festival (ATF) in Wolfville, Nova Scotia. During these periods TNL lay fallow. Grimes suggested a project whereby a production would be collectively created and mounted in a Northern Peninsula community. TNL's board of directors were supportive, and Grimes and stage manager Helen Himsl headed "down the coast" (that is, northward) to scout out possible locations in the late spring of 1995.

Grimes presented his ideas to the board as a first step in a template that would enact the regional theatre mandate of TNL and recreate the summer success of Stephenville, while developing the work of Newfoundland playwrights in a much more focused manner than either company had done before. Grimes envisaged a programme that would combine the community activism of the Mummers and the local popularity of the Summer in the Bight Festival. All of these four balls were to be juggled on a tiny budget siphoned from TNL's already meager operating grant for the fall season. Support from agencies like the Atlantic Canada Opportunities Agency (ACOA) would await results of the first endeavour.

Grimes and some of his fellow graduates at Sir Wilfred Grenfell College had already made an initial attempt at collective creation in 1994. For a piece entitled *Raspberries and Tinned Milk*, Grimes and a cast of young performers interviewed locals and collected their stories on tape. The actors took on the voices and behaviour of the interviewees during several weeks of rehearsals in which the structure and material were created for the show under Grimes's supervision. The show toured the southwest coast with funding support from Donna Butt. This proved a crucial step in Grimes's artistic maturation; he learned first-hand the mechanics of collective creation—as well as the challenges of producing a show several nights a week on the road in different communities and at venues of different sizes and configurations. Further, he now had a small, loyal group of talented performers skilled in Keith Johnstone-style improvisation techniques and collective creation. This initial company of actors helped forge a mutually beneficial association between the theatre training programme at Sir Wilfred Grenfell College and what was soon to become the fledgling Gros Morne Theatre Festival (GMTF), a link which continues to this day.

What Grimes and company needed at this point was the right *story*. Grimes was introduced to Ed English, a tourism officer for the west coast, whose father featured prominently in a famous piece of local history: the sinking in 1919 of the postal ship *S.S. Ethie* off waters near Sally's Cove. Grimes was intrigued by the story and asked his room-mate, Shane Coates, to draft a treatment of a play based on the story. Coates, an aspiring poet native to the peninsula, had never written a play. Working with the actors and using techniques borrowed from Boal, Bread and Puppet Theatre, and Chicago's Story Theatre, they created *Ethie*. According to Coates, "We never thought it would go, but it had a little motor in it. The audiences loved it. I kept trying to kill it, but each year it kept coming back."

Grimes contacted officials in Woody Point, Rocky Harbour, and Cow Head, three outports located as enclaves within Gros Morne National Park. Cow Head agreed to host the play at the Shallow Bay Motel. The owner, Darel House, stipulated two conditions: the play had to be produced as dinner theatre, ensuring him a profit regardless of box office, and it had to include Daniel Payne, a local musician. Grimes invited the teenaged fiddler to Corner Brook and found him to be a talented improviser, a powerful singer, and a brilliant fiddler. Payne, the eldest child in a family of talented artists, is now a key figure in the current renaissance of traditional music on the island. *Ethie* was produced for two nights in August 1995 to a total audience of 128 (TNL). Given that the published population of Cow Head is a mere 450, and that TNL had few resources to publicize the play to a potential tourist audience, the numbers represented a modestly successful beginning.

In 1996 Grimes returned to the region, determined to engage more communities along the peninsula's western coast. Rehired by TNL, he headed to Gros Morne Park for community-input meetings in Norris Point, Rocky Harbour, and Cow Head to determine the site of the festival's home and to set up local committees. All three communities were positive to these overtures, but only Cow Head was willing to commit to the process of establishing a festival. Norris Point, a more affluent community, and Rocky Harbour, the established tourist centre of the park, had little incentive to alter their approaches to tourism. Cow Head, set back from the Viking Trail highway and less ideally situated for tourist purposes, could benefit from such an attraction.

In providing the physical support critical to the establishment of the festival, Darel House perceived an opportunity for a business deal with benefits extending in three directions. The theatre would have a home and a base of operations, and Cow Head merchants would profit from the summer-long presence of actors, directors, and theatre-goers. House himself intended to develop the dinner theatre aspect of the operation for his own benefit, and would also profit from increased trade at the motel. An unused second-hand goods store beside his motel was leased to TNL for a dollar a year to serve as a conventional theatre and alternate venue to the dinner theatre taking place in the bar of the motel. House oversaw initial renovations to the building at his own expense. He took an active part in promoting the festival and was helpful in securing accommodation in Cow Head for half of the company's performers. The other half, led by Helen Himsl, decamped to Rocky Harbour (Buckle).

With his company of eleven performers and two stage managers, Grimes created a prototype season. All of the influences instrumental in the forging of modern Newfoundland theatre were to be included: a collective creation, a dinner theatre piece (*Ethie*), a variety night in the community-concert mold entitled *Neddy Norris Night* (after the name of the first recorded settler in the area), and a new play.

Grimes headed to the Centre for Newfoundland Studies at Memorial University to acquire recitations and music for *Neddy Norris*. When *Neddy Norris Night* opened with Grimes in the title role, it quickly became the signature creation of the festival. Coates revised his playscript for *Ethie* and, to their mutual surprise, the play became a huge hit. The local committees were utilized to find research contacts and accommodation for the company. Meanwhile, the cast, none of whom was older than 29, worked under Grimes's direction to create the collective *From Toxic Rock It Grows*. A regional playwright, Bob Pierce, was brought in to assist with the writing. As with the presence of mainland playwright Rick Salutin with the Mummers for *IWA* (Brookes 147–48), this created complications, as a solid nucleus was now disturbed by an outside entity. However, Grimes viewed Pierce's work as a valuable dramaturgical contribution, as the playwright observed patterns and created metaphors from outside the cauldron of the working process. The dialectical tension between historical fact and dramatic revision became an issue with the younger, idealistic actors, who were often reluctant to alter the first in order to achieve the second. This intense creative process was the foundation for the success of *Neddy Norris Night* as well. By this time the actors knew each other well and their improvisational skills were sharp from hours of use each day.

The final production of 1996 was not as successful. Grimes had perhaps unknowingly altered the working chemistry of the company in his desire to invite a director other than himself to direct a new play. *The Pasta King Of The Caribbean* was produced in Rocky Harbour to abysmally small houses. Directed by an inexperienced company member, and with Grimes's attention focused on his own work in a town some 43 kilometres away, the actors' confidence suffered and the production foundered. A perception amongst the company that Rocky Harbour was not as welcoming an environment as Cow Head took root, with implications for the future of the festival. Rocky Harbour would be left to its natural attractions, and Cow Head, spearheaded by local booster Darel House, would assume pride of place in TNL's summer operations.

At this point, with a successful first season accomplished, the TNL board of directors had begun to entertain the idea of a permanent home for the festival. The impression that Rocky Harbour, in Grimes's words, was too "PEI'ised" (a reference to the popular perception of neighbouring Prince Edward Island as placid and complacent) to actively promote a new festival led to the conscious decision to focus on Cow Head and to collaborate with Darel House in establishing the festival there. At this stage, Grimes had succeeded in enacting his personal vision of the festival. Though less political in orientation than the work of Brookes or Boal, the emerging festival had begun to distinguish itself with its celebration of local and regional culture and its use of emerging young artists from the area. According to Grimes, "It wasn't about making a dollar; it was about stealing a page from the park. They [park administrators] were about preserving wildlife. *Neddy Norris* is about preserving culture."

Cow Head is 30 kilometres north of Sally's Cove, where the Mummers staged their stand against the park. As Grimes departed TNL for mainland pursuits prior to the 1997 season, and the GMTF steadily increased its impact in the region, the irony was not lost on Grimes that the park was now serving as a home for theatre activity which complemented, rather than countered, its mandate. An exception to this was Stephen Drover's production of a collective play entitled *Layers In The Rock* in 1998, which tied together the history of the park with the people whose lives it changed forever—those residents forced to leave when the boundaries of the park were drawn and the enclaves enumerated.

In establishing a home for the festival Grimes the idealist and House the capitalist had found common ground. It was all, says Grimes, "about having a stake in it." House actively promoted the festival. In renovating the dry goods store donated by House and outfitting it, through ACOA funding, as a fully functioning theatre, TNL was signalling to the community that the festival was there to stay. Cow Head residents quickly embraced the festival, providing housing, goods, services, and hospitality to the ragtag band of young artists. On the one hand the artists managed to cope with issues such as a lack of fresh produce, while on the other the citizenry coped with an exuberant pack of urban youth enthusiastically rediscovering their Newfoundland roots.

A subsequent part of Grimes's plan had been for *Neddy* to travel, and an old van had been purchased for the purpose. The cast of *Neddy* was constantly changed to avoid a "star system" and to provide the casting flexibility needed to tour the show while *Ethie* played in Cow Head. House, however, chafed when *Neddy* was somewhere else on the coast and his bar was quiet. The board of directors worried quietly about the costs of travelling, especially as they pondered a commitment to large-scale renovation of the building donated by Darel House in Cow Head (Drover). Having taken the extraordinary risk of establishing a festival more than two hours' drive from their home community, the board's caution was understandable. [6] However, a van was eventually purchased and the touring aspect of the GMTF gradually became an integral part of its season (Buckle). [7]

"You dance with the one that brung ya," Grimes notes in describing the decision to commit full-time to a base of operations in Cow Head. The festival's visits to such communities as Parson's Pond, Daniel's Harbour, Norris Point, and Port au Choix were instrumental to its success when this writer became the GMTF's first Artistic Director, [8] not only in promoting the festival but in fostering a sense of ownership in the regional population and a perception that the GMTF was a guardian of local cultural tradition. Travelling with *Neddy Norris* and other shows would continue for three years after Grime's departure, but the seat of power had been firmly identified as being the House of House.

By the end of its second season the GMTF had attracted a total audience of 1377 people to its four shows (TNL). *From Toxic Rock It Grows* had been performed outside in a natural amphitheatre near the oldest part of the town known as "the Head." *Ethie* and *Neddy Norris Night* occupied the dining room and bar of the Shallow Bay Motel, and *Pasta King* had played in a motel in Rocky Harbour. At this point the warehouse, a small squat building, met fire code regulations and House suggested it as an alternative for productions not suitable for the motel, rather than the site used in Rocky Harbour. The TNL board began actively to apply for funding to renovate the building.

In early 1997 Jerry Etienne announced his resignation from TNL. The board, flush with the enthusiasm gained from a successful first full year with the GMTF, was now faced with an unstable situation. Fall and winter programming in Corner Brook was costly, and audiences had steadily diminished at the cavernous Arts and Culture Centre. On the other hand, the cost of establishing the festival, while not minimal, had been offset significantly by support from the Atlantic Canada Opportunities Agency, and audiences were not only increasing, but coming from across the province and from other parts of Canada. The situation of a dual season supported by single season funding was to continue under this writer's tenure as Artistic Director of both TNL and the GMTF from 1997 to 1999. Upon the hiring of Jeff Pitcher as TNL's Artistic Director in late 1999, the GMTF became the programming series with which TNL identifies itself to its sponsors and funding agencies.

Grimes, meanwhile, had decided to pursue his career outside the province. His vision for the company, though still evident, was becoming subordinate to the priorities of TNL and its board of directors. Popular enfranchisement and cultural experiments are easier to manage on a small scale, but with the increasing success of the festival came increased fiscal responsibility and the need for a "stable" product. Grimes is pragmatic with regard to the GMTF's direction: "All the actors coming out of the theatre school should be able to stay in Newfoundland. That part still works. The unknowable, the collective—why lose it just because it's a risk or it doesn't make money? But my vision couldn't be sustained—once you do it, you move on."

Grimes is probably overly pessimistic in his assessment. The GMTF continues in many ways to live up to the objectives he had in mind at its inception. The commitment to interaction with the community remains integral to its success. Collectives continue to be produced periodically. The theatre spaces have become more conventional and the touring has diminished, but the festival's influence on Newfoundland theatre has only grown. It has achieved this while remaining popular within its community and region, something Grimes had always envisaged.

With the departure in 1997 of the festival's driving force and TNL's Artistic Director, the GMTF faced new challenges. A mainland director took hold of the artistic reins, and the renovation of Darel House's old warehouse building resulted in the GMTF's attractive, 90 seat theatre. The number of shows produced increased, along with the number of people employed by the festival. The increase in audience since 1996 has been exponential. From its initial 128 patrons in 1995, the GMTF reached, in the 2002 season, a total attendance of 9100 people (TNL).

Fittingly, the Artistic Director of the GMTF from 2000 to the present is another artist with a stake in the legacy of the Mummers Troupe. Jeff Pitcher, former Stephenville theatre student, Mummer, and performer with Rising Tide, has stewarded the organization through a remarkable period of artistic and financial growth. In 2002 houses were 100% full and, more remarkably, over 3200 people were turned away (Buckle). Plans are afoot for the development of a second theatre space in Cow Head (Pitcher). Pitcher's extensive theatre background all over the island uniquely qualifies him as a spokesman for TNL and the GMTF in terms of funding and arranging reciprocal artistic and production deals with other Newfoundland companies. He has continued and expanded the commitment of the festival to new plays and regional artists, and the GMTF is now active in the workshopping and development of Newfoundland material. This too accords with Grime's vision of the festival as a developmental facility for artists and community alike. As well, the artistic leadership of TNL has recognized the need for the festival to retain its local appeal and not outgrow its surroundings (Drover). Mistakes made at festivals such as the ATF, where fiscal over-reach and an outdated mandate unrelated to the community resulted in massive debts, seem unlikely to occur in Cow Head.

Newfoundlanders are increasingly confident in their culture and in representing it to the global community. When this writer arrived at the Shallow Bay Motel in 1997, the presence of Newfie joke books, plastic lobsters, and other stereotypical paraphernalia was a distressing sight. Neither Varrick Grimes nor myself were interested in perpetuating the "Newfie" stereotype in the work of the festival. Today, however, as playwright and current TNL Artistic Director Jeff Pitcher notes, the "rubber boot issue" has been put to rest (Pitcher). By this Pitcher means not that the stereotype has disappeared: his series of plays based on the characters of "Ed and Ed," featured annually at the GMTF, play to the stereotype and have proven to be popular with audiences. Perhaps they have not been put to rest so much as taken over by the former victims of this stereotyping. The unapologetic stance and confident skill with which various elements of Newfoundland history are put into play at the festival discourages any lingering uncritical association of such stereotypes with the population of the region.

The production of *Tempting Providence* by Robert Chafe, which was commissioned by TNL in 2003 and directed by Jillian Keiley, provides another example. The play is an adept amalgam of effective, lyrical theatricality and Newfoundlanders' view of themselves as a hardy lot where outsiders, such as Myra Bennett, can come and make a new life for themselves. As a result of successes such as Grimes's creation of *Neddy Norris Night,* this writer's production of Michael Cook's *The Fisherman's Revenge* (1998, 1999), and Keiley's production of *Tempting Providence,* the GMTF is now established as the second largest festival in the province, and is a major contributor in the revival of the west coast economy and culture. In a few short years, the vision of Varrick Grimes and the hard work and dedication of TNL and its supporters has borne fruit on rocky soil.

The development and rapid evolution of the Gros Morne Theatre Festival is an apt metaphor for the rapid growth in professional theatrical activity in the region as a whole since 1992. With a clear and often conscious nod to the old traditions of mummering and the community concert, theatre artists have created a thoroughly modern theatre culture which reflects contemporary approaches without losing the distinctiveness which marks theatrical performance in Newfoundland. The burgeoning Summer in the Bight Festival in Trinity Bay has been joined by the Gros Morne Theatre Festival as hotbeds of local theatrical creation and activity. Other festivals have sprouted along the coastline of the province over the past ten years, but none has achieved the national and international success of the GMTF.

In St. John's a theatre community has developed which can fuse disparate theatrical influences into distinctive expressions of local culture. Collective creation continues in various independent productions; in December 2005 a collective entitled *No Mummers Allowed In!* was directed by Andy Jones at the LSPU Hall. The title and subject of the piece, a playful murder mystery utilizing various well-known elements of the mummering tradition, testifies to the importance of Newfoundland's cultural past as artists go about creating its future. Notably, the play also featured four performers who together create anarchic sketch comedy as the Dance Party of Newfoundland. Sara Tilley, a [Richard] Pochinko-trained clown who has started her own theatre company in St. John's, was also in the cast. Within this production, directed by one of the most respected members of what is now Newfoundland theatre's "old guard," one could find elements of the collective creation, community concert, and mummering traditions, with outside modern influences such as clown thrown in for good measure.

In the 1970s the Mummers began to bring the outports and the capital city together, in rediscovering old practices and creating theatre in towns outside St. John's. CODCO brought Newfoundland to the world and returned, its experienced members bearing gifts. Rising Tide validated the indigenous-oriented festival model.

The Gros Morne Theatre Festival, in borrowing successfully from all of these progenitors, has established itself as a distinctive voice of Newfoundland culture.

(2004)

Notes

¹ In writing this article, interviews were conducted with individuals who were primary figures in the first efforts to establish a theatre festival in Gros Morne National Park and with those who took primary roles in establishing and maintaining the festival. In addition, conversations of a more casual nature took place during my tenure as Artistic Director at TNL with various members of the board of directors involved in starting up the project; with Darel House, the motel owner who became an instrumental part of the festival's early success; and with artists and residents in Cow Head. In all cases every effort has been made to corroborate opinions and confirm the details of events.

² The "six mile" rule was promulgated in 1637. Although it was suspended in 1677, liberalization of the settlement laws were resisted by the fish merchants and new restrictions were added regularly. In 1671 laws were added explicitly forbidding the keeping-up of gardens. Furthermore, O'Flaherty notes settlers were not to "erect or make any houses, buildings, gardens, etc." or "fell, cut down, root up, waste, burn, or destroy any wood, or timber trees" (40–41). This would seem categorical.

³ As commentators have noted, the term "indigenous" is problematic with regard to Newfoundland history, given the presence of at least three aboriginal peoples before the European colonizations in the eleventh and seventeenth centuries. James Tuck points out that both mainland Labrador and the island of Newfoundland were covered by glaciers until about 13,000 years ago (11). Groups such as the Maritime Archaic Indians, Recent Indians, and Thule Inuit arrived after substantial migrations. They can therefore claim to be First Nations but not truly indigenous. Given that the word is defined in the Concise Oxford Dictionary as "originating or occurring naturally in a particular place," I believe the word describes both those first nations peoples born subsequent to the migration of their people to the area of Newfoundland and Labrador and those, such as the European settlers, who came after and stayed to produce new generations.

⁴ As detailed in the social anthropology data collected by the contributors to *Christmas Mumming in Newfoundland* (see Halpert; Story, "Mummers"), outport residents do not knock on each other's doors when visiting. This practice may well have changed in recent years but the drama of Newfoundland is rife with references to the strangeness of a knock on the door.

5 Soper says the first production took place in 1938 (12), but the organization's initial meeting took place October 2, 1937 (17). It is fascinating to read in Soper's account the view that the St. John's Players were a group devoted to experimentation; this may be true given the arid context of the contemporary drama scene in St. John's in 1937. Soper draws links with the Players and the "little theatre" movement associated with Antoine and Brahm in France and Germany—pretty heady company; but Antoine's performers, after all, were all amateurs as well, and untrained amateurs at that.

6 Similar sentiments from various board members were made known to me during my first year as Artistic Director of the GMTF, in 1997.

7 Under Jeff Pitcher, the TNL/GMTF's current Artistic Director, the emphasis has shifted from touring locally to an increasingly successful national and international profile.

8 This writer assumed the dual roles of Artistic Director of TNL and of the GMTF in April 1997, continuing until August, 1999. Grimes remained an Artistic Associate at TNL while he did the work necessary to create the Gros Morne Theatre Festival.

Works Cited

Brookes, Christopher. *A Public Nuisance.* St. John's: ISER, Memorial University, 1988.

Brunner, Astrid. "Summer Festivals in Atlantic Canada: Balancing Love and Money." *Canadian Theatre Review* 45 (1985): 56–62.

Buckle, Gaylene. "Re: GMTF Article." Emails to M. Devine. 29 August 2002, 8 September 2002, 11 September 2002.

Cell, Gillian. "The Cupids Cove Settlement: A Case Study of the Problems of Colonisation." *Early European Settlement and Exploitation in Atlantic Canada: Selected Papers.* Ed. G.M. Story. St. John's: Memorial University, 1982. 97–114.

Coates, Shane. Private conversation. St. Anthony, Aug 1997.

Cook, Michael. *Colour the Flesh the Colour of Dust.* Toronto: Simon & Pierre, 1974.

———. *The Head, Guts, and Sound Bone Dance.* St. John's: Breakwater, 1975.

———. *Jacob's Wake.* Vancouver: Talonbooks, 1975.

Drover, Stephen. Telephone interview. 12 October 2002.

Filewod, Alan. *Collective Encounters: Documentary Theatre in English Canada.* Toronto: U of Toronto P, 1987.

Grimes, Varrick. Personal interview. Toronto, 20 September 2002.

Halpert, H. "A Typology of Mumming in Newfoundland." *Christmas Mumming in Newfoundland*. Ed. H. Halpert and G.M. Story. Toronto: U of Toronto P for Memorial University, 1969. 34–61.

Lynde, Denyse, ed. *Voices From the Landwash*. Toronto: Playwrights Canada, 1997.

Major, Kevin. *As Near to Heaven by Sea: A History of Newfoundland and Labrador*. Toronto: Penguin Books, 2001.

O'Flaherty, Patrick. *Old Newfoundland: A History to 1843*. St. John's: Long Beach P, 1999.

Peters, Helen, ed. *The Plays of CODCO*. New York: Peter Lang, 1992.

———, ed. *Stars in the Sky Morning: Collective Plays of Newfoundland and Labrador*. St. John's: Killick P, 1996.

———. "Summer in The Bight Festival." *Canadian Theatre Review* 89 (1996): 76–78.

Pitcher, Jeff. "Re: GMTF Article." Emails to M. Devine. 7 October 2002, 9 November 2002, 12 March 2003.

Rose, Clyde. "Foreword." Russell 1–6.

Russell, Ted. *The Holdin' Ground: a Radio Play*. Toronto: McClelland & Stewart, 1972.

Skinner, Chesley. "Drama in Newfoundland Society: The Community Concert." Diss. Michigan State University, 1984.

Soper, Lloyd. *The St. John's Players: The Little Theatre in Newfoundland 1949*. St. John's: St John's Players, 1949.

Story, G.M. "Newfoundland: Fishermen, Hunters, Planters, and Merchants." *Christmas Mumming in Newfoundland*. Ed. H. Halpert and G.M. Story. Toronto: U of Toronto P, 1969. 7–33.

———. "Mummers in Newfoundland History." *Christmas Mumming in Newfoundland*. Ed. H. Halpert and G.M. Story. Toronto: U of Toronto P, 1969. 165–85.

———, ed. *Early European Settlement and Exploitation in Atlantic Canada: Selected Papers*. St. John's: Memorial University, 1982.

TNL (Theatre Newfoundland Labrador), Archives, Corner Brook, Newfoundland.

Tuck, James. *Newfoundland and Labrador Prehistory*. Ottawa: National Museum of Man, 1976.

Yeo, Leslie. *A Thousand and One First Nights*. Oakville: Mosaic P, 1998.

Afro-Gynocentric Darwinism
in the Drama of George Elroy Boyd [1]

by George Elliott Clarke

Preliminary (Playful) Polemic

Nationalism and fascism begin at home, and take their sustenance from the family undergoing a crisis, particularly one of identity. Given the brutal tragedy of the four-century-long African slave trade (with its bloodily efficient exploitation, sexual and economic, plus often liquidation, of its human capital), its diasporic survivors, especially intellectuals and artists, focus necessarily on the situation—read *plight*—of the Black family. *Certes*, the nouns *family*, *identity*, and *crisis* are virtual synonyms in the literature of the African Atlantic, a cultural geography that includes Canada (as much as it does the better known "Neo-African" spaces of the United States, the Caribbean, Latin America, and Western Europe). Of course, a signal balm for these familial identity crises involves the efficacy—and risks—of cultural nationalism. Thus, two dramas by African-Nova Scotian—or Africadian—playwright George Elroy Boyd depict Black familial strife that provokes acts congruent with nationalism—and fascism. Boyd's teleplay, *Consecrated Ground* (1983, 1996), relates the struggle of a Black woman, Clarice, to bury her dead infant son in Black community space despite the objections of a white-controlled metropolis. His play, *Gideon's Blues* (1996), narrates the events that prod a Black mother to murder her adult son and only child. Boyd examines the African-Canadian family and its race, class, and gender issues to excavate the tensions between an attractively protective cultural nationalism and a sorrowfully deranging, self-destructive fascism.

Boyd traces trajectories—dramatic arcs—always patent in New World African scholarship. Hence, introducing the collection, *Colored Contradictions: An Anthology of Contemporary African-American Plays* (1996), co-editor and African-American scholar Harry J. Elam, Jr., scrutinizing plays utilizing the theme of "The Black Family in Crisis" (12), insists that "[e]xternal and internal forces threaten the security and the values"—that is, identities—"of the families in each of these works" (12). Elam's perception confirms the perspicacity of Paul Gilroy's insight that "the trope of family which is such a recurrent feature of [African-American] discourse is itself a charac-teristically American means for comprehending the limits and dynamics of racial community" (Gilroy 191). Elam's rhetorical strategies produce, then, not "Africentricity," but what "might be more properly called Americocentricity" (191). Such scholarship contributes, alleges Gilroy, to "the great ethnocentric canon of African-American literature" (186) and "the lure of ethnic particularism and nationalism" (4).

Throughout *The Black Atlantic: Modernity and Double Consciousness* (1993), Gilroy wars perpetually against the "ever-present danger" (4) of "African-American exceptionalism" (4) and "ethnic absolutism" (5); yet, his fear that African-American cultural nationalism may morph into narrow particularity is apt. Twentieth-century history shows that nationalism regresses, potentially, into fascism, that ideology claiming "to fulfill both the aspiration of the 'left' for an egalitarian community and the demand of the 'right' for order and authority" (Hatlen 148). Explains American literary scholar Burton Hatlen, fascism seeks "a principle of community" founded upon "the nation" (149), thus fusing "a 'socialist' egalitarianism with a 'conservative' authoritarianism" (150). The peril inherent in Afrocentrism, then, is that it may assume fascist hallmarks such as "militarism" and attempts "to recover authentic community and legitimate authority..." (Gilroy 152). Specifically, for Gilroy, cultural nationalist worry regarding the strife of Black males may drive advocates to adopt fantastic, fascistic "panaceas." Gilroy is wary, then, of speech wherein "the social and economic crises of whole communities become most easily intelligible ... as a protracted crisis of masculinity" (194).

Almost as if to flout Gilroy's liberal nervousness, Elam uses the rubric "Black Men at Risk" (that is, in *crisis*) and comments that the plays denominated "explore issues of black male identity" (5).[2] Elam commits, then, in Gilroy's eyes, a grave sin: "The integrity of the race is thus made interchangeable with the integrity of black masculinity" (194). Nevertheless, African America is not the only site where "the contemporary political and economic crises of Blacks... are [portrayed as] crises of... self-identity" (194). Black cultural nationalism, in its racialist and patriarchal modes, also thrives in Canada.

Boyd's plays engage, profoundly, with the supposedly American trope of *family* and its "familiars" of *identity* and *crisis*. They demonstrate that, in Canada too, *pace* Gilroy, "the symbolic reconstruction of [Black] community is projected onto an image of the ideal heterosexual couple" (194). Here, too, "[t]he patriarchal family is the preferred institution" (194). Indeed, African Canadians, like African Americans, address an existential dilemma that American literary critic Robert Bone describes as the alternation of our "deepest psychological impulses between the magnetic poles of assimilationism and Negro nationalism" (4). African-Canadian writers and intellectuals also balance what Gilroy cites as "the unsatisfactory alternatives of Eurocentrism and black nationalism" (186). Still, Boyd's dramas articulate both an American-style racial chauvinism and a Canadian dissent therefrom.

While the plays bemoan the absence of strong, self-empowered, race-identified Black males, they stress the presence of strong-willed, self-empowering, Black females—or, to employ the anachronistic designation of a century ago, "race women," those who work for the "uplift" of Black people. Boyd thus fulfills the general tendency of Canadian literature, in contrast to that of the United States, to emphasize "the weak male/strong-female syndrome" (64), as American sociologist Seymour Martin Lipset terms it in *Continental Divide: The Values and Institutions of the United States and Canada*. Citing Gayle McGregor's idea that "'the Canadian literary hero seems to demonstrate a distinctly [female] gender aspect,' while the American is mas-culine" (qtd. in Lipset 64), Lipset agrees that "'[t]he Canadian heroine… is strong' and dominant within the family, while the reverse is true in American fiction" (64). Lipset also points to a study of "the story content of English-Canadian films" that finds, "[t]hrough many different scenarios… 'the radical inadequacy of the male protagonist—his moral failure, especially, and most visibly, in his relationships with women'" (qtd. in Lipset 64). In contrast, females possess "'greater authenticity,' having 'the power to love and trust and commit themselves without adding up the cost'" (64). While Boyd adumbrates an African-American-style cultural nationalism, he differs by foregrounding women, not men, as its primary exponents. His plays enact, then, an Afro-gynocentric Darwinism, in which Black women represent "the survival of the fittest," while the primary Black male characters appear as sly, cringing, obsolete sell-outs.

The Playwright

Born in Halifax, Nova Scotia, in 1952, and raised as a member of the more than two-century-old Africadian community, journalist George Elroy Boyd first achieved national prominence in Canada as the anchor of CBC (Canadian Broadcasting Corporation) *Newsworld* in 1992. His first play, *Shine Boy*, treating the life of Africadian pugilist George Dixon, debuted at Halifax's Neptune Theatre in 1988 to fine reviews. His teleplay version of *Consecrated Ground*, which deals with the destruction of the sesquicentarian Africadian community of Africville in the 1960s, has never been produced, but a stage version played Halifax's Sir James Dunn Theatre to great acclaim in 1999. A published version of the stage play was nominated for a Governor-General's Literary Award for English-language Drama in 2000. Boyd's *Gideon's Blues*, a play delineating the consequences of the development of a crack cocaine *cum* prostitution economy in inner-city Halifax, among members of the Black community in the 1980s, was produced under the auspices of Upstart Theatre and presented at the now-defunct Cunard Street Theatre in Halifax in 1990.

Boyd is an African-Canadian playwright of the first rank, and his staged demesne—marginalized, Black urban Nova Scotia—constitutes a major, distinct form of African-Canadian culture, namely, that which may be classed as the classically Unitarian. Given this fact, his decision to populate his plays with stern women, meeching men, absent fathers, and dead babies exhibits an unsparing, sociological account of contemporary urban African Canada. *Our* reality, according to Boyd, is communal disintegration, a fate expressed through the collapse of Black male loyalty to the self, the family, and the "nation."

Boyd's Black "Boys"

Boyd's teleplay, *Consecrated Ground*, opens with the sounds of a "howling, snow-cluttered" wind and "a baby crying, weakly" (12). This contrast between a mighty,

white-shaded wind and a frail Black infant—Tully, the baby boy of Clarice and Willem
Lyle—foreshadows other imagery emphasizing the emasculation of Black males and
the masculinization of Black females, within the inclement context of a white male-
dominated society. Thus, while viewers of the teleplay hear, over the opening credits,
the hymn, "Faith of our Father[s]," we see, ironically, not a man but a woman, Clarice,
"pumping vigorously"—in a parody of male coital performance—to draw water from
a well. [3] However, an ominous futility—or sterility—is figured by her production of
only a "trickle of water" from the phallic "spout" of the pump. "The Faith of our
Father[s]"—despite the best efforts of a literal mother—has almost run dry—right
beside the "bleak, sea-scraped landscape" in which Africville is situated (12). This
image of ironic aridity foresees that moment when, during a battle with her husband
that dissolves into "crying in wild embraces and kisses" (29), Clarice does not yield to
him in love, but, rather, tells him to leave: "Willem... I don't... I don't wantcha here,
anymore" (29). Clarice's first words in the teleplay, spoken during a blizzard, accent
her frustrating position as a Black mother in a snow-white environment where the
faith of the ancestral patriarchs cannot produce enough water to provide sustenance
for the new—and last—generation of Africville residents:

> Momma's comin', Tully. Momma's comin'. I'm just gettin'
> some water for your formula, baby. Momma's comin'... (13)

Tully is, in truth, the last of the line. He is an only child, born in a Black community,
located on the extreme north end tip of peninsular Halifax, that is being slowly razed
by bulldozers representing white urban planning and social engineering, forces that
have declared Africville a "segregated slum" and ordered its demolition. Thus, when
Clarice, responding to the final, shattering wails of her hungry, infant boy, runs into
her house and sees a "shadow dart away from the top of [Tully's] crib" and rats
"scurry" (13), these pests that have fatally bitten her child appear as kin to the
bulldozers ripping apart Africville itself: "A rat, perched atop a pile of debris, scurries
away as a bulldozer starts and idles nearby" (16). Truly, the rats' white teeth that
penetrate Tully's Black flesh mirror the bulldozers—"Those destroyin' creatures"
(19)—tearing through Africville residents' homes. Too, in the instant just before
Clarice retrieves her dead—or dying—son, "A rat runs between her legs" (13), an
action that anticipates the later motion of a bulldozer passing "through the frame"
(16) of a shot of Africville. Both images reflect the violation—or desecration—of the
community. Just as rats "reap"—or "rape"—the final offspring of the Africville
patriarchs, so do bulldozers violate the homes that, as Clarice says of her own,
"Granddaddy built ... with his bare hands" (24).

But only Clarice resists the aggression of the bulldozers. Her husband, Willem,
recognizes that official Halifax "ain't buildin' no monuments. They tearin' the
memories down" (21). But he is more a foe to Clarice—or Leasey as he calls her—
than ally. To frustrate her plan to bury their son in Africville, he secretly sells their
property to the City of Halifax (23). In vivid contrast to his forceful wife, whose name
evokes that of a "masculine" horror film heroine, [4] Willem is deceitful and weak-
willed. [5] Though Africville matriarch Sarah James tells Willem, "[Clarice] needs you.

She needs your strength, son. Now you got to be strong. Strong enough for the both of ya" (18), and though Willem infantilizes Clarice by calling her "baby" incessantly, it is she who displays "determination" (19). When she tells the white city employee Clancy, "They're scared of you and yer bulldozers. They're plain scared, and that's why they signed their land away" (26), she embodies communal courage. Boyd submits, in his prologue, that the teleplay is "the story of a proud and strong woman, who refused to acquiesce..." (11). Clancy, too, soon knows that Clarice can "feel... strongly" (27).

Clarice's strength contrasts with Willem's capitulation to white authority. Clarice wants Tully buried in Africville, but Willem protests that, because Clancy objects (19), this cannot be done. Willem is cowed by "the white man," who has his "ordinances... and... by-laws—and [...] the police behind him" (19). Intriguingly, Willem conflates the phrases "white man" and "the man" (20), thus implying that manliness and its popular attributes—power, determination, strength—are consonant with whiteness. [6] He lectures Leasey, "the man say you gotta have consecrated ground to bury someone. And there ain't no consecrated ground in Africville" (20). His declaration—the proof he has internalized marginality—summons this answering sermon from Clarice/Leasey:

> No consecrated ground!? *(long pause)* No consecrated ground? What is Africville if it ain't consecrated ground? [...] My ancestors, they consecrated this ground. All the baptisms down at the beach [...] I watched 'em consecrate it. This is where they lived and died... where... where they LOVED, Willem. Surely... *(starts to cry)* ...NO ONE!! AIN'T NOBODY ON THIS EARTH TELLIN' ME AFRICVILLE AIN'T CONSECRATED GROUND!! (19)

Following these exclamations, Clarice scorns white-male power: "Ain't no Mister-Clancy-city-white man tellin' me. I saw it... I lived it... Africville is consecrated ground" (20). Clarice backs up her sentiment, both by throwing "Willem's jacket at him" (20) and by briefly, metonymically, demonizing Clancy as "murderin' hands" (21). She brands him a killer: "You killed my child. You killed Tully the day you [the City of Halifax] built that dump on our doorsteps" (26). She also deems Clancy "the devil" (25) whose bulldozers are "desecratin' the land, tearin' up people's lives. You and your machine's desecratin' their souls" (26). She then affirms that "Tully's gonna be buried in Africville where he belongs" (21). Others flee; Clarice fights.

For all her swagger and energy, though, Clarice is nearly thwarted by her spineless husband. Constantly belittling himself and other Blacks, Willem feels he must give way to the city's "big plans" involving "big industry" (22). His cowardice seems a form of "penis envy." The white phallus—pictured as lucre, bulldozers, and "the man" himself—seems indomitable. Thus, in the flaccid posture of bowing his head "as if in prayer," Willem is "seduced" into signing over his wife's ancestral land to Clancy (23). The "Quit Claim Deed" that Clancy then hands Willem symbolizes the latter's surrender, and his abjection is emphasized by his signing of the papers on, as Clarice notes, "our baby's casket" (28). He has been dispossessed twice: once by rats, now by laws; he and Clarice are now "a childless couple" (23), and landless, and soon homeless.

When Clarice learns how fully she has been dispossessed by her husband's *treason*, "a look of dreaded realization possesses her face" (27), and she confronts the Bible-reading, church deacon Willem, calling him a "black... bastard. You black, ungrateful, sonofabitch" (28), here utilizing race-sex epithets that, metaphorically, accent his bastardized status as childless father and unsexed husband. Willem retaliates by denouncing Clarice as a "stupid, goddamned bitch" (28), but she attacks him physically, and he does not resist: "*Clarice lashes at him, repeatedly slapping his face. Willem takes it, not raising a hand to defend himself*" (28). Here, too, Clarice seems masculine, symbolically unmanning her husband by "slapping him." He is "feminine," remaining passive. Clarice's assault on Willem culminates in her raced dismissal of his behaviour: "the white man takes advantage of stupid niggers and you are a stupid nigger, Willem" (28). This comment positions the white man as *man* and Willem as his antithesis, a non-man, a "stupid nigger." Thus, even when blows melt into caresses, Clarice does not accept her husband again, but rather, says, "I want ya to leave... to go..." (29). Although Clarice allows herself a rare statement of defeatism, "Don't be ashamed of us, Willem [...] we all... they allow us to be..." (29), she ejects her husband from their marital bed—and from the land she has inherited but that he has surrendered over the body of their heir apparent.

In the final scene of the teleplay, the Lyle family is reconstituted in the instance of Clarice's triumphant burial of her dead son, his body wrapped only in a blood-soaked blanket, with Willem helping her to dig the grave with their "bare hands" (31).[7] Yet, the burial occurs secretively, at night, with a bulldozer growling, threateningly, in the near-distance. This "triumph" is, then, empty, for the Lyle heir is dead and Africville is dying. Ironically, the teleplay's opening hymn, "Faith of our Fathers," plays again in the background (31). Although Reverend Miner,[8] the Black Baptist minister who conducts an impromptu burial service, proclaims, "I do consecrate this holy and sacred ground" (32), his words are almost "*drowned*" out by the "*noise of the bulldozer*" (32). Reciting Psalm 8, Miner intones, "Out of the mouths of babes and sucklings thou hast ordained *strength*, oh Lord, because of thine enemies" (32; emphasis added), but his words apply best to Clarice, not Willem. Her strength is what survival requires. She affirms the principle of Sarah's nostrum: "I guess, really, if yer a nigger in this country—ya gotta learn how to be agile or you'll perish" (31).

In the end, the Promised Land of Africville becomes a dumped-on graveyard, a ghost town of memories. If the ending conjures up John Milton's *Paradise Lost*, we do not see here Adam and Eve, "Our ling'ring parents," with the "World... all before them," "hand in hand with wand'ring steps and slow,/Through *Eden* [taking] thir [*sic*] solitary way" (12. 638, 646–48), but, rather, two childless parents, Clarice and Willem, "digging" a grave at night with their bare hands in likely very cold, very hard soil. Boyd shows us a diabolical paradise. In Milton's epic, Adam learns that, though he must quit Eden, he "shalt possess/A paradise within thee, happier far" (12. 586–87). In Boyd's teleplay, Sarah tells the Adamic Clarice, "Africville lives in here (*gestures to her heart)....* And you'll see, baby, Tully'll live in here too" (31). But it's a bleak vision of a post-mortem Eden. Worse, the Black male "Adam" in this story of a failed Paradise, where "[t]he sun sets majestically on the... Africville [garbage] dump" (16), is a philistine father and a eunuch husband. Clarice—Leasey—is—or will be—better off without Willem, who stands exposed as a cowardly gravedigger of "the race."

Boyd's *Consecrated Ground* closes with a funeral that precludes any continuance of the Lyle patrimony, but *Gideon's Blues* opens with one that signals the termination of the second-generation of the currently three-generation-established Steele clan. Indeed, when Louise[9]—Momma-Lou—Steele reflects on the burial of her murdered adult son, Gideon,[10] she remarks, in her prayer to her deceased husband and Gideon's father, "The rain, Poppy, it drooled all over our baby's grave, all over Gideon's coffin, and pooled black, into that dark, gleamin' hole where they put 'em... my lovely baby, Poppy, our only, lovely-est chile..." (37). Like *Consecrated Ground*, *Gideon's Blues* begins with a parent mourning the loss of an only child, a dead baby. However, here the funeral occurs first, with the play unfolding in panoramic flashback. Nevertheless, this play is, even more than *Consecrated Ground*, a harsh study of Black male failure and the compensating necessity for Black matriarchal assertion to preserve—or conserve—"the race."

Commenting on his creation of the character, Bigger Thomas, in *Native Son* (1940), African-American novelist Richard Wright saw that his homicidal, naïve revolutionary was "an American product, a native son of this land [who] carried within him the potentialities of either Communism or Fascism" [qtd. in Gilroy 163]. Boyd addresses this dualism but accents, strikingly, the "fascistic" possibility. Wright's poor, and poorly educated, Bigger lands a legitimate job that, indirectly, lands him in jail, with two grisly murders of women, white and Black, on his conscience. On death row, under the tutelage of his Communist Party lawyer, he rejects nihilism and accepts socialist existentialism. In contrast, Boyd's colleged, bourgeois-aspiring Gideon Steele finds employ as a Machiavellian drug dealer, who is slain shortly after he slays his shifty brother-in-law, Seve. While Gideon comes to practice vampirish gangsterism in Halifax's "hood,"—that is to say, the economically depressed North End, defined by Gottingen Street—it is his mother, Momma-Lou, who accepts, in the end, a doctrine of racialist fascism to "cleanse" away Gideon's criminality. Vitally, then, where Wright's novel opens famously with the "*Brrrrrriiiiiiiiiiiiiiiiiinng!*" of an alarm clock (3), our first glimpse of Gideon occurs after his sister, Cherlene, "calls... 'GIDEON!! FOR GODSAKES, GIDEON, WILL YOU WAKE UP!!? GIDEON!!'" (39). Bigger's "awakening" triggers, eventually, his attainment of a socialist consciousness, but Gideon's own awakening prefaces his dismal death and his mother's *reactionary* radicalization. While *Consecrated Ground* may be described as a *Black* comedy, with its (temporary) reunification of now-ghoulish parents, *Gideon's Blues* is an unstinting, *Black-on-Black* tragedy.

To begin, Gideon matures as a fatherless child, whose "Poppy," dies when he is a boy. His mother, Momma-Lou, the "family matriarch" (36), becomes his nurturer and provider, but, in reality, the funds to raise Gideon—and later to support him,

Cherlene, and their two children, Wendolyn and Pauli, derive from "Poppy's pension" (49). Although Poppy is a vanished father, his name is a slang variety of Papa, or Father—or God, a paternalist being also apparently absent. [11] Nevertheless, just as Poppy's death benefits assist the surviving Steeles, so does Poppy-as-pseudo-God, [12] as a constant interlocutor for Momma-Lou in her prayers, provide psychological succour to her as matriarch. Despite her intimate conversations with her providential overlord, however, Momma-Lou must manage, all alone, her son, daughter-in-law, and grandchildren, all who live under her roof.

Still, she seems soldierly or police-like in demeanour. [13] Momma-Lou recalls, "I had ammunition for Mr. Gideon's butt when he was young" (39). When he lazed in bed, she would beat on the headboard so hard with a *billy club* that "[p]oor Gideon used to think it was the second coming of Queen Nzinga" [14] (39; emphasis added). (Note that she refers here, not to a male military figure, but a female one.) Later, when Gideon argues with his wife and his mother, Momma-Lou warns, "Don't you know you're outnumbered here?" (51). Remembering her marriage to Poppy, Momma-Lou says pointedly, while speaking with Cherlene's wayward sister, Baye, "I was bigger than him" (58): "Look, girl—there was a time I was ready to kick his little ole black behind! He gave me my baby and wanted no… watcha call it?… 'responsibility?' I say, 'don't [sic] go down that-there dirt road, Poppy—been there—done that! U-turn!'… And we worked it out" (58).

Momma-Lou is a feisty, "take-no-prisoners" dictatrix. In politico-sexual terms, too, she is "bigger" than Poppy—and Gideon, who admits that she used "to beat the blue-blazes out of me" (68). Though she practices the "feminine" pursuit of "needle-point," she is also capable of "brandishing a walking cane" (67) or "menacingly grab[bing] an old cane" (99), or "retrieving a rifle" (111) and threatening to shoot her only child (112). Too, her needles, cane, and rifle are all phallic markers of her masculine attributes of daring, "guts," and macho survivalism (an ideology Sarah references in *Consecrated Ground* [31]). Remarking on Gideon's search for work, Momma-Lou states, "People don't 'preciate how much stamina and persistence a black person need to even apply for a job in this here white town [Halifax]" (43). Bearing in mind Hatlen's assertion that "fascism finds its logical fulfillment in a militarism directed against the enemy without (151)," Momma-Lou's folksy combativeness in her relation to "white" Halifax is neither benign—*nor improper.*

Momma-Lou is confident and mighty: not Gideon. In Act One, scene two, Cherlene dubs him "Mister Tired-butt" (39) and "Mister sleepy head" (40), names suggesting a dopey and somnambulant masculinity. He sleeps through his children's departures for their maternal grandmother's house but, finding a note left by his son, Pauli, "the little big man" (41), registers that he has been commanded to "[t]ake care-a Mommy for me Daddy!" (41). The boy is more alert to "male" responsibilities than his father. Considering his daughter, Wendolyn, and her interest in art, Gideon says, "I hope she won't depend on her old man to put her through school" (42). Defeatism scores his personality (just as it does that of Willem in *Consecrated Ground*). Thus, preparing for an interview in a bank, Gideon predicts the act's futility: "Now how many niggers are loans officers in a bank in Nova Scotia?" (42). When he succeeds in failing, Gideon still tries to assert his manhood, telling his mother, "you don't have to pay for this family—I'm the man of this house" (49). His mother contests this claim: "You may be the man of the house, but I got Poppy's pension. That make HIM the man of the house!" (49). (Later, Momma-Lou complains to Poppy, "it seemed to me like society did nothin' but use that boy… lied to 'em, used 'em til they used him up! Nobody will ever make me believe that they didn't just goad our Gideon into playing some deadly game he couldn't win" [61].[15])

Gideon only enjoys a macho independence while dealing drugs for Grebanier, a satanic, Québécois criminal. Soon, his desire for Cherlene is rejuvenated, and he transforms from "Mister Tired-butt" (39) to "a butt man" (71), sexually excited, virile, and wanting his wife: "The mother of my two beautiful kids, her man strongly indicating that he is just one stroke from ecstasy" (71). At the height of his violent profit-making, Gideon aspires to imitate Grebanier, "[t]he godfather" (36), that is, his worldly Pappy/Poppy, even telling an associate, Amos, "I'll BUY ya Newfoundland" (93). By playing his own Mafia-style "godfather," Gideon constitutes his own (absent) father, but one as corrupt as Shakespeare's Macbeth. When Cherlene discovers the source of his flashy wealth, she yells, "I HATE YOU!" at her "whore of a husband" (95). Then, in an echo of Clarice's attack on Willem in *Consecrated Ground* (28), Cherlene "slaps Gideon" (95). This act upsets him deeply: "She slapped me man. We never laid a hand on one another before this" (96). Castrated figuratively, then arrested briefly (106), Gideon requires "correction." So, Momma-Lou levels "Poppy's rifle" (111) at her son while renaming him "boy" (111): "That's how you been acting. Just like a child Pauli's age. You think I raised you to be a boy? I raised you to be a man! A bright, proud black…" (111). Despite his mother's threatening entreaties, Gideon executes Grebanier's order to murder Seve, Gideon's own brother-in-law, by cutting his throat (115).

This murder caps the multiple infractions and immoralities plaguing the Haligonian Black community. Cherlene opines, "We got women prostituting themselves, our men becoming junkies. Dope! COCAINE…. Crack is eatin' this community" (78). Momma-Lou avers that "[c]rack don't like mortar" (78). Tracing the responsibility for this *dégringolade* back to Gideon, Momma-Lou, disguised as a gargoyle during the Halifax Mardi Gras (staged on Halloween), designs to commit "carnage" by shooting Gideon to death (121). She stalks him, lures him into an alleyway, and executes her son for his unmanly refusal to "do the right things." Before this drastic event, Momma-Lou, as "Gargoyle," preaches to Gideon on Black history: "The things you be fightin' against be as old as the plains of Kenya—don'tcha understand? I hadda fight 'em. Poppy hadda fight 'em and Pauli and Wendolyn—they gonna have to fight em too" (122).

Gideon rejects this moral "lecture," damning it as irrelevant for "the street" (122). But Gargoyle-Momma-Lou exclaims, "WE'RE STANDIN' IN THE JUNGLES—A KENYA!! WE'RE RIGHT IN THE MIDDLE OF THE PLAINS!" (122). For her, Halifax's streets and alleys are a wilderness-battlefield, where her son, by harming other Blacks and refusing to combat white racism, becomes a race traitor (akin to Willem in *Consecrated Ground*). Momma-Lou's rebuke of her son exhibits a stark, Darwinist fascism: "It's the plains, boy. And on the plains it's survival. Survival of the fittest. The wee animals? The poison animals? 'Gotta be culled from the herd" (122). Here, Boyd recapitulates the argument of African-American playwright Charles Fuller's Pulitzer Prize-winning play, *A Soldier's Play* (1981), whose "tragic hero, Sergeant Vernon C. Waters, takes upon himself the role of saviour of all African Americans in a racist society" (Macon 301). Problematically though, Waters is a crypto-fascist—who drives another Black, a Mississippi blues man, C.J., to commit suicide because his lack of sophistication marks him as expendable, as an animal to be "culled from the herd." Waters's speech justifying his fascistic oppression of C.J. seems premonitory of Momma-Lou's "execution speech":

> Them Nazis ain't all crazy—a whole lot of people just can't fit into where things seem to be goin'—like you, C.J. The black race can't afford you no more.... The day of the geechy [poor Southern black] is gone, boy—the only thing that can move the race is power. It's all the white respects— and people like you just make us seem like fools. And we can't let nobody go on believin' we all like you! You bring us down—make people think the whole race is unfit! (Fuller 38)

In *Gideon's Blues*, of course, Gideon's own mother deems him expendable because his "lack of manhood," his refusal to resist white power positively, has led him to prey on his brethren and sistren. Thus, Boyd revises Fuller by transferring the locus of tragedy from the murderous, "improve-the-race" fascist (who is, in Fuller's play, "executed" by a vengeful Black) to the victim—namely, Gideon [16]—of a homicidal, "family values"-styled campaign for moral (and racial) "hygiene." Too, Gideon's executioner is exonerated. Before she shoots her "baby," her "only-est child" (37), Momma-Lou-Gargoyle reminds him that, as a Black person—and as a man—he has failed to do what a Black person must, that is, persevere: "you walk... you WALK!... It's [white racism is] a crime against Black humanity, but a crime does not cancel a crime... you stooped too low..." (122). After slaying Gideon, Momma-Lou sheds her Gargoyle costume, dons mourning clothes, and cries to Poppy about how death has taken "our baby's heart... our baby's soul" (124). Gideon's decadent, failing Black masculinity necessitates his destruction.

While rats, bulldozers, and white liberals like Clancy represent evil and the demonic in *Consecrated Ground*; in *Gideon's Blues*, it is crack cocaine, prostitution, and Grebanier who do so. Indeed, Gideon's doom may be eternal, for Grebanier is an image of Satan. When Momma-Lou is sitting alone doing needlepoint in Act One, scene nine, she senses the presence of "some all-seein' invisible evil," and, we read, "The spectre of Grebanier is raised in the background" (77). When Grebanier next interrupts Momma-Lou's needlepoint, (in Act Two, scene ten), she calls him "a agitatin' devil—a Shango" (116). Grebanier responds simply, "I have been called worse. I am but the broker for the supplier of demands" (116), a self-justification Beelzebub himself could have coined. When Gideon is buried, "light"—hellish—

"*seems to be emitting from the grave itself*" (37). Blight is not just supernatural in origin however. In *Consecrated Ground*, bulldozers and social workers annihilate Africville, but, in post-Africville Halifax, in *Gideon's Blues*, "every brick, every stone, rock and pebble that my parents put together to build this community is dissolvin'… meltin' away," notes Momma-Lou, thanks to crack addiction (78). In both Boyd plays, then, future Black generations are in jeopardy. In *Consecrated Ground*, Clarice tells Clancy angrily, "Ya ain't happy, until ya feed the little black babies to [the rats]" (27). The next generation of Africvillers either die or leave. In *Gideon's Blues*, Seve's prostitute-and-crack-junkie girlfriend, Baye, symbolizes the destruction of children: "This baby, formin' in my belly… my little baby's a junkie" (56). The fetus perishes: Seve "beat her so bad […] she miscarry his chile… she dropped that baby-to-be" (99). The children of Cherlene and Gideon survive the murderous violence that claims Gideon, Seve, and Baye's fetus. However, by the end of *Gideon's Blues*, Cherlene becomes, like Momma-Lou, a widow-matriarch in the household. Once again, as in *Consecrated Ground*, the female survives the misguided male's self-destructiveness.

A Conclusion

In *Consecrated Ground*, in an opening shot, the camera highlights a sign that warns residents of "CONTAMINATED WATER" to be boiled before drinking (13). The implicit allegory is clear: Africville is already "contaminated"—or weakened—by "corrupt elements," even before the assassin-bulldozers arrive. In *Gideon's Blues*, too, pollution and its attendant connotations of moral impurity are extended to human beings. The drug addict-prostitute and expectant mother, Baye, spreads contamination (51) and "contagion" (57); and illegal drugs, distributed by Gideon, corrode the bonds of community and family. Moreover, the invasive, disease-laden rats that kill Tully in *Consecrated Ground* are equivalent to the drugs that poison Halifax's "hood"—and Baye's fetus—in *Gideon's Blues*. This proto-fascistic "naturalism," expressed first in the circulation of vermin and "toxins" and later in fratricidal and filial violence, underlines Boyd's problematizing of a discourse of moral hygiene ("kill the hoods, the cowards, and the traitors among us") that promotes racial eugenics ("only the fit should live"). Importantly, the Afro-gynocentric Darwinism that makes Black males expendable and Black females "heroes" is a crucial matrix for the issuing of any valid, contemporary, Afro-North American, social realist drama. Boyd's unsettling plays possess this virtue; thus, they champion urgent concerns. For instance, how is the (Canadian) Black community nurtured and developed when its putative individual constituents are permitted to jettison it in favour of furthering only, liberally, selfishly, themselves? That question spotlights the absurdity of the desperate speculation articulated by Gilroy and others that we are, in any area of the Black Atlantic, free of the guilty pleasures of nationalism—or worse…

(2004)

Notes

1   A version of this essay was presented to the Theatre and Exile Conference at the Graduate Centre for the Study of Drama, University of Toronto, on 22 March 2002. I dedicate this essay to Vera Cudjoe, an African-Canadian woman of British background who established black drama in Toronto in the 1970s and 1980s.

2   Elam also cites Kobena Mercer's relevant proviso that "identity becomes an issue when it is in crisis, when something assumed to be fixed, coherent, stable is displaced by the experience of doubt and uncertainty" (qtd. Elam 5).

3   Another "phallic" image associated with Clarice occurs when Reverend Miner, a black minister, embraces her prior to the funeral for her son: "she's stiff as an anchor" (27).

4   In the popular US film, *Silence of the Lambs* (1991), actress Jody Foster plays Clarice Starling, an FBI agent "masculine in both manner and career," whose serial-killer "prey" is an "effeminate" man who wishes to be a woman (Clover 233). Boyd's Clarice is similarly "masculine" and faces off against an "effeminate" husband. Even if Boyd does not intend to refer to *Silence of the Lambs* and its "feminist" protagonist, Clarice is still a relevant and valid choice of name for his own "hero," given that it means, in French, "little brilliant one" (Dinwiddie-Boyd 262). Boyd's Clarice may be less physically imposing than her husband, but she is far superior to him in both intellect and "fire."

5   Note that Willem is likely derived from William, which, in German, means "resolute protector" (Dinwiddie-Boyd 161). Willem does not play any such role for Clarice. He is the very spirit of uncertainty: "He moves hesitantly toward the door, not wanting to enter, but knowing that he must" (17).

6   Boyd recognizes the validity of this argument. In his Author's Note, he remarks that, in the destruction of Africville, "'the man' was dictating the African-Nova Scotian community's fate; once again 'the man' was lying…. Once again, …I was reminded of the cultural insensitivity of 'the man'" (7). "The man" is automatically white—and empowered, and so black "men" are reduced to "boys."

7   This observation contrasts ironically with Clarice's remembrance of her "Granddaddy" who "built their place with his bare hands" (24).

8   Miner's name suggests he is "minor"; thus, his faith cannot overcome modernity's bulldozers.

9   Louise, the female version of Louis, means, in French, "Famous warrior" (Dinwiddie-Boyd 317). Boyd's Momma-Lou is certainly a warrior. Note, too, that her two-part name combines both feminine and masculine gender connotations.

10   Gideon is named ironically; for this Biblical name of Hebrew derivation means "one who cuts down" and refers to "a judge of Israel who won great battles through faith

in God" (Dinwiddie-Boyd 68). While Boyd's Gideon does "cut down" his wife's brother, he is also "cut down" himself, and cannot be said to triumph in any way. Given that this "unusual name" was used by "free blacks in the 19th century" and is "obsolete" among African Americans now (Dinwiddie-Boyd 68), Boyd may be signaling that Gideon has no place in contemporary Nova Scotian/Canadian/North American/Western society.

[11] Poppy's name may also refer, ironically, to the poppy flower, a symbol of valiant military death, but also of opium, a narcotic. Thus, "Poppy" suggests, not only God, but also "sleep" and "death."

[12] Momma-Lou notes, for instance, "Poppy's listenin' and the Lord Jesus Christ—" (49).

[13] See note 9.

[14] Momma-Lou refers here to the "great 17th-century African warrior" and queen who was also a brilliant "administrator and organizer" (Dinwiddie-Boyd 403).

[15] Momma-Lou believes that the black community is in a "war" that is practically genocidal. Here, though, the police "let the niggers kill themselves" (75) with drug overdoses. She also preaches that "[y]ou got police arresting our kids for pimpin'— they slam their black asses in jail! The little white girls, though, they get all the social workers and the Children's Aid they need. But what about our boys?" (78).

[16] Tragedy is also marked here by the failure of the second-generation Steeles to fulfill Cherlene's dream, after the fashion of the Youngers in African-American playwright Lorraine Hansberry's *Raisin in the Sun* (1959), to find suburban prosperity: "Just think—my own dishwasher. My washer and dryer. And to live out in one of them high-falutin' suburbs" (42). *Gideon's Blues* is a tragedy, and so Cherlene will end her days as a widowed single-parent dodging prostitutes and drug pushers amid a "war-zone."

Works Cited

Bone, Robert A. *The Negro Novel in America.* New Haven, CT: Yale UP, 1965.

Boyd, George Elroy. "Author's Note." Boyd, *Two, By George!* 7.

———. *Consecrated Ground.* [Teleplay] 1992. Boyd, *Two, By George!* 9–33.

———. [as George Boyd]. *Consecrated Ground.* [Play] Winnipeg, MB: Blizzard, 1999.

———. *Gideon's Blues.* Boyd, *Two, By George!* 35–124.

———. *Two, By George!* La Have, NS: Stage Hand, 1996.

Clover, Carol J. *Men, Women, and Chain Saws: Gender in the Modern Horror Film.* Princeton: Princeton UP, 1992.

Dinwiddie-Boyd, Eliza. *Proud Heritage: 11,001 Names for Your African-American Baby.* New York: Avon, 1994.

Elam, Harry J., Jr. "Colored Contradictions in the Postmodern Moment: An Introduction." *Colored Contradictions: An Anthology of Contemporary African-American Plays.* Ed. Harry J. Elam, Jr. and Robert Alexander. New York: Plume-Penguin, 1996. 1–15.

Fuller, Charles. "A Soldier's Play." 1981. *Classic Plays from the Negro Ensemble Company.* Ed. Paul Carter Harrison and Gus Edwards. Pittsburgh: U of Pittsburgh P, 1995. 1–53.

Gilroy, Paul. *The Black Atlantic: Modernity and Double Consciousness.* Cambridge, Mass: Harvard UP, 1993.

Hansberry, Lorraine. *Raisin in the Sun.* 1959. New York: Signet-New American, [1966?].

Hatlen, Burton. "Ezra Pound and Fascism." *Ezra Pound and History.* Ed. Marianne Korn. Orono, ME: National Poetry Foundation, 1985. 145–72.

Lipset, Seymour Martin. *Continental Divide: the Values and Institutions of the United States and Canada.* New York: Routledge, 1990.

Macon, Wanda. "Charles H. Fuller, Jr." *The Oxford Companion to African-American Literature.* Ed. William L. Andrews et al. New York: Oxford UP, 1997. 301–02.

Milton, John. *Paradise Lost: A Poem in Twelve Books.* 1674. New York: Odyssey, 1962.

Silence of the Lambs. Dir. Jonathan Demme. Orion Pictures, 1991.

Wright, Richard. *Native Son.* 1940. New York: HarperCollins, 1998.

Out of this newly broken silence, the two plays speak eloquently; but hesitations, elisions, and their own silences mark the difficulty of finding appropriate forms and protocols with which to articulate what in some ways, at the time, remained unutterable. As a non-Aboriginal, reading and seeing the plays, I was struck by their wrenching power and pain, and by how much the playwrights do *not* say in their attempts to negotiate trauma from contrasting perspectives—male and female, Native and white, participant and observer—utilizing starkly different theatrical strategies. Lill, neither Catholic nor Aboriginal, focuses on three white nuns who work at a residential school in Nova Scotia. The nuns in *Sisters* talk about the Native children and sometimes hear them offstage or in memory, but the audience never sees them onstage. Highway's tragicomedy examines a group of Native men on a Northern Ontario reserve, some embracing the missionary practices of the Church and others wanting to resurrect traditional customs. A Cree who attended Catholic residential school himself, Highway exposes the pervasive influence of Catholicism in *Dry Lips Oughta Move to Kapuskasing* without making any explicit reference to the residential school experience.

Although a great deal of critical attention has been paid to *Dry Lips*, no one has yet examined either play's engagement with the specific historical impacts of the Church or its schools on First Nations individuals and communities. [5] A wide range of residential school literature confirms the quasi-documentary veracity of *Sisters*, particularly student recollections of the school on which the play is based, published in Isabelle Knockwood's *Out of the Depths* (1992) three years after the play first appeared. *Sisters* was a timely and important historical exposé and, for me, an affecting theatrical experience, yet the question of why Lill chose not to give voice and embodiment to the school's Native victims remains vexatious. Understanding the ideological and historical circumstances that shaped her writing makes sense of her theatrical choices. In giving sympathy and subject position to the nuns who helped perpetrate the atrocities, however, Lill seems to engage in what historian and trauma theorist Dominick LaCapra calls "the dubious appropriation of the status of victim through vicarious or surrogate victimage" (71), compromising her response to the historical trauma at the centre of the play.

Residential School History: "A Deluge of a Misery"

Canadian residential schools were established soon after the Indian Act of 1876 gave the federal government jurisdiction over Aboriginal education. Nicholas Flood Davin (himself a playwright) proposed the system to Sir John A. MacDonald in 1879 after studying the industrial schools set up for Aboriginal Peoples in the United States. Day-schools had proven inadequate to reshape Native children, Davin argued, "because the influence of the wigwam was stronger than the influence of the school" (1). He insisted that "[i]f anything is to be done with the Indian, we must catch him very young" (12) and remove the child from the invidious orbit of the family. "The importance of denominational schools" in the civilizing process lay in the need "to take away [the children's] simple Indian mythology" (14). The ensuing arrangement

from "God of the Whiteman! God of the Indian! God Al-fucking-mighty!": The Residential School Legacy in Two Canadian Plays [1]

by Jerry Wasserman

> The most potent kind of art is that which is inseparable from religion.
> —Tomson Highway (1990)

The long, sad tale of Canadian residential schools continues to unfold. In 1993, the Royal Commission on Aboriginal Peoples received 60,000 formal complaints of residential school abuse (Fournier and Crey 49). A decade later, the issue of compensation for victims of the "Schools of Shame" remained unresolved (Frank). Meanwhile, the body of material chronicling the experience and its damages grows ever larger. A selective bibliography published in 2002 for the National Archives exhibition *Where Are the Children?: Healing the Legacy of the Residential Schools* lists over 150 books, articles, testimonials, theses, videos, and plays (Fisher and Lee). Almost all have appeared since the late 1980s when the long-suppressed story of the schools burst into public view; but missing from the bibliography are two major writers whose works illuminate some of the darkest corners of the residential school experience and reveal the personal and political challenges facing those who first attempted to bring its legacies to light. When Tomson Highway's *Dry Lips Oughta Move to Kapuskasing* and Wendy Lill's *Sisters* premiered in the spring and summer of 1989, staging plays about the residential schools and their traumatic aftermath involved tricky negotiations of race and gender issues, personal anguish, and cultural politics. [2] In 1998, Highway's autobiographical novel/residential school exposé, *Kiss of the Fur Queen*, would confront more directly the relationship between Aboriginal Canadians and the Catholic Church. [3]

[…]

Two important books published the previous year helped lay the groundwork for the plays. Basil H. Johnston's *Indian School Days* (1988), the first Native residential school memoir in 15 years, "initiated an explosion of writing about residential schools in Canada" (Rymhs 58). [4] Celia Haig-Brown's *Resistance and Renewal: Surviving the Indian Residential School* (1988) was the first academic study to give voice to Native peoples' own memories of the schools. Until then, Dian Million argues, "'abuse' as an issue did not inhabit the narratives written by academic scholars" about Native life; indeed, the "'Indian Problem' in Canada had been 'unspeakable' for most of Canada's history" (99–100).

between the government and the churches would prove mutually profitable: "By essentially subcontracting the responsibility for Indian education to the church denominations the federal government could save money. Further, the incorporation of a religious component in the curriculum… undoubtedly would speed up the process of assimilation. For their part, the missionaries took advantage of the apparatus of the state to advance their own form of religious colonization" (Furniss 12).

[…]

The Catholic residential school in Nova Scotia known as "Shubie" seems to have been one of the most brutal: "By the early 1950s the school's reputation had spread throughout the Native community, so that on many reserves, 'Don't do that or you'll be sent to Shubie,' was a standard threat to children" (Knockwood 88).[6] In a poem called "Hated Structure: Indian Residential School, Shubenacadie, N.S.," former student Rita Joe memorializes the place as "a deluge of a misery/of a building" (75). Alumna Isabelle Knockwood chronicles a nightmarish history of the institution in which life for Mi'kmaw students consisted largely of deprivations and chastisements administered by often sadistic priests and nuns. For speaking their Native language students suffered beatings. Bed-wetting, a chronic problem in residential schools, met with humiliating punishments. Runaways were pursued with tracking dogs like escaped criminals or fugitive slaves (Millward 177, 184, 187). Knockwood relates that "Runaways were brought back in a cop car by the RCMP. Their heads were shaved and they were kept in the dark broom and soap closet, sometimes for several days and nights. They were strapped and fed only dry bread and water. In one case, the boys were tied to a chair and left there for two days" (88). She recalls with amazement the "depths of some nuns' hatred for the children" (47). In 1986, the abandoned school building burned down in a suspicious fire.

Wendy Lill and *Sisters*: "Because it Destroyed All Our Lives"

Soon after the fire, as accounts of abuses at Shubie became public, artistic director Mary Vingoe of Ship's Company Theatre in nearby Parrsboro commissioned Wendy Lill to write a play about the school. Lill had written the award-winning film *Ikwe, Daughters of the Country*, about Métis women, for the National Film Board, as well as a number of successful stage plays including *The Occupation of Heather Rose* (1986), a powerful drama about a young white nurse's experience on a northern reserve. Lill's residential school play, like *Heather Rose*, would focus not on the Native subjects but on the white women used by the system to administer to them: "I was asked by the Ship's Company to go past the stereotype of the 'nasty nun' and the victimized Indian children. I wanted to get past those images, get underneath them" (Lill, Interview 39). She felt that whites no longer needed to write about Native culture "with people like Thomson [sic] Highway out around…. I wanted to tell the story from the other side. I wanted to see how these nuns could do what they did" (qtd. in Enright 14).

Sisters, set in 1969, revolves around a once-idealistic nun who has grown mean-spirited and violent during her two decades at the now-closed school, which she has just burned down. [7] A memory play, *Sisters* shifts back and forth in Sister Mary's mind between the frame narrative, where she is interrogated by a court-appointed lawyer, and earlier scenes (where she is sometimes Young Mary, played by another actress) at home with her boyfriend or at the school with free-spirited Sister Gabriel and Sister Agnes, her superior. The brutalities inflicted on the students take place offstage, indicated only in the nuns' conversations and by sound cues.

The onstage action, what Mary remembers, emphasizes the sisters' own spiritual and emotional difficulties. In choosing to become a nun and renounce worldly love, Young Mary struggles to repress her natural vivacity for the asceticism of the convent. Coming from a large family, she is attracted to the surrogate family structure the Church seems to provide. As Sister Agnes explains, "Father Martin is our principal and our confessor. The Lord is our master. The Government is our employer and someday, I'm going to be Mother Superior" (19). The rhetoric of mothers, fathers, and sisters evokes a warm family circle; but the reality is a hierarchical system in which the nuns must enforce policies imposed on them by men, from the local priest and the Indian agent to bureaucrats in Ottawa and the Pope in Rome. The contradictions in the Church's family model become clearer when Mary descends into a lengthy spiritual crisis. Sister Agnes assures her that she will feel God's love, but "only if you let go of emotions and desires and human attachments" (48). In denying the necessity for emotional attachment, Mary will betray her relationships with the Native children and her surrogate sister, Gabriel.

At first, Mary is shocked by the inhumane treatment that school policy demands she adopt towards the children, especially her favourite, Alice Paul, who reminds Mary of her "little sister" (34). [8] When Alice is caught wetting her bed, Sister Agnes orders Mary to organize the humiliating sheet parade: "Line them up with their wet sheets over their heads outside the mess hall door…. Once on the sheet parade, they'll move heaven and earth not to wet their beds again" (35). Mary reluctantly obeys, but as her crisis deepens she overcompensates, hanging onto Church rules like a spiritual life raft. When Alice is forbidden to go home to visit her dying father because Indian Affairs thinks she might "revert to type" (41), she runs off anyway with Sister Gabriel's help. As the dogs track her down and Gabriel looks to Mary for sympathy, Mary turns her back on them both: "Don't come to me. Go to God. It was wrong to help Alice!" (50). Allowing her own spiritual drama to supercede the needs of the others, Mary betrays them and herself.

Over time, Sister Mary becomes increasingly stern, whipping her students and setting dogs after the runaways, yet all the while deluding herself that the children love her. Near the end of the play, she is devastated by a letter from Alice Paul, now grown up, recalling the nuns as "empty vessels of meanness, Sisters of the Dark House" (82). As well, 1960s liberalization has ironically reversed the policies of government and Church that Mary, against her better nature, had taken as gospel. Feeling empty and undermined, she finally tells her lawyer why she torched the school: "Because I went there to love and I ended up…. Because I HATED IT! Because it destroyed all our lives" (94–95). Again the play foregrounds the nun's anguish; the Native children's suffering is subsumed in the phrase "all our lives."

A powerful condemnation of the residential school's destructive policies and the nuns' complicity in them, *Sisters* exposes many of the institutional horrors of the school. It echoes the non-fictional accounts of atrocities such as the "sheet parade," the treatment of runaways and use of dogs, and the general atmosphere of repression and denial. In addition, by presenting the play through Mary's non-Native perspective, Lill invites her non-Native audiences to understand their own complicity and responsibility for the tragedy of the schools. No one had done this before on the stage. Lill effectively portrays how the nuns were victimized and made victimizers in turn: "I'm trying to illustrate that the nuns in the residential schools were suffering from their own level of oppression. They were certainly oppressed by the Catholic church: they were the workhorses! They were doing the bidding of the government too. They were stultified by the set of rules imposed upon them. They had to turn away from the compassion that they knew was needed by those kids in the schools" (Lill, Interview 40).

The theatrical absence of "those kids in the schools" proved controversial. Reviewing the 1990 Winnipeg production of *Sisters*, Doug Arrell praised Lill's attempt to explore the subject of church-run residential schools "without polemics and without turning the nuns into monsters," but worried that "we remain somewhat in the dark as to just how bad things are and just what the experience of the children is" (32–33). When the play reached Vancouver in 1997, critic Colin Thomas was more caustic: "*Sisters* trivializes the tragedy of the Indian residential school system.... Lill's approach feels insulting—like recounting the story of the Nazi concentration camps from the point of view of the guards, with only passing reference to the horrors visited upon the inmates" (63).[9]

Sisters certainly appears to shift the subject position of victim from the Native children to the white nuns. "Historical trauma is specific," Dominick LaCapra argues, "and not everyone is subject to it or entitled to the subject position associated with it" (78). The roles Sister Mary assumes in the trauma narrative include historian, or "secondary witness," and perpetrator. The memories she conveys to her lawyer comprise a history of the school, and in that capacity as witness/historian Mary experiences what LaCapra calls the "desirable affective" quality of "empathic unsettlement"; but, he adds, the unsettled empathetic witness should not "confuse one's own voice or position with the victim's" (78). Additionally, Mary may suffer from having perpetrated crimes against the children. Perpetrator trauma, too, according to LaCapra, "must itself be acknowledged and in some sense worked through.... Such trauma does not, however, entail the equation or identification of the perpetrator and the victim" (79).

Lill's appropriation of victim status for Mary appears, ironically, to have resulted from the playwright's attempt to avoid appropriating the Native position in other ways. Just as the residential school story was breaking, a series of controversies over artistic appropriation was raging among Canadian women writers. In June 1988 at the

Third International Feminist Book Fair in Montreal, Lee Maracle had confronted novelist Anne Cameron about her writing in the Native voice, arguing that "stories about women of colour written by white women are riddled with bias, stereotype and intellectual dishonesty" (185–86). In August 1988, Women's Press rejected three stories for an anthology called *Imagining Women* "on the grounds that the writers in question, all white, had drawn on and used the voices of characters from cultures and races other than their own" (Nourbese Philip 19). The press split over the issue and the resulting debate climaxed in May 1989 at an uproarious meeting of the Writers' Union of Canada where complaints about censorship were countered by accusations of racism: "The danger with writers carrying their unfettered imaginations into another culture—particularly one like the Native Canadian culture which theirs has oppressed and exploited—is that without careful thought, they are likely to perpetuate stereotypical and one-dimensional views of this culture" (Nourbese Philip 22).

Non-Aboriginal representation of Native stories remained a high-profile issue throughout 1989. In June, Toronto's Committee to Re-establish the Trickster, a Native cultural organization which counted Tomson Highway as a charter member, presented a workshop called "Whose Story is it Anyway?" to examine the question: "Who has the right to speak or write?" (Godard 185; cf. *Books in Canada*). That question was at the heart of *The Book of Jessica* (Griffiths and Campbell), in which Métis activist Maria Campbell accused white playwright Linda Griffiths of artistic appropriation in their collaborative stage adaptation of Campbell's autobiographical memoir *Halfbreed*, a charge subsequently relevelled by academic critics (Hoy). In September 1989, a month after the premiere of *Sisters*, CBC aired *Where the Spirit Lives*, a TV movie about a residential school, written by a non-Aboriginal partly from the perspective of the Native children. It received a mixed reception from Natives and non-Natives alike (Miller). Ojibwa poet Lenore Keeshig-Tobias was unequivocal: the movie and other works by white writers who told Native stories amounted to "culture theft, the theft of voice" (71).

Undoubtedly aware of this growing political storm as she considered how to approach the topic of the Shubenacadie residential school in 1988–89, Wendy Lill chose a strategy that allowed her to deal with the nuns' oppressive experience while exposing the horrors of the school without either appropriating the Native children's voices or totally ignoring their stories. Understanding Mary as a trauma victim, Lill embodies her story in the theatrical form typically used to explore the emotional architecture of father-daughter sexual abuse. She follows the paradigm that stages the internal drama of traumatized women survivors in accordance with clinical and therapeutic texts such as Judith Herman's *Father-Daughter Incest* (1981) and Ellen Bass and Laura Davis's *The Courage to Heal* (1988). Like other "incest plays," *Sisters* uses a memory structure in which a split protagonist, played by two different actresses, attempts to re/member her dismembered life. The narrator-victim alternatively identifies with and rejects the offending father and complicit mother. She intensely desires to reconcile with her "child within," the damaged younger self she feels guilty of having betrayed (Wasserman, "Daddy's Girls"). The surrogate family structure of the residential school provides all the necessary roles here, with the patriarchal Church as the violator and the Native girl, Alice, as Mary's abused inner child.

Containing the play entirely within the non-Native subjectivity of Sister Mary's memory allowed Lill to avoid appropriating the Native voice, as contemporary pressures demanded, and still dramatize the school's abusive institutional structure; yet as Keeshig-Tobias reportedly complained about *Where the Spirit Lives*, "the mental agony is among the white characters, not the Native ones" (qtd. in Miller 75–76). *Sisters* privileges the agony of the theatrically immediate white women, whose lives the play stages as tragedy, even to the point where Mary's repressed homoerotic feelings for Sister Gabriel supercede, in her final cathartic confession, her concern for the Native children. When the lawyer asks again why she burned down the school, Mary blurts out, "Because I broke Gabriel's heart" (94). The residential school, like Mary herself, burned for Gabriel, not for the children they helped abuse.

[…]

Conclusion: After the Poison

[…]

As one of the first writers to address in fictional form the emerging revelations of abuse in the Church-run schools, Wendy Lill imagines a nun who indirectly admits her wrongdoing and, in a way, calls herself to account; but the transformation of the residential school horror into the personal tragedy and catharsis of Sister Mary mitigates the effectiveness of Lill's theatrical response in addressing the crimes committed against Native children. Responding to the temper of the times, trying not to violate the new rules by which a playwright of conscience might address the wrongs done to people not of her own culture, Lill writes a powerful play vividly memorializing the suffering of those who did the Church's dirty work. In the larger historical picture the anguish of the nuns who worked at these schools seems a kind of collateral damage. The primary victims suffer offstage in *Sisters*, their stories mere second-hand accounts, theatrical rumour. The mostly anonymous Native children remain theatrically absent. [10]

(2005)

Notes

[1] The excerpt included here contains Wasserman's discussion of Wendy Lill's *Sisters*. Wasserman's discussion of *Dry Lips* has been excluded—Ed.

[2] *Dry Lips Oughta Move to Kapuskasing* premiered at Toronto's Theatre Passe Muraille in April 1989, co-produced by Native Earth Performing Arts, and was lavishly remounted at Toronto's Royal Alexandra Theatre in 1991. Subsequently performed in Winnipeg, Ottawa, and Vancouver, and more recently in Tokyo, it won the Chalmers Canadian play award and has been widely anthologized. *Sisters* was first staged in August 1989 by Ship's Company Theatre in Parrsboro, Nova Scotia, where it was remounted in 2001. It has had professional runs in Winnipeg, Whitehorse, Ottawa, Vancouver, and San Francisco, as well as numerous university productions. *Sisters* was broadcast on CTV's Stage on Screen series in 1991.

[3] Although Anglican, Presbyterian, and United Church clergy administered some Canadian residential schools, more than 70% were run by the Catholic Church (Frank 38). Even today, according to the Church, half the total funding of Catholic missions in Canada "assists our First Nations people to celebrate their Catholic faith within the richness of their own cultural heritage and traditions" (Ancker).

[4] Deena Rymhs points out that a residential school memoir, *Geniesh: An Indian Girlhood*, by Jane Willis, had appeared as early as 1973 but received little attention and soon went out of print (68nl).

[5] Critical discussions of Highway's plays have focused primarily on issues of gender, cultural hybridity, and reception, but hardly at all on the historical relations between First Nations and the Catholic church. For a bibliography of Highway criticism through 2000, including *Dry Lips* reviews, see Wasserman, *Modern Canadian Plays* (398–400). Two of the best subsequent discussions of the play are Lundy and Shackleton. Although she has had eight major plays produced, Lill has received little critical attention. Only Bennett and Heald seriously address her work overall, and analyses of *Sisters* appear mainly in reviews. For a bibliography of Lill through 2000, see Newman and Grace.

[6] The invocation of residential school as a standard threat to Native children seems to have been commonplace across Canada. In Northern Ontario, Basil Johnston recalls, "From the tone in which statements like, 'You should be in Spanish!' or 'You're going to Spanish! Mark my words!' were delivered, we knew that 'Spanish' was a place of woe for miscreants, just as hell and purgatory were for sinners" (6). BC Native Ron Hamilton has similar recollections: "When I was particularly mischievous or poorly behaved, Mama, and at times my older brother and sisters, would scold, 'behave yourself or I'll send you to the boarding school!'…. We thought of it [the Alberni Indian Residential School] as the ultimate punishment" (qtd. in Nuu-chah-nulth Tribal Council xxi).

[7] Lill changes the date of the actual Shubenacadie fire from 1986 to 1969 in *Sisters* to make the school's destruction more immediate to Sister Mary's tenure there. Nine Canadian residential schools were destroyed by arson between 1936 and 1944 (Miller 368, 382).

8 In *The Occupation of Heather Rose*, Lill's nurse Heather measures her failure by the death of the young Native girl Naomi, who at one point Heather thought "was going to be just like my little sister" (72).

9 The 1997 production of *Sisters* at Vancouver's Firehall Theatre, directed by Donna Spencer, attempted to complicate the issues of race and victimization in the play by casting Native actresses in the roles of both Sister Mary and Young Mary.

10 My thanks to Cynthia Zimmerman, Louise Forsythe, Maureen Hawkins, and Ric Knowles for their valuable responses to a version of this essay presented to the Association for Canadian Theatre Research in May 2004 in Winnipeg. Thanks also to *Journal of Canadian Studies*' three referees. The original paper was given at the Civil War(s) in Contemporary Performance Arts conference at the University of Rennes, France, in May 2002.

Works Cited

Ancker, Kathleen. "About Catholic Missions in Canada." Catholic Missions in Canada, 2003. http://www.cmic.info/ofpce01/Offlce/aboutCMIC2003.htm.

Arrell, Doug. "McCaw's Last Stand." *NeWest Review* 16 (February/March 1991): 32–33.

Bass, Ellen and Laura Davis. *The Courage to Heal: A Guide for Women Survivors of Child Sexual Abuse.* New York: Harper, 1988.

Bennett, Susan. "The Occupation of Wendy Lill: Canadian Women's Voices." *Women on the Canadian Stage: The Legacy of Hrotsvit.* Ed. Rita Much. Winnipeg: Blizzard, 1992. 69–80.

Books in Canada. "Whose Voice Is It Anyway?" 20 (January/February 1991): 11–17.

Davin, Nicholas Flood. *Report on Industrial Schools for Indians and Half-Breeds.* Ottawa. CIHM 03651, 1879. Early Canadiana Online, National Library of Canada. http://www.canadiana.org/ECO/mtq?doc=03651.

Enright, Robert. "The Explorer of Human Emotions: An Interview with Wendy Lill." *Border Crossings* 10 (January 1991): 12–17.

Fisher, Amy and Deborah Lee. *Native Residential Schools in Canada: A Selective Bibliography.* Ottawa: National Library of Canada, 2002. www.collections canada.cu/native-residenttal/index-e.litml.

Fournier, Suzanne and Ernie Crey. *Stolen from Our Embrace: The Abduction of First Nations Children and the Restoration of Aboriginal Communities.* Vancouver: Douglas and McIntyre, 1997.

Frank, Steven. "Schools of Shame." *Time* (Canada), 8 July 2003: 30–38.

Furniss, Elizabeth. *Victims of Benevolence: Discipline and Death at the Williams Lake Residential School, 1891–1920.* Williams Lake, BC: Cariboo Tribal Council, 1992.

Godard, Barbara. "The Politics of Representation: Some Native Canadian Women Writers." *Canadian Literature* 124–25 (1990): 183–225.

Griffiths, Linda and Maria Campbell. *The Book of Jessica: A Theatrical Transformation.* Toronto: Coach House, 1989.

Haig-Brown, Celia. *Resistance and Renewal: Surviving the Indian Residential School.* Vancouver: Tillicum Library, 1988.

Heald, Susan. "Wendy Lill and the Politics of Memory." *Canadian Dimension* 29 (April–May 1995): 54–56.

Herman, Judith. *Father-Daughter Incest.* Cambridge, MA: Harvard UP, 1981.

Highway, Tomson. *Dry Lips Oughta Move to Kapuskasing.* Saskatoon: Fifth House, 1989.

———. *Kiss of the Fur Queen.* Toronto: Doubleday, 1998.

Hoy, Helen. "'When You Admit You're a Thief, Then You Can Be Honourable': Native/Non-Native Collaboration in *The Book of Jessica.*" *Canadian Literature* 136 (1993): 24–39.

Joe, Rita. *Song of Eskasoni: More Poems of Rita Joe.* Charlottetown: Ragweed, 1988.

Johnston, Basil H. *Indian School Days.* Toronto: Key Porter, 1988.

Keeshig-Tobias, Lenore. "Stop Stealing Native Stories." *Borrowed Power: Essays on Cultural Appropriation.* Ed. Bruce H. Ziff and Pratima V. Rao. New Brunswick, NJ: Rutgers UP, 1997. 71–73.

Knockwood, Isabelle with Gillian Thomas. *Out of the Depths: The Experiences of Mi'kmaw Children at the Indian Residential School at Shubenacadie, Nova Scotia.* 3rd ed. Lockeport, NS: Roseway, 2001.

LaCapra, Dominick. *Writing History, Writing Trauma.* Baltimore: Johns Hopkins UP, 2001.

Lill, Wendy. Interview with Judith Rudakoff. *Fair Play: 12 Women Speak.* Ed. Judith Rudakoff and Rita Much. Toronto: Simon & Pierre, 1990. 37–48.

———. *The Occupation of Heather Rose.* In *NeWest Plays by Women.* Ed. Diane Bessai and Don Kerr. Edmonton: NeWest, 1987. 63–94.

———. *Sisters.* Vancouver: Talonbooks, 1991.

Lundy, Randy. "Erasing the Invisible: Gender Violence and Representations of Whiteness in *Dry Lips Oughta Move to Kapuskasing.*" *(Ad)dressing Our Words:*

Aboriginal Perspectives on Aboriginal Literatures. Ed. Armand Garnet Ruffo. Penticton, BC: Theytus, 2001. 101–23.

Maracle, Lee. "Native Myths: Trickster Alive and Crowing." *Language in Her Eye: Views on Writing and Gender by Canadian Women Writing in English.* Ed. Libby Scheier, Sarah Sheard, and Eleanor Wachtel. Toronto: Coach House, 1990. 182–87.

Miller, Mary Jane. "Where the Spirit Lives: An Influential and Contentious Drama about Residential Schools." *American Review of Canadian Studies* 31 (2001): 71–84.

Million, Dian. "Telling Secrets: Sex, Power and Narratives in Indian Residential School Histories." *Canadian Woman Studies* 20 (2000): 92–104.

Millward, Marilyn. "Voyages Home: Running from the Shubenacadie Indian Residential School, Nova Scotia." *Voyages: Real and Imaginary, Personal and Collective.* Ed. John Lennox et al. *Canadian Issues* 16. Montreal: Association for Canadian Studies, 1994. 175–90.

Newman, Shelley and Sherrill Grace. "Lill in Review: A Working Bibliography." *Theatre Research in Canada* 21.1 (2000): 49–58.

Nourbese Philip, Marlene. "The Disappearing Debate, or How the Discussion of Racism Has Been Taken Over by the Censorship Issue." *This Magazine* 23 (July–August 1989): 19–24.

Nuu-chah-nulth Tribal Council. *Indian Residential Schools: The Nuu-chah-nulth Experience.* [Port Alberni, BC]: Nuu-chah-nulth Tribal Council, 1996.

Rymhs, Deena. "A Residential School Memoir: Basil Johnston's *Indian School Days.*" *Canadian Literature* 178 (2003): 58–70.

Shackleton, Mark. "Restoring the Imprisoned Nation to Itself: Resistance, Repossession, and Reconciliation in the Plays of Tomson Highway." *Reconfigurations: Canadian Literatures and Postcolonial Identities.* Ed. Marc Maufort and Franca Bellarsi. Brussels: PIE-Peter Lang, 2002. 203–14.

Thomas, Colin. "Victims' Voices Silenced in Residential-School Drama." *Georgia Straight* 6–13 November 1997: 63.

Wasserman, Jerry. "Daddy's Girls: Father-Daughter Incest and Canadian Plays by Women." *Essays in Theatre* 14.1 (1995): 25–36.

———, ed. *Modern Canadian Plays.* 4th ed. Vol. 2. Vancouver: Talonbooks, 2001.

TheatrePEI: The Emergence and Development of a Local Theatre

by George Belliveau, Josh Weale and Graham Lea

Despite the province's long history of theatrical production and the presence of a major Canadian theatre festival (The Charlottetown Festival), TheatrePEI—which was inaugurated in 1980—was the first formal theatre organization dedicated to the development of distinctly local theatre on Prince Edward Island (PEI). The history of its creation lies in an opportune synergy between Canadian theatre history and PEI political activity. In this article we explore how a shared interest in localism among theatre artists and an activist Progressive Conservative government led to the creation of TheatrePEI in the early 1980s. In the context of this essay we define localism as the expression of issues relevant to a particular community.[1] In examining specific PEI productions, as well as the conditions from which these productions emerged (and in certain cases the reception of the work), we explore the possible impact and meaning of TheatrePEI within the province.

In *Reading the Material Theatre*, Ric Knowles presents a desire to develop "modes of analysis that consider performance texts to be the products of a more complex mode of production that is rooted, as is all cultural production, in specific and determinate social and cultural contexts" (10). Knowles's theoretical lens is informed by a combination of cultural materialism and semiotics. Robert Wallace, for his part, uses feminist and postcolonial theories in *Producing Marginality* to develop a frame-work to study theatre and social history by looking at "ways in which theatre both responds to and affects cultural and political imperatives in communities" (29). These two Canadian scholars emphasize the importance of understanding and studying the social, historical, and political contexts from which the theatre under investigation emerges—rather than solely focusing on, or analyzing, the resulting productions. As we investigate the emergence and development of TheatrePEI in this essay, a close analysis of the social, historical, and political conditions guides our exploration of the company's various initiatives and productions. Specifically, we examine how the socio-political context largely shaped the creation of the company, and then how particular productions, with local themes and issues, were deliberately aimed to create relevant theatre for PEI communities.

The Years Leading up to the Creation of TheatrePEI

Looking through the theatre archives at the Confederation Centre of the Arts in Charlottetown, it becomes quite clear that until the 1970s theatre on PEI existed almost solely in the form of out-of-province touring companies or foreign plays (mainly from the U.S. and England) produced by local theatre groups.[2] There was a decrease in touring after the 1970s, yet productions of scripts from outside of Canada continued to take place in PEI. Nonetheless, a noticeable shift began to emerge in PEI, as in other parts of Canada, during the 1970s (and earlier in some regions) when a growing interest in producing theatre with local themes took place, moving from "colonialism to cultural autonomy" (Filewod vii). According to scholars, this national cultural shift in theatre was in part prompted by a change in the political climate, which saw "a groundswell of interest in Canadian history, culture, and institutions" (Benson & Conolly 85). The "Alternative theatre movement," as it came to be called, was named as such "because it was perceived to oppose the system of publicly subsidized civic theatres established across Canada in the late 1950s and early 1960s" (Filewod vii). This important movement in Canadian theatre history "may be said to have begun with [George] Luscombe's founding of Theatre Workshop Productions in 1959" (20). Over the next decade it progressively gained momentum and arguably peaked in the early 1970s when in "the 1972–73 season nearly 50% of the plays produced by subsidized theatres in both English and French were in fact Canadian" (Wasserman 18).

As has been extensively documented, the Alternative theatre movement in Canada was assisted by new federal funding models, such as the Local Initiative Program and Opportunities for Youth grants. These funding sources encouraged artists to explore regional identities, and, as a result, theatre groups writing and producing plays about political, social, and historical issues rooted in local Canadian contexts emerged in various parts of the country. On the production side, dramatic techniques such as documentary storytelling and collective creation became staples of this theatre movement, partly as a reaction to the general lack of indigenous playwrights and/or plays, but also because these methods were ideal for the telling of stories grounded in the history of a local community.

One of the seminal examples of this form of collective and consciously local theatre is, of course, Theatre Passe Muraille's 1972 production of *The Farm Show*. This show was viewed as groundbreaking from the perspectives of both dramatic technique and subject matter. According to Don Rubin, artistic director Paul Thompson turned Passe Muraille into a "Canadian experimental house, [in that of] the 50 or so productions done at Passe Muraille between 1970 and 1973, about 90 percent were new plays by new writers from various parts of the country" (315). The collective creation process in *The Farm Show* required the creators to study local characters, to listen to local stories, and to work the land. In some ways *The Farm Show* turned localism into art, in that Thompson saw this development of indigenous theatre through exploration of place as a means of asserting local autonomy in the face of colonial influences. Thompson suggested in an interview that *The Farm Show* was a conscious exploration of localism as a defence against cultural imperialism (Johns 31).

During the 1970s on PEI the most significant examples of this type of collective style of theatre with local themes came in the form of two significant dramas: *The Chappell Diary* (1973) and *The Road to Charlottetown* (1977). *The Road to Charlottetown* was the product of a collaboration between PEI poet Milton Acorn and actor/musician Cedric Smith. Although initially produced in Ontario for a prison tour, the play was brought to the Confederation Centre of the Arts in the summer of 1977. Through the poetry of Acorn, *The Road to Charlottetown* is thoroughly grounded in the land and people of PEI. Co-creator Smith had been involved in a number of collaboration projects with Luscombe at Toronto Workshop Productions, which had included composing the music for the documentary drama *Ten Lost Years* (1974) based on the book by Barry Broadfoot. Smith's experience with collective creations, and the agrarian sensibilities he shared with Acorn, helped foster a non-linear drama that weaves back and forth in historical time. Described by Smith as a "People's Passion Play," *The Road to Charlottetown* "is a fantasy based on the tumul-tuous truth of the Island Land Struggle, by tenants victimized by landlordism." The play tells the story of Islanders, working on the land, who had to pay hefty rents to often absentee landlords. Through a series of 20 vignettes, the heroism of everyday Islanders against the promises of "eternal tenantry and toward socialist ideals is played out" (Acorn, Program notes). The chorus written by Smith that bookends the show and is sung by the entire cast suggests this relationship between character and place:

> We came from the sea, we were swept to the shore,
> And we cling to the land like our ancestors before,
> And we work with the nets, and we work with the plough
> As the seasons pass and the centuries bow.
>
> The brooding hills at our back, the swollen sea in our face,
> We have carved a slender hold in this unprotected place,
> And we harvest hills and harvest the swollen sea,
> To our sons leave a trace of where we used to be.
> And we came from the sea. (10)

The 1977 production of *The Road to Charlottetown* offered Prince Edward Islanders one of the first examples of theatre's potential for bringing to life a distinctly Island story grounded in the local landscape. Unfortunately, it proved to be a disappoint-ment at the box office,[3] and according to Ron Irving this dissuaded the Charlottetown Festival from further experimentations with this style of local documentary theatre. A re-mounting of *The Road to Charlottetown* at the Victoria Playhouse in 2003 will be discussed later in this article.

Work on *The Chappell Diary* began in 1973 as a collaboration between Island theatre artist Ron Irving, Island historian/activist Harry Baglole, and a group of actors who, for a number of years, were referred to as the Hall Players. (The actors took on that name because this show and others they worked on were designed to tour across PEI, playing in various small community halls.) Irving led the group of actors to create a drama based on the diaries of early Island settler Benjamin Chappell. The historical subject matter was complemented by the collective approach, and the drama explored the struggle of eighteenth-century British settlers engaged in the creative act of transforming a wild landscape on PEI's north shore into a pastoral one.

What becomes quite apparent after analyzing both *The Road to Charlottetown* and *The Chappell Diary* is the sense of nostalgia within the texts, a romanticized and idealized view of local history (particularly in *The Chappell Diary*). This approach differs from *The Farm Show* where artists in the Passe Muraille collective were in a number of ways creating history by interviewing locals and then theatrically representing and documenting their lives and stories on the stage. The PEI plays were based on documented, archived research, and in the case of *The Chappell Diary* the actors were primarily from the local area re-telling and re-imagining their history. In the case of *The Farm Show*, the actors were largely from urban Toronto and they were trying to capture the lives of rural farmers. As a result, a certain anxiety permeated the creative processes—as they tried to "get it right"—as becomes quite evident in Michael Ondaatje's documentary film *The Clinton Special: A Film about the Farm Show* (1974). Through various scenes in the film it becomes apparent that the actors seemed desperate to have "the farmers 'like' the show" (Harrison 1). Because the play was meant to be both about and for the farmers, a pressure to please, versus a critique of the farmers' lives, was placed upon the actors. *The Chappell Diary* and *The Road to Charlottetown* depict nonliving characters, and as a result the actors/creators were given freedom to re-imagine and creatively construct idealized characters. Consequently, these PEI plays inherently hold a nostalgic perspective, with a certain romanticized depiction of the past for their contemporary audience.

The Genesis of TheatrePEI: Socio-political Climate

Throughout the 1970s, when PEI theatre artists and activists were beginning to explore the stories of their agrarian past, the abandonment of this way of life was being accelerated by the 15-year development program of modernization introduced by the Liberal government of Alec Campbell. While many aspects of this program, such as the development of infrastructure, were seen in a positive light, by the late 1970s a backlash was beginning to mount against the social reorganization that had accompanied this modernization. In general, this backlash focused on the amalgamation of services, the centralization of power, and the industrialization of agriculture and fisheries. This process was widely seen to be manifesting itself in the weakening of traditional local communities (MacLean 230).

Throughout the 1970s an activist group known as the Brothers and Sisters of Cornelius Howatt began protesting this centralizing program. They were named after Island politician/farmer Cornelius Howatt, who had vehemently opposed PEI's entrance into Confederation and the loss of local autonomy it would precipitate. This group of farmers, artists, and activist constituted a political wedge that would lead to full blown political backlash by the end of the 1970s. In 1980 former MP and blueberry farmer Angus MacLean's Progressive Conservatives came to power on a platform of "Rural Renaissance." His campaign, which was supported by several members of the Brothers and Sisters, was based on fiscal responsibility, self-sufficiency, and reinvigorated local communities (MacLean 238). In regards to cultural development, MacLean's government favored a decentralized approach and saw the province as a community of communities.

Seizing the opportunity that this political development represented for theatre artists, a group of Island citizens, including Harry Baglole (who had been active in both the Brothers and Sisters of Cornelius Howatt and MacLean's election campaign), submitted a proposal for the creation of a Community Theatre Program on PEI. Throughout the proposal the authors consciously appealed to the desire of the government to foster a more localized sense of community. The proposal, written by Baglole in 1980, began by appealing directly to the stated mandate of the new government:

> We believe this program to be precisely in line with the cultural policy of the present Island Government, as articulated before, during, and since last year's election. There have, for example, been commitments to decentralize the arts by encouraging the revival of cultural activity in small halls and community centres in all parts of the Island, and to encourage the celebration of the Island spirit in traditional music, dancing, literature, and other forms of cultural expression. (1)

This mandate to stimulate activity in small halls and community centres was one that bore a resemblance to the localized focus of the Alternative theatre movement. It was therefore a mandate that the promotion of this brand of theatre could help to fulfill. In this spirit, the proposal also attempted to differentiate theatre as a medium from mass media in terms of both commercialism and social organization:

> We live in a passive age. For entertainment, most of us depend on slick, innocuous (or sometimes not so innocuous) media programs concocted mostly in the United States and delivered to us courtesy of Anacin, General Motors, Coca Cola, and the purveyors of assorted deodorants and breath sweeteners. We no longer very often gather with friends and neighbours to share stories; less often do we perform plays for each other; almost never do we attempt to create our own dramas, telling of our own lives and communities. (1)

In making a case for the creation of a Community Theatre Program, Baglole differentiated the more participatory nature of the theatrical medium from the passive, consumptive mass media. He also invoked the anti-American nationalism that was near the heart of the Alternative theatre movement of the 1970s. The explicit arguments were that theatre is a form of communication more conducive to localized social organization than the mass media of film or television. The proposal also went on to describe the types of theatre productions and activities envisioned by its authors. In general, these could be divided into two groups: telling their own stories and solving their own problems. In describing the need for Islanders to tell their own stories Baglole appealed to the new government's agrarian sensibilities:

> We Islanders are a strangely inarticulate people. This past generation has
> seen the passing almost of an entire way of rural life, and although there
> has been much anguish, the experiences of those thousands of families
> who moved from farms has not found expression in a single highly
> memorable play, novel, poem, or short story. We anticipate that the
> Community Theatre Program will help Islanders to find their own
> individual and unique voices; to speak and to act. (1–2)

Similarly, in outlining the activist uses of theatre, the proposal also described the
desire to enable small communities a forum for engaged localized communication:

> Dramatic techniques are powerful tools of communication. The
> resources of the Community Theatre Program will be available to com-
> munity groups who may wish to educate and inform about issues such
> as drug abuse, land use, the problems of the handicapped, etc. (3)

The proposal was accepted and the Island Community Theatre was incorporated
in 1980. Ron Irving accepted the position of executive director and would serve as
advocate, educator, and artistic director in fulfillment of the organization's diverse
mandate. The name of the organization would soon be changed from Island
Community Theatre to TheatrePEI in order to avoid being viewed as an amateur
theatre group when seeking Canada Council funding. In the role as artistic director,
Irving and his successors Elizabeth Muir and Rob MacLean (son of premier Angus
MacLean) produced a body of work that focused on both telling Island stories and
creating a forum to discuss social problems.

TheatrePEI: Productions and Initiatives

During its twenty years of producing theatre—from 1981 to 2001—TheatrePEI
mounted dozens of original theatre productions and served as the only year-round
producer of professional theatre on PEI. The company staged several productions on
educational topics ranging from racism to environmentalism, with the majority of
them touring PEI schools. Some of these touring plays included *Mother Earth Blues*
(1982), *Water Wise* (1984), *May the Forest be with You* (1985), and *Racist! Who Me?*
(1995). Practically all of these shows were collective creations and offered young local
actors a first opportunity in writing and acting for the stage. The collective approach
was also used to create special interest shows including *The Venerables* (premiered
1984), a long-running play performed by seniors about the foibles of aging, *The Postal
Show* (1992), which dealt with cutbacks to Canada Post's rural service, and *The
Patronage Show* (1998).

TheatrePEI also produced mainstream shows that dealt with issues pertinent to
the community. One example was a production of David Mamet's *Oleanna* in 1995,
which played in the midst of a highly publicized case of sexual assault that occurred
on the University of Prince Edward Island campus. This production invited the

community to participate in the dialogue initiated by the presentation by holding mediated discussions with the audience, actors, and director after each performance.

Plays by established PEI writers such as Adele Townshend, Michael Hennessey, and David Weale were also produced by TheatrePEI. Notable examples include Townshend's *For the Love of a Horse*, which had received a glowing review by Dora Mavor Moore in the 1968 Canadian Playwriting competition, yet had not received a full scale production until it was mounted by TheatrePEI in 1986. Michael Hennessey's *Trial of Minnie McGee*, which tells the story of the last woman sentenced to death on PEI (and bears a strong resemblance to Sharon Pollock's Lizzie Borden play, *Blood Relations*) was successfully produced by TheatrePEI in 1983. Island folk historian David Weale's drama *A Long Way from the Road* was produced by TheatrePEI in 1994. Weale's production spawned a revival of local storytelling across PEI, and in many ways encouraged other artists to share local stories through this long-time tradition on the island. TheatrePEI also developed the New Voices Playwriting contest, through which it encouraged and workshopped new theatre pieces, some of which were eventually developed into full productions. These various TheatrePEI initiatives encouraged theatre activity within the province, and the subject matter of the productions frequently fulfilled one of the organization's stated mandates, that of telling our own stories. It should be noted that the cited productions are not an exhaustive list; instead they represent the type of themes represented in TheatrePEI productions. [4]

Despite the apparent success of TheatrePEI in the fulfillment of its mandate, the organization's budget was severely cut in the late 1990s, which, coupled with an accumulated debt, forced the organization to stop acting as a producer (Binkley). [5] While TheatrePEI continues to promote new play development through playwriting contests, staged readings, community festivals, and workshops, it is hard to see the end of production as anything but a major setback to the organization's vitality. Fortunately, among the final plays that TheatrePEI staged before they ended production were perhaps two of the most effective new works in terms of its founders' desire to address issues relevant to the community: *Rough Waters* by Melissa Mullen and *Horse High, Bull Strong, Pig Tight* by Kent Stetson.

Rough Waters was initially workshopped in 1997 during an intensive three-week play development program within the auspices of TheatrePEI s New Voices competition. With the guidance of Bruce Barton as dramaturge and the actors who participated in the workshop, Mullen refined her family drama for its 1998 semi-professional Charlottetown production and an eventual PEI tour. Less than three years later *Rough Waters* was part of Neptune Theatre's main season, and the Halifax, N.S. production received "strong reviews and even stronger public response" (Barton 342).

Rough Waters is a family drama that uses the gradual abandonment of a traditional way of life in the fisheries as its backdrop. The story's central conflict is between a father and son. The father, Gordon, has inherited his own father's conservative approach to fishing, while the son, Jamie, hopes to start a fish farming business with his more entrepreneurial uncle Wayne. Within this generational divide we see the progression from viewing the fisheries as a way of life to its status as an industry. Further, we see the inner conflict within the father between his desire to preserve this way of life, which his daughter Carrie so admires, and his desire to provide the financial security for his family that his brother Wayne enjoys. While the play does not seek to pass any finite judgment on this notion of progress, it does portray the tension that this type of profound cultural shift inevitably precipitates.

Although the play contains a sense of nostalgia in terms of what the fishing industry "used to be like," Mullen refrains from sensationalism in that there are "no extended political manifestos or declarations on the plight of beleaguered fishers" (Barton 343); as a result, the play distinguishes itself from other works from the Maritime provinces that often sensationalize the hardships of fishing, farming, or mining communities. Instead of creating a romanticized depiction of a fishing community, Mullen manages to depict characters in *Rough Waters* who possess "an earnest engagement with the personal, social, and cultural forces that shape a significant portion of rural Maritime lives" (Barton 343).

In internationally acclaimed playwright Kent Stetson's *Horse High, Bull Strong, Pig Tight* we get a more one-sided, yet no less complex perspective on the abandonment of agrarian life. Stetson's one-person show, which received the Wendell Boyle Award for theatre and heritage in PEI, premiered in 2001 in Charlottetown before touring parts of PEI, New Brunswick, and Nova Scotia. Despite its limited productions to date, the play was well received in Charlottetown according to critic Sarah Crane, as "the audience was left roaring several times" by the phrases and self-recognition (8). Stetson invites the audience to witness the abandonment of agrarian life through the eyes of one Peter Stewart. Over the course of the play, Stewart displays an almost holy reverence for the work of the farmer. And, most interesting, Stetson consciously counter-balances contemporary life with a nostalgic sense of the past:

> Young Jimmy—
> The Fool's bo—
> Steps away from his computer screen,
> Walks out the door…
> He might as well be on Mars
> For all he knows of the red Island soil
> Them "made in Japan" sneakers lands on.
> "The kids is born here," says Harry.
> "They eat and sleep and go to school here.
> But their souls are made in America.
> The almighty dollar is their Heavenly Father these days.
> Their father which art in Washington"
> Harry was not fond of the Yanks. [6]
> He'd make you wonder.
> Our own Island youngsters,
> Threatenin' to blow up Colonel Grey,

And shoot each other for wearin' the wrong brand name.
Like they seen on the T.V.
America's Most Wanted?
I think it's the souls of our children
God bless America, wha?
My soul grew in the fields and barns and kitchens.
My computer was a one room school.
My television was a fiddle or a card party.
Or Harry Muttart's store Saturday night after barn work.
I knew the same songs and stories as my neighbors.
I knew their children, and their parents.
And their parents.
I knew every house and who was in it for miles in each direction.
Our Heavenly Father lived in St. Columba's Presbyterian Church.
Right there.
And He was a farmer.
A good farmer just like us. (399)

Throughout the above passage (and the play) Stetson creates a character in Peter Stewart who has developed an uncompromising belief in the connection between the land and the "soul" Stewart clings to the past with roots so deeply connected to the land that he would rather die than sever the link. In one of the most memorable passages of the play Stewart quotes his beloved Lily, who actually describes the connection in physical terms:

When you're born on the Island
The second they cut your umbilical
Another cord sprouts out 'a your navel.
Shoots right out and plants itself in the soil
Takes root in the bedrock.
You're attached to P.E.I. forever.
It's made outa'... well, ah... light.
Golden-red light.
It's right-flexible, eh? Tough. Right elastic.
You can go pretty much anywhere on the earth
And it's still there,
Sprouting outa' yer belly
Attached to the red rocks of home.
Anywhere but Toronto.
Starts to fray the minute you get off the bus in Toronto. (413)

Indeed, Stewart is so thoroughly connected with the land—and, in particular, his land—that in the end his very life is connected with the fate of the farm. When all hope seems to be lost, and doom to both Stewart and his land seem inevitable, Stetson, in a wonderful act of optimistic imagination, has Stewart's grandson use his computer and the interactive powers of the Internet to save the family farm from the clutches of the agri-business corporation Margate Farms. The complexity of Stetson's tale largely results from the redemption of this new media that Stewart had blamed for his sons and grandson's alienation from the land.

Stetson's play differs from Mullen's in its depiction of nostalgia, in that *Horse High, Bull Strong, Pig Tight* romanticizes, to a certain extent, "the way it used to be." The overt political statements in Stetson's play on current commercial enterprises overtaking small PEI farms directly addresses the plight of contemporary farmers. The protagonist is presented as an individual caught between "the modest, Island way of life he used to know, and the threatening encroachment of technology, big business"—particularly large agricultural enterprises that overtake smaller farms (Crane 8). This depiction of Stewart, rooted in an idealized past, differs from the characters in *Rough Waters*, who seem to defy the stereotypical portrayal of the "long lost days of the past." The romanticized history alluded to in Stetson's play through Stewart's clutching of a semi-idealized past reflects the notion of a created stereotypical culture which serves to sell (to tourist audiences in particular) a romanticized view of PEI.

While agriculture remains a significant portion of PEI's economy, "tourism […] seem[s] set to overtake agriculture as the province's economic leader. The working rural landscape that had defined Prince Edward Island for Islanders [is] now equally important as a tourist attraction" (MacDonald 382). In an article in 1986, Elizabeth Mair commented that the work of TheatrePEI had enabled "Island theatre […] to emerge at last from the shadow of the Charlottetown Festival, and to be finding a genuine island audience. But as long as theatre stays dependent on tourist tastes […] there will remain a split in focus" (22). The increasing importance of the tourist trade to rural PEI is perhaps best highlighted in *The Road to Charlottetown*. In the scene entitled "Tourist" a tourist is confronted by a group of "land activists" who are posing as road workers:

> OLD JOHN: Tell me, sir, would The Island be quaint enough for ye, then?
> ANGUS: Ah, the blessings of fresh ocean air! A place of leisure and contentment.
> DAVEY: Where the sun shines every day and tomorrow's problems never arrive.
> OLD JOHN: A dreamy never never land (31).

With this, the "Islanders" have summarized much of the manner in which PEI has been marketed to tourists. This idyllic version of "The Island" is not completely accurate, as the tourist soon discovers:

> TOURIST: [But the brochure] also said that the Islanders were a gentle, friendly people.
> OLD JOHN: Indeed, for the most part, sir. But we keeps a few around what ain't for when the situation needs it!!! (31)

The contrast between what is shown for tourists and the actual lives of people takes on a heightened meaning when presented in PEI communities where this takes place. This short scene recognizes the dual existence of the local audience as they struggle to live their own lives and to accommodate the tourists who help drive the economy. At the same time, the scene reminds the tourist audience of the sanitized view of reality presented to them.

Residual effects of TheatrePEI

Although TheatrePEI no longer directly produces theatre, its impact and legacy continue to be felt in the development of new works, along with an audience eager for local theatre. There has been a great deal of theatrical activity resulting both directly and indirectly from the organization's existence, and there continues to be interest in telling and hearing local stories. In the years since TheatrePEI slowed its production, a number of independent producers have sought to capture a local audience through indigenous productions. For instance, the Victoria Playhouse, which traditionally produced a typical mix of light summer stock fare, has had at least one locally created play in each year since TheatrePEI stopped producing. Since the late 1990s, they have staged two comedies by Island writer Pam Stevenson (*Conjugal Rites* in 2000, *The Haunting of Reverend Hornsmith* in 2001), a period drama by Lars Davidson (*Adrift* in 2002), a storytelling show by artistic director Erskine Smith (*The Most Amazing Things* in 2000), and two runs of New Brunswick playwright Charlie Rhindress's *Maritime Way of Life* in 1999 and 2001.[7]

As part of its goal to produce more local theatre, The Victoria Playhouse remounted Acorn and Smith's *The Road to Charlottetown* in 2003, directed by Cedric Smith himself. The theatre's setting in the tiny fishing and farming village of Victoria, PEI offered a beautiful compliment to the play's agrarian themes. Smith gave the play an added touch of localism by using props scavenged from the villages shoreline: driftwood served as prop pistols, pitchforks, benches, and shillelaghs, sandstone served as coins, costumes were sewn with shells and seaweed. The show opened with the blowing of a conch shell that had served as a doorstop in a Victorian home for close to a century.

In exploring the emergence and eventual development of TheatrePEI from a social, political, and historical perspective, this essay has aimed to offer insights and perspectives on an important theatre initiative on Prince Edward Island. In discussing the political climate that led to TheatrePEI and examining particular productions, we have tried to demonstrate how the company's intended mandate was partially realized. The intentions of TheatrePEI remained closely focused on creating theatre about and for local audiences. How these intentions were received and the impact the localist approach has had on communities in PEI is beyond the scope of this essay (although worthy of further inquiry). To conclude, we turn to Knowles once again. He proposes that we consider "theatrical performances as cultural productions which serve specific cultural and theatrical communities at particular historical moments"

(10). TheatrePEI emerged at a time when theatre in many parts of Canada was expanding and (re)inventing itself, when the Conservative PEI government wished to look at ways to celebrate the small and capitalize on the strengths of its individual communities. Given these conditions, it seems reasonable to consider TheatrePEI's cultural legacy as a theatre that aimed, developed, fostered, and produced work relevant and meaningful about and for locals on PEI.

(2005)

Notes

[1] See Filewod 21–22 for a further discussion on localism and theatre.

[2] An earlier article published in this journal [*Theatre Research in* Canada] provides an historical perspective on PEI theatre activity. See Peake.

[3] During the 1977 Charlottetown Festival season, aside from the usually crowd-pleasing and successful production of *Anne of Green Gables: The Musical*, the Festival premiered *The Legends of the Dumbells* about entertainers during WWI, and restaged *By George!*, a pastiche of Gershwin songs. These three successfully produced musicals overshadowed the more experimental *Road to Charlottetown* in terms of attendance.

[4] All information about TheatrePEI productions was accessed through programs, posters, and media advertisements found in storage boxes in the TheatrePEI office in Charlottetown and through personal interviews with TheatrePEI's general manager Dawn Binkley and former artistic director Ron Irving.

[5] Irving's desire to maintain high production standards and quality performances, along with theatre rental (TheatrePEI had no home theatre) and/or touring costs, made it nearly impossible to operate on the meager existing budget.

[6] A familiar instance of anti-American Canadian nationalism.

[7] It is worth pointing out the importance of Rhindress's comedy, despite its not being from PEI, in the sense that the playwright adopts a unique satirical and critical perspective on the romanticized and idealized self-presentation that makes its way into a number of Maritime plays.

Works Cited

Acorn, Milton. Program Notes for *The Road to Charlottetown* (1977). Rpt. Victoria Playhouse Program, 2003.

Acorn, Milton and Cedric Smith. *The Road to Charlottetown.* Ed. James Deahl. Hamilton: UnMon Northland, 1998.

Baglole, Harry. "Community Theatre Proposal." PEI Department of Community Affairs, 1980.

Barton, Bruce, ed. *Marigraph: Gauging the Tides of Drama from New Brunswick, Nova Scotia, and Prince Edward Island.* Toronto: Playwrights Canada, 2004.

Benson, Eugene and L.W. Conolly. *English-Canadian Theatre.* Don Mills, ON: Oxford UP, 1987.

Binkley, Dawn. Personal interview. July 2004.

Crane, Sarah. "Meaning of Island Life: Review of *Horse High, Bull Strong, Pig Tight.*" *The Buzz* January 2001: 8.

Filewod, Alan. *Collective Encounters: Documentary Theatre in English Canada.* Toronto: U of Toronto P, 1987.

Harrison, Flick. Review. "The Clinton Special: A Film About the Farm Show." 7 May 2006. http://www.vivelecanada.ca/article.php/20031022111115356/print.

Irving, Ron. Personal interview. July 2004.

Johns, Ted. "An Interview with Paul Thompson." *Performing Arts in Canada* 10.4 (1973): 31–33.

Knowles, Ric. *Reading the Material Theatre.* Cambridge, UK: Cambridge UP, 2004.

MacDonald, Edgar. *If You're Stronghearted: Prince Edward Island in the Twentieth Century.* Charlottetown: Prince Edward Island Museum and Heritage Foundation, 2000.

MacLean, Angus. *Making It Home.* Charlottetown: Ragweed, 1999.

Mair, Elizabeth. "Theatre: Who's it For?" *Canadian Theatre Review* 48 (1986): 19–22.

Mullen, Melissa. *Rough Waters.* Barton 341–88.

Ondaatje, Michael. *The Clinton Special: A Film about the Farm Show.* Toronto: Mongrel Media, 1974.

Peake, Linda M. "Establishing a Theatrical Tradition: Prince Edward Island, 1800–1900." *Theatre Research in Canada* 2.2 (1981): 117–32.

Rubin, Don, ed. *Canadian Theatre History: Selected Readings.* Toronto: Playwrights Canada, 1996.

Smith, Cedric. Director's Notes for *The Road to Charlottetown*. Inserted Victoria Playhouse Program, 2003.

Stetson, Kent. *Horse High, Bull Strong, Pig Tight*. Barton 393–423.

Wallace, Robert. *Producing Marginality: Theatre and Criticism in Canada*. Saskatoon: Fifth House, 1990.

Wasserman, Jerry, ed. *Modern Canadian Plays*. Volume 1. 4th ed. Vancouver: Talonbooks, 2000.

Building Bridges: English & French Theatre in New Brunswick

by Glen Nichols

In 1996 Mary Vingoe commented about how far Atlantic theatre had come since the 1970s when "[a]nything else worth looking at came from elsewhere. Most people wanted to be elsewhere. [...] We are deaf if we live in a place where the voices of our own artists are not heard. In the Maritimes, we have begun to cast off our deafness—life is a great deal richer because of it" (21). While Vingoe's outlook might be true for Nova Scotia where a number of professional theatre companies produce a range of innovative and original plays, the same cannot be said for English-speaking New Brunswick; however, there is change on the horizon.

It is impossible to speak "generally" of theatre in New Brunswick; there are really two distinct theatre worlds here: English-language and French-language theatre. The histories, styles, repertoires, and infrastructures are strikingly and, perhaps sadly, different and separated. What is perhaps ironic at first glance is that the demographic minority, the francophone population which comprises approximately 33% of the New Brunswick total, has produced the theatre companies, artists, and repertoire with a greater presence than those of the English-speaking majority. This paper will explore the unique conditions of contemporary theatre production in New Brunswick as context for a closer look at several recent French-language plays. The conclusion will reveal a few hopeful signs in English-language theatre activity in the province.

French-language theatre in New Brunswick is currently driven by three professional companies. The oldest is Théâtre populaire d'Acadie (TPA) which has been based in Caraquet in the north-east corner of the province since 1974. With over 100 productions to its credit, TPA's repertoire, while including important original Acadian creations, has tended to emphasize an international and classical repertoire. TPA has developed a strong tradition of collaboration with Quebecois and international theatre companies. Théâtre l'Escaouette was formed by a few of the first graduates of the drama program at the Université de Moncton in 1978 and has been based in Moncton ever since. Dedicated originally to works for young audiences which it toured to schools across the province, Théâtre l'Escaouette has shifted to works for a more general audience in the past dozen years, but has not diluted its mandate for creating original plays. The repertoire has been dominated by new works by Herménégilde Chiasson, but has also been enriched by frequent co-productions with companies from central Canada such as the National Arts Centre, Théâtre de la Vieille 17 and Le Théâtre du Nouvel-Ontario. The company does some touring, particularly in Quebec and central Canada. For example, its remount production of Chiasson's *Pour une fois* was performed in Toronto (February 2004) in a co-production with TPA. Théâtre l'Escaouette was instrumental in the purchase and renovation of a new multi-million-dollar performance space which opened in Moncton in the fall of 2004. This highly anticipated facility fills an important gap in the city's theatre and performance infrastructure.

The newcomer on the professional theatre scene is Collectif Moncton Sable, created in Moncton in 1996. This highly innovative design-based physical-theatre company began by staging works developed in collaboration with poet France Daigle, but in 2002 they produced the stunning text, *Empreintes*, by the young poet and film-maker, Paul Bossé. A special year was 2005 because Moncton Sable brought two productions to the stage—*Linoléum* and *Alors, tu m'aimes*—works that continue to expand the experimental approach of the company. The first was another text by Paul Bossé, which again wove together several time periods and explored the revelation of past mysteries linked to the gradual uncovering of layers of flooring in a Moncton apartment by its current occupants. The other, by first-time playwright Monique Snow, introduced four young actors (Annie LaPlante, Brigitte LeBlanc, Anika Lirette and Marie-Pierre Valay-Nadeau) newly graduated from the Université de Moncton. Like most Moncton Sable productions, *Alors, tu m'aimes* was more lyrical than narrative, more exploratory and evocative than definitive. Built around the theme of love, the fragments or parts of fragments often repeated in later moments with different intonation and different contexts (the actors each played a variety of roles only identified by numbers in the script).

An overview of French-language theatre cannot avoid including Le Pays de la Sagouine, the theme park based on Antonine Maillet's works and located just outside of Moncton in the seaside village of Bouctouche, Maillet's hometown. The site produces highly popular summer theatre and employs a large number of artists. The texts they use include some original sketches each year by Maillet, as well as dinner theatre and street performances. A colossal spectacle entitled *L'Odysée*, also written by Maillet, was created in 2004 (and remounted in 2005 and 2006) as part of celebrations marking the 400th anniversary of the first French settlement in North America and the founding of Acadie. The show, involving dozens of volunteer performers and a number of professionals, commemorates significant events from the long history of Acadie.

There is the major conservatory program at the Université de Moncton. Since the 1970s the department has become renowned for high quality training and has been the source of the vast majority of Acadian theatre professionals at work in New Brunswick and beyond today. The impact of the Université de Moncton on the professionalization of Acadie in general, as well as in the theatre, cannot be understated. For the fine arts, and the theatre in particular, the university has provided not only modern training, but also an ever-expanding audience for arts which speak to an increasing diversity of Acadian voices.

New play development takes place at all three companies. Of note, Théâtre l'Escaouette, through their biennial Festival à haute voix, has attempted to cultivate new theatrical voices. The 2005 version of the festival featured nearly a dozen new plays reflecting a broad range of styles and forms. The direct impact of this initiative has been remarkable. Already noted above is Monique Snow's *Alors, tu m'aimes*, produced by Moncton Sable, but there also has been the phenomenal success of Mélanie F. Léger's *Roger Roger*, and the award-winning Emma Haché has had pieces developed in the series. Works coming out of the festival have gone on to be produced independently in the region and beyond in both theatre and film.

English-language theatre in New Brunswick on the other hand, despite the fact the English population is double the size of the francophone minority, is produced by only two professional companies. First is the self-named "provincial" company, Theatre New Brunswick (TNB), which has been based in Fredericton since 1969. TNB is mandated to tour its shows across the province, which it continues to do despite rising costs and shrinking audiences. TNB also supports a young company that tours to provincial schools with theatre for young audiences. In addition, there is an in-house theatre school for the general public. Rather than developing collaborations with other national or international companies, Theatre New Brunswick focuses on its own productions, and does not tour outside the province.

Live Bait Theatre, based in Sackville in the south-east corner of the province since 1988, has been largely a summer and seasonal dinner theatre company, but it has been noted for some regional collaborations, especially in recent years. The company is expanding its season and has recently (2004) opened a new permanent performance space in Sackville.

There is no professional conservatory theatre training offered in English in the province, although the three English-language universities, Mount Allison, St. Thomas, and the University of New Brunswick, all support drama concentrations including practical courses within their English degrees. While the university towns of Sackville and Fredericton do seem to support a high degree of arts and cultural events, a factor undoubtedly related to the presence of the students and faculty in the area, this has not translated into a strong indigenous theatre culture in either city.

Beyond the basic differences in infrastructure, the various theatres in New Brunswick also divide along differences in repertoire, design approaches, and relationship with the community.

The 2003–2004 Theatre New Brunswick season featured four main-stage plays that toured the province: Kim Selody's adaptation of *The Hobbit*; Norm Foster's latest comedy, this one for the Christmas market, called *Dear Santa*; Maureen Hunter's *Vinci* and Dan Needles' *Wingfield on Ice*. With the exception of the Hunter piece, the season is clearly built around plays with easy accessibility and a high degree of audience familiarity. Only *Vinci* took the audience beyond the well-known and comfortable, but even there, the season flyer touted the play as "Wittily poking fun at religious zealots, [… it] depicts a strong sense of sacrifice and unwavering hope," comments emphasizing the play's appeal to a general audience. The season that just finished (2005–06) looked very similar, with Norm Foster's newest piece, *Here on the Flightpath*; a children's Christmas special, *Pinocchio*; a winter musical, *I Love You, You're Perfect, Now Change*; and Michel Tremblay's *For the Pleasure of Seeing Her Again*.

Design at TNB focuses on elaborate sets and costumes emphasizing realism and linear "believability." The company's regular use of a turntable set frame, for example, enabling rapid set changes when plays call for multiple locations, is indicative of the generally realistic approach.

Live Bait's dinner theatre and summer season in 2003–04 featured *Beach Party* by local playwrights Jane & Dave McClelland, *Class of '73: Reunion*, by Live Bait founders and co-artistic directors Charlie Rhindress & Karen Valanne, and J.J. McColl's musical, *Menopositive*. Their summer and Christmas fare has remained consistent since then, satisfying an important and dependable audience base. Demonstrating the new and exciting directions the company is taking, Live Bait also produced Don Hannah's *Fathers and Sons* in its first production in Hannah's home province, and an original play by Sackville teacher and playwright, Mark Blagrave, *We Happy Few*. Set in a convalescent hospital during the First World War, the play dealt with questions of "the artist's responsibility to society and the human fallout of war," to quote the company publicity. The play successfully used innovative environmental staging and non-theatrical lighting to engage the audience in the play's world.

In the fall of 2005, Live Bait produced the world premiere of Jenny Munday's *Relatively Harmless*. Sean Mulcahy's expressionistic set emphasized the surreal aspects of the script, which portrayed the return of a woman to her family home after many years absence to attend the funeral of her father, who had been wheel-chair bound for ten years after suffering a stroke. The play weaves several timeframes as the woman and her family come to terms with the effects of the father's illness and death on each other and their relationships. The play was theatrically demanding and one can only hope it inspires more productions like it.

On the English side, connections with the community are tenuous. TNB, especially, has been through a notably difficult time in recent years with diminishing audiences and serious financial short-falls. While the worst of that seems to be in the past thanks to generous donations from private and public sources, and audiences are returning, links with the various communities the company tours to vary widely. Live Bait, however, has an enthusiastic following and enjoys solid, if variable, houses. The shift to more demanding plays, though, requires a bit of adjustment. The opening night audience at *Fathers and Sons*, for example, perhaps because the play was offered late in the summer season, dearly anticipated a rollicking comedy and started out laughing at scenes that were not really funny and took awhile to get into the play's tone. At the subsequent production of *We Happy Few*, though, the audiences were still at capacity. There is a strong community connection with the company, which I believe will be enhanced as Live Bait continues to offer a wider variety of theatre options.

On the francophone side, the Théâtre populaire d'Acadie 2003–04 season began with the Canadian premiere of *Le collier d'Hélène* by Quebec playwright Carole Fréchette; the second TPA-only production was *La sortie au théâtre*, a montage of cabaret sketches by 1920s German expressionist playwright Karl Valentin. The TPA season also featured two plays for young audiences created in co-productions with Théâtre de Papyrus from Belgium: *Hulul* and *La petite ombre*. This second also involved collaboration with Les Gros Becs from Quebec, a truly multi-dimensional project, described in company publicity as "theatre of surrealistic images inspired by the universe of a haunted ship." The company tours its shows across the province and well beyond New Brunswick with the majority of performances increasingly taking place in Quebec, central Canada, and across Belgium and France. The latest season, 2005–06, continued this trend by featuring two in-house shows, both by the young Acadian Emma Haché, *Les défricheurs d'eau* and *Murmures* (which toured extensively), and hosting four general-audience productions and two for young audiences, all by Quebec companies.

With all the preparations for their new building, Théâtre l'Escaouette only produced two shows in 2003–04, both in co-production. The first was Herménégilde Chiasson's newest play, *Le Christ est apparu au Gun Club*, produced with the Théâtre français of the Centre national des arts. The second was a new play called *Willy Graf* by franco-Ontario playwright Michel Ouellette. This one was produced with the Centre national des arts again, as well as with Théâtre de la Vieille 17 in Ottawa. Half the cast and crew were Escaouette personnel and half were from Ottawa. The rest of the season at Théâtre l'Escaouette was filled out with shows on tour from Quebec and France: *Prophètes sans Dieu* by Slimane Benaissa (Theatres… l'Été, TILF, Groupe des Vingt and l'Adami); *Le Bible*, a giant puppet show by Théâtre du Sous-Marin Jaune and Théâtre la Bordée; and, finally, *Zazie dans le métro* by Raymond Queneau (Théâtre des Fonds de Tiroirs). Despite the preoccupations of the renovations and transition, since 2004 the company remounted *Le Christ est apparu au Gun Club* in 2005, which has since toured extensively across Canada. Another play by Chiasson, *La grande seance*, was produced in 2004 (with Théâtre français du Centre national des arts and Théâtre populaire d'Acadie), the 400th anniversary of the founding of Acadie. The play depicts a theatre company preparing to stage an historical pageant to mark the anniversary.

Design-wise, the French-language theatre companies explore various styles and approaches from the 1920s expressionism of Valentin to a subtle orientalism of *Willy Graf* which featured sliding paper walls and Japanese-inspired woodcut designs. TPA, especially, is known for developing classically-inspired performances drawn from diverse sources such as commedia dell'arte and French neoclassical drama. Meanwhile l'Escaouette (alone and in co-productions) pushes the limits of imagistic theatre in plays like *Pour une fois* and, to a lesser degree, *Le Christ est apparu au Gun Club*. Moncton Sable is, of course, renowned for its innovative design concepts. The earlier thematic treatments of Daigle's work made particular demands. One memorable example was the production of *Foin* (Hay) in which the theatre space was filled with dozens of bales of straw, providing both the audience seating and the setting environment (paper tissues were supplied!). A truly sensory experience, indeed (if one has ever sat on a bale of hay, for any length of time!).

For the French-language companies the connection with their communities seems solid, deep, and dedicated. There is a vibrant commitment exhibited by consistently full houses. TPA plays in Moncton at the large Capitol Theatre, for example, and enjoys audiences of several hundred spectators at each performance. There is also large corporate and government support.

From this necessarily superficial overview, it is apparent that New Brunswick contains two independent theatre systems with little to compare except the accident of sharing a geographical space. How does one explain this difference? That is a problem I have asked many times in my ten years in the province, with little satisfactory explanation. And how does one begin to overcome these differences in developing a more complex and sophisticated theatre system for the English-speaking theatre audience in New Brunswick?

One of the ways of beginning an understanding of or at least an exploration of the differences between the two theatre systems was suggested by Brian Crow's description of post-colonial theatre: "In such post- but neo-colonial contexts dramatists have created theatre for a variety of urgent cultural functions. They have often been concerned to use the stage to define and affirm their people's cultural "personality"—in the face of continuing cultural, economic, and political subjugation—by recovering the past, freed from the biases of metropolitan or mainstream history" (17). What struck me was how this could describe the French theatre of New Brunswick, but not that of the English community. In an odd and perhaps ironic way, the doubly colonized francophone minority of the province is creating theatre from a more evolved post-colonial position than is the English majority.

One can trace contemporary Acadian dramaturgy through several primary post-colonial models suggested in *The Empire Writes Back* by Ashcroft, Griffiths, and Tiffin. The first model is that of nationalistic and self-conscious myth-building (16–18), which can be seen in the plays of Antonine Maillet and other pioneers of Acadian theatre concerned with constructing a unified national identity through facial and historical re-centering. It is interesting that she is still writing in that historical mode as demonstrated by the productions at *Le Pays de la Sagouine*. Next is the comparative model that looks at the relationship of two or more colonial positions (18–20). We see this in the later works of Herménégilde Chiasson where he is concerned with the exoticisation of Acadie as seen from Montreal, the neo-colonial centre of French Canada. Finally, the model of hybridity and syncreticity (35–37) is demonstrated in the enthusiastic embracing of co-productions and the internationalism of the repertoires of Acadian theatre companies as well as the interest in historical deconstruction and interrogation of national myths in the plays.

In all honesty, none of these models can be perceived in the English-language theatre repertoire. Part of that may be due simply to the small number of indigenous New Brunswick plays in English. Other than the extremely prolific and popular Norm

Foster, whose work shows greater affinity in style and content to Neil Simon and London's West End than to anything recognizably New Brunswickian, other plays in English do not have the critical mass to establish trends or patterns. Plays like Jenny Munday's adaptations of Herb Curtis's novels, *The Americans are Coming* and *The Last Tasmanian*, and Charlie Rhindress's *Maritime Way of Life* spring to mind as significant high points, but without a strong continuity it is impossible to draw much sense of identity.

One explanation is that the English community, despite its position as the dominant majority, exhibits the effects of colonization. The historical roots of English New Brunswick in the loyalist diaspora, and the contemporary marginalization of New Brunswick at the geographical and metaphorical margins of a Canadian and North American hegemony, point to a highly colonized positionality. But, and this is crucial to the differences in New Brunswick dramaturgies, the nature of that position is radically different from that of Acadie.

Ashcroft, Griffiths, and Tiffin, among others, cite two fundamental types of colonial constructions which affect post-colonial reactions: that of the settler/invader and that of the conquered. The first seems to be the model of English New Brunswick. Settler/invader colonies displace or eliminate any indigenous peoples and set about establishing a piece of the "mother-country" in the context of and in resistance to the new foreign home. According to Helen Gilbert, "Settler histories do not simply replicate the master narrative's characteristic tropes; instead, they are often concerned with replicating authenticity for a society dislocated from the imperial centre and, simultaneously, alienated from the local land and indigenous culture" (113). The Loyalist-founded English community of New Brunswick, with a triple alienation, seems to exhibit, at least in the theatre, some hesitancy in developing an indigenous cultural identity. The system, repertoire, and aesthetics of theatre remain stolidly borrowed from the centre (or centres: London, New York, and central Canada), replicating the authenticity of a lost "homeland" or revered metropolis, with only a glimmer of interest in addressing the lack of regional voices.

This lack of indigenous dramaturgy may also have to do with the ability of the English community of New Brunswick to "imagine" itself. While both English and French are small populations spread thinly across a wide area, English New Brunswick does not have the advantage of an identifiable common face, regardless how clichéd or problematic that face might be. The Acadians have the story of the "deportation" mythologized and a source of national narrative, around which to have begun their collective trip back from a colonial past. As of yet, English New Brunswick has not constructed or been able to imagine that sense of commonality/identity. In its place is a sense of precarious dominance in a marginal landscape.

In addition, the dynamics of the relationship between the two principal communities also inflicts a kind of subtle self-doubt on the English in New Brunswick. On one hand, the incredible gains in economic and cultural security experienced by the Acadians over the past four decades have rebalanced the social fabric of the province, increasing the self-inflicted sense of precariousness in portions of the English community. Compounding this, claims of uniqueness or identity sometimes get confused with reactionary racial or linguistic retrenchment such as that promoted by the late CORE party. The mantra might be, "It is better to be invisible than be mistaken for being rude," so English theatre has tended to disappear inside itself: not sure "who" it is, not able yet to imagine a "self," afraid of offending, and being to some degree intimidated by the Acadian miracle around it.

While the French Acadian community was originally also a settler/invader colony, it experienced an entirely different history of settlement, expulsion, and return under the English as colonial masters. The result is a society more akin to the model of a conquered people striving to accommodate a mythologized and idealized past in resistance to the presence and domination of an English majority. In addition one could even say Acadie has been colonized from within by the myth of its past. Citing Helen Gilbert again, "plays and playwrights [in conquered societies] construct discursive contexts for an artistic, social and political present by enacting other versions of the pre-contact, imperial, and post-imperial past on stage [...]. Reconstructing the past in this way usually heralds the emergence of new voices and new tools for understanding that past" (106). This is exactly the source of the most contemporary Acadian dramaturgy by the likes of Emma Haché and Paul Bossé, as well as Herménégilde Chiasson's later pieces.

In a paper Chiasson himself presented to the Assemble generale annuelle de la Fédération culturelle canadienne-française in June of 1996, entitled, "Comment traverser le tain de notre miroir pour atteindre le paradis de la visibilité," he explained at length the difficulty Acadian culture has in combating neo-colonial images produced by an externally-controlled media that often has an agenda contrary to the interests of Acadie. The real problem comes when Acadians themselves begin to suffer from the irreconcilable differences between the reality they are living and the images of themselves they begin to believe in. As he explains,

> Les Acadiens domiciliés au Québec nous ont donné une image folklorique qui fait recette dans les médias et qui les a rendus visible sur le territoire de l'Acadie, au point où une grande majorité des Acadiens s'identifie maintenant à cette vision exotique fondée beaucoup plus sur le mythe que la réalité. (10–11)

Chiasson's 1999 play, *Pour une fois*, which was in the active repertoire of Théâtre l'Escaouette as late as 2004, exemplifies the most sophisticated deconstruction of Acadie's self-obsession with a mythologized past and the battle against the internal and external forces of colonisation. The episodic plot involving Charles Lanteigne, a would-be historian, and his family is a metaphor for the history of Acadie from its beginnings with Samuel de Champlain through to an uncertain date in the (near?) future. The combination of domestic, contemporary characters and historical allusion is Chiasson's vehicle to foreground the troubled connections between history and contemporary life in Acadie. The play's exploration of Charles's gradual alienation from his community and family becomes a metaphor for the collective alienation of contemporary Acadians from mythologized and internalized elements of historical identity of Acadie promoted and re-enforced by the outside world. This play thus depicts the two forces of post-colonial resentment in modern Acadie. Charles Lanteigne's insistence on the historical and cultural priorities of Acadie constantly bump into the more rationalist and economic preoccupations of those around him. Although he ends up marginalized for the actions he takes, the political maturity espoused by the Parti Acadien victory can be seen, partly at least, as a product of his convictions and their effect on those around him. Meanwhile, the multiplicity and hybridity of language layers in the play, coupled with the episodic structure and meta-theatrical framing, imply the complexity of Acadian identity, countering the simplistic mediatized image of neo-colonial Acadie as a unified cultural entity that emphasizes folkloric stereotypes. The integration of collective, individual, theatrical, and thematic aspects marks the maturity of the play as it achieves significance through self-conscious integration of particular, regional material.

A second play of Chiasson's, *Aliénor*, originally created in 1997, was recently (2003) produced in English translation by LIVEWIRE Theatre in Moncton. This poetic play depicts Étienne's unjust accusation of sexual assault of his daughter Aliénor. The interplay of Étienne and Aliénor creates a powerful allegory for the creation of a post-colonial Acadie, forward looking, but conscious of its foundations. Étienne, like oppressed Acadie, avoids destruction first by escaping from the world to live in the woods, then later by taking on the wrath of the world in a martyr-like resistance to injustice. Aliénor, engendered by her martyred past, becomes a kind of post-colonial Evangeline, a new symbolic paradigm: although raped by the intruders she is able to survive and defeat her opponents by refusing to flee or to be martyred, insisting instead that "We will be avenged, father, by life" (246). In the end it is Aliénor who prevails. She believes that in building a new world on the ashes of the old "I will never betray the history of our suffering" (246), but "We must bury the past. We must write it down in a book and bury the book. And the dead will read that book and they too will finally be able to sleep" (245).

In September of 2002, Moncton Sable produced *Empreintes* by first-time playwright Paul Bossé, an award-winning poet and film-maker. The remarkable play weaves three plots involving an Australopithecus who sacrifices his life to save his wife and child, a modern-day anthropologist who saves a gorilla from death by boredom, and a Chiac-speaking robot who rescues David from the machinations of his techno captors in a future world. From the dawn of prehistory and the first human family, to the present day, to a future when computers have taken over the world, the complex narrative of *Empreintes* explores the traces of human compassion across the millennia. In effect, it is a play within a play within a play: we watch David watching Lucie watching the ancient events, the three stories folding into each other like contrapuntal strains in a symphony.

The play is remarkable for situating Acadie on a global, pan-historical stage without pretension or apology. Acadie is normalized as an imagined player on a global scale; it is perfectly natural that the researcher in Antarctica should call upon the Centre d'études acadiennes to find a talking-walking robot to help solve his murder mystery. A central feature of the play is the clash of dialects within and beyond Acadie. Again, Chiac, the particular dialect of southern New Brunswick, is treated as the normal means of discourse while other dialects of French, especially standardized French, are treated as "other." The play responds to the internal and external colonization of Acadie, as a place both real and imagined, with a re-centering of language and space that shows a sophisticated post-colonial evolution. The world of the play neither compares itself to otherness, nor expresses any kind of resistant frustration in the face of a minority position. Acadie simply is what it is, and what it is in the play is an intensely complex, self-conscious, imaginative space, acknowledging but not subordinating itself to its connections with the past, its neighbours, and a fictional global future.

The evolution of modern Acadian drama first constructed a common identity through the self-conscious imagining of an idealized, mythologized past. The raising of history in this way in the plays of Maillet, Jules Boudreau, and Calixte Duguay, for example, served to create an important racial and national identity, but, because the images remained aloof from the reality of Acadian life, it became a kind of hegemonic albatross around the Acadian neck, erasing differences, complexities, and modernizations. Consequently, the theatre has become a site of interrogation of that constructed commonality, exploring the inherent contradictions between the myth and the complex realities of contemporary Acadie. This re-imagining of the social and aesthetic space was achieved by integrating the myths and the way they function into the images of contemporary life and thought. The force of this hybridization laid the foundations for a global confidence that now enables Acadian dramaturgy to reach out to the world and bring the world to Acadie, not as backward colony seeking some kind of justification or approval, but as partner and participant.

On the other side, for the English theatre system to move forward, there is first and foremost the underlying need to imagine a common identity. The English community of New Brunswick, and the theatre that serves it, is split between three rival urban centres and a broad rural hinterland, each with competing needs. There are the constant inter-relations with the French minority within the region and with the larger business and cultural forces from outside the region. While these factors are crucial in the shaping of English culture in the province, so far English theatre has only just begun to deal with or build bridges among these aspects of New Brunswick reality, but has not yet grasped the necessary role it must eventually play in the construction of this identity.

When this paper was first written in the winter of 2003, Scott Burke had recently been appointed the new Artistic Director of Theatre New Brunswick and had made overtures to organize a roundtable or mini-conference to bring together English and French theatre personnel from across the province. This kind of face-to-face exchange could have been an important first step in shrinking the gap that currently exists between practitioners in the two systems. Alas, such a meeting never took place and Burke left TNB after only two years. His successor, Claude Giroux, only remained in the office for one season and, as of the spring of 2006, Leigh Rivenbark, former

Associate Artistic Director, is filling in. Once this period of instability, which reaches the administrative levels as well, is in the past one can hope for renewed leadership from TNB.

Live Bait Theatre, though, has shown the stirrings of a sleeping giant lately. With a new performance space and the beginnings of a winter season, the company is building on its interest in new play development. While original play creation is not new to Live Bait, the recent extensive and extended collaborations with Playwrights Atlantic Resource Centre, including the writer-in-residenceship of Jenny Munday, shows a seriousness and integration with tremendous promise for New Brunswick theatre development, both in terms of dramaturgy and audience building.

Equally exciting is the NotaBle Acts Summer Theatre Festival in the capital city of Fredericton. The festival is entering is fifth successful year, having doubled its length to two full weekends in July and August. Dedicated to the development of original plays, the festival provides a range of mechanisms for emerging and established writers, including showcase productions, contests for short plays and one-acts, workshops, public readings, and audience feedback sessions. Since the demise of the Brave New Words program at TNB a number of years ago, new play development in English has been very limited, making the emergence of NotaBle Acts a very promising sign. The festival is building not only a strong reputation but also an important body of new works. One can only hope that, like Théâtre l'Escaouette's Festival à haute voix, this work will begin to translate into new companies and full productions, and will begin to have an impact upon the shaping of an identity for English New Brunswick and its culture.

Finally, the Capitol Theatre in Moncton, although primarily a roadhouse, has established a bilingual theatre school to complement, eventually, the kind of conservatory training offered at the Université de Moncton. Underlying the foundation of this school are important collaborative links in both linguistic communities, as well as with business and the municipality, within and beyond the region. The timeline for the full implementation of the school is not yet confirmed, but if it does come to fruition it will be a crucial element in the long term growth of indigenous professional English language theatre in the province.

(2005)

Works Cited

Ashcroft, Bill, Gareth Griffiths, and Helen Tiffin. *The Empire Writes Back: Theory and Practice in Post-colonial Literatures.* London: Routledge, 1989.

Chiasson, Herménégilde. *Aliénor. Angels and Anger: Five Contemporary Acadian Plays in Translation.* Ed. and Trans. Glen Nichols. Toronto: Playwrights Canada, 2003. 199–255.

———. "Comment traverser le tain de notre miroir pour atteindre le paradis de la visibilité." Internet site for the Galerie d'Art de l'Université de Moncton. Accessed 15 April 2000. http://www.umoncton.ca/gaum/findex.html.

Crow, Brian with Chris Banfield. *An Introduction to Post-colonial Theatre.* Cambridge: Cambridge UP, 1996.

Gilbert, Helen. *(Post) Colonial Stages: Critical and Creative Views on Drama, Theatre and Performance.* Hebden Bridge, West Yorkshire: Dangaroo, 1999.

Vingoe, Mary. "This is Not my Curriculum Vitae." *Canadian Theatre Review* 87 (1996): 19–21.

Can I Get a Witness? Performing Community in African-Nova Scotian Theatre [1]

by Maureen Moynagh

In his introduction to *Nation and Narration*, Homi Bhabha reminds us of the extent to which ambivalence "haunts the idea of the nation," fracturing efforts to imagine unity and coherence, so that narratives of nation remain partial and incomplete (1). Alan Filewod echoes and extends this idea in his claim that "Canadian theatre can as a whole be considered as a meta-performance that enacts crises of nationhood" (xvii). If those crises of nationhood may be understood to include the place of racialized and sexualized "others" in the nation and the place of the "regional" within an imagined national culture, then African-Nova Scotian theatre enacts the ambivalence, the crisis of nation(hood) of which Bhabha and Filewod speak. In fact, many African-Nova Scotian plays intervene in what Bhabha terms "those justifications of modernity— progress, homogeneity, cultural organicism, the deep nation, the long past—that rationalize the authoritarian, 'normalizing' tendencies within cultures in the name of the national interest or the ethnic prerogative" (4). In part, this intervention is made through an abiding concern with history in the work of playwrights as diverse as George Elliott Clarke, George Boyd, Walter Borden, David Woods, Louise Delisle and Lucky Campbell, who cover the spectrum from professional theatre to the grassroots. But whether the play has a historical or contemporary focus, the interventions these plays make in the ways Canada is imagined are enabled by a performative structure of witnessing that forges a politically alternative community at the scene of the performance.

Freddie Rokem draws on Brecht's "The Street Scene" to argue that, in performing history, the actor may be seen as a witness to the historical event in a way analogous to that of the actor in epic theatre who models the behaviour of any eyewitness to a traffic accident, demonstrating what has happened to those assembled on the scene (8–9). To function as witness, the actor, Rokem suggests, "need not have witnessed the events directly" (9); rather, it is the attitude of the actor to the events he or she performs that is key:

> As a witness the actor does not necessarily have to strive toward complete neutrality or objectivity in order to make it possible for the spectators, the "bystanders" in the theatre, to become secondary witnesses, to understand and, in particular, "to form an opinion" about the forces which have shaped the accidents of history. (9)

It is the partiality of the actor as witness, in other words, that enables a critical relationship to the historical events depicted in the play and that similarly invites a critical response from the audience. If "theatrical performances of and about history" seem particularly geared to "reflect[ing] complex ideological issues concerning deeply rooted national identities and subjectivities and power structures" (Rokem 8), I hasten to add that it is possible for the actor to function as witness in relation to contemporary events as well, even if those "events" are entirely fictional, provided that the character's relationship to a particular socioscape also invites the audience to take up a critical relationship to the scene of the performance.

Andrew Parker and Eve Kosofsky Sedgwick help to make clear how this theatrical witnessing might work in their deconstruction of Austin's notion of performativity. Taking what is arguably Austin's key example of the performative, the "I do" uttered in the context of a marriage ceremony, Parker and Sedgwick point out that the speaking, acting subject interpellates those present as witnesses through an appeal to state [or church] authority and an implicit appeal to heteronormativity. Yet "[t]he marriage example... will strike a queer [witness] at some more oblique angle or angles" (10). That is to say, not all witnesses to this particular performance will subscribe to a heteronormative ideology, nor will they all necessarily occupy a straightforward (pun intended) relationship to state authority. [2] While witnesses may occupy an ambivalent relationship to the discourse by which the performance hails them, disavowal is an unconventional response, Parker and Sedgwick remind us. As they put it, "Negative performances tend to have a high threshold" (9). The witness typically constitutes the performance, and thus, as against Austin's claim that theatre hollows out a performative utterance, Parker and Sedgwick argue that the relationship between performance and witness(es) takes us "to the topic of marriage itself *as theatre*—marriage as a kind of fourth wall or invisible proscenium arch that moves through the world... continually reorienting itself around the surrounding relations of visibility and spectatorship" (11).

I want to draw several things from this discussion. First, consider the ideological nature of any performance and its power to invite the audience to witness according to the terms set out, not merely by the individual actor, but by the dominant discourses invoked by the performance. What happens when actors invite the audience to constitute a performance that disavows the dominant discourse? Or to put it differently, What about queer performativity and performance? Presumably, this sense of a performance that "queers" state authority and its supplementary narratives is what Rokem is interested in when he speaks of a Brechtian mode of witnessing. It is also what I am interested in with respect to African-Nova Scotian theatre. Benedict Anderson identifies the novel and the newspaper as the key "forms of imagining" associated with the emergence of the nation as imagined community. What these forms offer is the experience of "homogenous, empty time," a sense of belonging (both of characters and readers) to a shared socius at a given moment in time, even if most of the members of that society remain unknown to one another (24–26). The theatre creates that sense of belonging by bringing the actors and the audience together at the scene of the performance and by implicitly or explicitly articulating what occurs onstage with the world outside the theatre. The threshold of performance is raised, to invoke Parker and Sedgwick once more, when this performative structure operates against the grain, bringing actors and audience together in a critical relationship to dominant conceptions of the socius to which they are meant to "belong." I am arguing that the historical sensibility of African-Nova Scotian theatre and such key tropes as the restoration of loss and the quest for identify and place offer just this mode of alternative witnessing to the dominant narratives of nation.

Representing historical events in performance has to do not only with what Richard Schechner calls the "restoration of behavior," a feature of all performance, but also with what Rokem describes as a restoration of loss. That is, the performance may be understood as "recreating something which has been irretrievably lost and attempting, at least on the imaginative level and in many cases also on the intellectual and emotional levels, to restore that loss" (13). In the case of African-Nova Scotian theatre, as in the case of the performances about the Shoah that Rokem discusses, the onstage performances take place in the context of community efforts to mourn and restore loss outside of the theatre. This mode of witnessing is particularly in evidence in plays about the destruction of Africville, in plays about slavery and in plays about judicial injustice. Of course, literal restoration is impossible, as Joseph Roach has pointed out, since nothing is performed exactly the same way twice (46); the citation or reiteration of historical events in performance allows for invention and intervention in ways that return us to the notion of witnessing that I have been discussing. These plays cast the performers in the role of witnesses to historical practices, institutions, events, and invite audiences similarly to become partial, to witness on behalf of African-Nova Scotian communities in the present.

Africville[3] resonates powerfully among African-Nova Scotians as a cautionary tale about racialized economic and political violence. At the same time, Africville has come to represent the spirit of African-Nova Scotian community broadly conceived and to constitute a source of political consciousness. As members of the Africville Genealogical Society continue to press the city government for compensation, artistic efforts to "restore the loss" of Africville emphasize its transmutation into a symbolic force. The best known play about Africville is undoubtedly George Boyd's *Consecrated Ground*. Produced by Eastern Front Theatre in 1999, *Consecrated Ground* intervenes in Canadian national narratives by "lay[ing] bare the raw wound of the only Canuck, anti-black racism most Canadians know about" (Clarke, "Making" 393). The impact first of municipal neglect of Africville and then of its expropriation is portrayed through the growing marital conflict between Clarice and Willem. Boyd's figuring of the destruction of the black community is also gendered, as Clarke points out: Clarice assumes the role of defender of the community, and, in his betrayal of his wife and of Africville itself, Willem is emasculated ("Making" 395). Seduced by the promise of modern housing and access to schools for his son, Willem signs over his wife's property, embracing the liberal-welfare model that ultimately betrays them both. In the end, the couple comes together in a burial ceremony for their son, and for Africville, that consecrates the ground on which the community stood for so many generations—ground made sacred, Clarice insists, by the community itself:

> Canuck, my ancestors, they consecrated this ground… the kids laughing and playin' in Kildare Field consecrated it! The funerals, the hymns at the church, consecrated it…. All the baptisms down at the beach, Willem, they consecrated the ground. This is where they lived and died… where… where they cried… where they loved, Willem… *loved.* (461)

The audience is witness to the consecration that closes the play, silently joining in the mourning for the community that has been lost and restored through the commemorative act of the play itself. Rachael von Fossen confirms that in this, as in his most recent play *Wade in the Water*, Boyd "insist[s] upon the importance of historical subject matter as contemporary testimony" (92).

David Woods has written two plays about Africville: the radio play *Part of the Deal* was produced by CBC Radio in 1992 and *Once* (1996), which mixes poetry and music in an evocative commemorative piece, was performed by Voices Black Theatre Ensemble in Halifax and aired on CBC Radio in 1996. In *Part of the Deal*, Woods offers the audience a complex structure of witnessing by presenting as protagonist a young black man, George Pilgrim, who is ashamed of both his Africville[4] roots and his blackness: "It is always your own that drags you down." He works for the city as "Assistant Relocation Officer for the Resettlement of the Negroes from the Unsavoury Area"; it is his job to persuade residents to sign over their property to the city. In the course of his job, he meets and befriends a resident who takes him on a tour of Africville one night. Through the tour, George witnesses aspects of the Africville story he has not encountered before: His companion insists that "home was never as bad as the newspapers made it look" and attests to Africville's natural beauty: "You should see this place in the fall, man! Just about sunset the whole sky be filled up with colours—red, yellow and orange—just hangin' over the water. It be like lookin' up at heaven!" He also witnesses the racial violence of the municipality, a violence in which he is implicated, as firefighters engaged in training exercises neglect to check an apparently empty dwelling before setting it ablaze and then dousing the flames, only to learn too late that the house was not empty. While George is only partly weaned from his comprador position by what he sees in the company of his new friend, he comes to be haunted, literally, by what he has witnessed, and the audience is invited, through its witnessing, to take up a position that is simultaneously critical of the assimilationist politics he represents and of the municipal government's attitude toward Africville as represented by George's boss, Mr. Le Grou, and the firefighters. We are invited, in other words, to complete the transformation George partially undergoes through seeing what was positive in Africville and see what was corrupt in the municipality's dealings with the community. Like *Consecrated Ground, Part of the Deal* effectively invites the audience to become part of a political community gathered in solidarity around what Africville has come to mean. In Clark's words, "[T]he community persists as an act of memory and an act of witness, one that deems the Africville Relocation an act of injustice—and of racism" ("Making" 393).

Performance is also a means of bearing witness to the legacy of slavery, a history that has a particular resonance for Canadians, in light of narratives that construct the nation as "the promised land," the terminus of the Underground Railroad. The trope of unfulfilled promises that implicitly haunts plays about Africville acquires a very particular resonance in African-Nova Scotian plays about slavery, from George Elliott Clark's *Beatrice Chancy* to George Boyd's *Wade in the Water*, from Louise Delisle's *A Slave's Day in Court* to Lucky Campbell's *A World of Our Own*. In testifying both to the fact that slavery was practiced in Canada until 1834 and to the precariousness of the "freedom" accorded those fleeing either slavery or the U.S. Fugitive Slave Act (1850), these plays challenge the moral rectitude that characterizes popular representations of Canada's role in the hemispheric history of slavery. Here diasporic identification challenges and enlarges upon narrowly national modes of imagining.

Beatrice Chancy cites both the history and the literary iterations of the Cenci to stage a tragedy about the sexual and racial violence at the heart of the Canadian colony.[5] The nation's insistence that, when it came to slavery, Canada was a place apart is here confronted with its role in the trans-American institution. Appropriately, slavery is presented as a family affair in *Beatrice Chancy*: Francis Chancy is an Annapolis Valley planter and Beatrice his mixed-race daughter by a slave mother. Beatrice's admission to the national family is made contingent on her renunciation of blackness; when she falls in love with another slave, she loses her precarious status as Chancy's daughter, her access to whiteness. He rapes her, consigning her to slave status and driving her to murderous revenge—the spark for a slave revolt that further redeems Beatrice's crime. As is frequently the case in representations of Beatrice, the audience is asked to see her act of patricide as justifiable under the circumstances, and thus once again, our witnessing situates us in an ambivalent relation to dominant narratives of nation.

George Boyd's *Wade in the Water* similarly puts Canada back into the trans-American history of slavery, despite the fact that the experience of slavery itself is set in the more familiar terrain of a southern U.S. plantation. As Rachael Van Fossen points out, it would be a mistake to "see *Wade in the Water* as dealing with primarily American subject matter" since "to do so would be to deny... the historical movement of Black Loyalists to Canada" (104). In fact, the trajectory of the journey that is sketched out in *Wade in the Water* is particularly resonant with African-Nova Scotian history, as the protagonist moves from the United States to Nova Scotia and then on to Sierra Leone.[6] While Canada is scripted as a haven from slavery in this play, it also ultimately is found wanting as a home(land). In this way, Boyd rehearses what Diana Brydon has characterized as "ambivalently utopic expectations of Canada, [and] ambivalently nostalgic longings for Africa" (105).

A similar ambivalence haunts the grassroots drama of Lucky Campbell and Louise Delisle. In *A World of Our Own* (1994), Campbell depicts the tribulations of an ex-slave named Liberty, who fought on the side of the British in the American revolutionary war in exchange for freedom and land in Nova Scotia. Liberty soon learns he must also fight for the land he was promised; as he puts it, "we were last in line for all of the promises" (1). Delisle's play "*A Slave's Day in Court*" echoes this suggestion that even where justice is ultimately done, injustice is the norm for African-Canadians and freedom is precarious. As Clarke puts it in his Foreword to Delisle's collection of plays, "[T]he theme of trust and its violation… scores most of [Delisle's] plays" ("Dramatic Entrance" 8). Ambivalence about Canada-as-haven in these plays works to expose the often racist reception blacks have received in the nation, whether slave or free, newly arrived or native born; together they offer a historical counter-narrative that encourages the audience to make connections between then and now.

Plays that foreground the trope of a quest for identity and place offer an equally ambivalent articulation of belonging in the nation. Walter Borden's *Tightrope Time* explores identity by focusing on the struggle for revaluation of those devalued by gendered and racialized social conventions. In Borden's one-man show, the audience is taken on a tour of the "many mansions" in the mind of the Host, offering us "multifarious perspectives of blackness by touring one black man's polyphonous consciousness," as Clarke puts it in his introduction to the play ("Walter" 474). The Host denounces social classification at the outset, declaring that "[boundaries and labels/Are debilitating limitations/Which at best serve only to lock us/Within the convenience of others" (483). The characters we meet over the course of the play do their best to escape those limitations, to flout conventional conceptions of value, and none more evidently than those whose gender and sexuality combine with race to consign them to the margins: Ethiopia the Drag Queen, Adie the Hooker, and Chuck the Hustler. In making these characters facets of the Host, Borden implicitly incorporates them into the broadly encompassing notion of identity he is presenting in the play. The Minister of Health and Welfare affirms the capacity of human beings perpetually to exceed prescribed social categories: "Well, this celebration is not so much a historical documentation of the quest by a people for a place in the Nova Scotia or indeed the Canadian mosaic, as it is an illumination of the resiliency of the human spirit" (491). He explicitly encourages the audience to identify with emotions that unite across boundaries of race, gender, sexual orientation and nation, affirming that "the human spirit has no special resting place. It will find a lodging wherever it is received" (491). The black, gay, transgender, female, old and young voices summon a community defined by a politics of identification rather than by identity polities. Rather than accommodating exclusionary narratives of nation, in other words, Borden argues for re-imagining community.

Whylah Falls also offers a utopian re-imagining of community that is explicitly wrested from a history of suffering and injustice. Like the plays about Africville and about slavery, *Whylah Falls* restores a historical loss: it was inspired in part by the 1985 murder of Graham Norman Cromwell near Weymouth Falls, NS, and the acquittal of his killer by an all-white jury. The performance bears witness to the injustice of Cromwell's death and invites the audience to bear witness to the place that death occupies in a broader pattern of violence and injustice, including sexual violence. In tribute to the community of Weymouth Falls, Clarke uses the theatre to imagine a place that "ain't undramatically real," a cosmopolitan rural community peopled by vernacular poets like X's beloved Shelley and her blues-strumming brother Othello, a community that teaches the exiled poet-figure X how to love and how to craft poetry that will speak to the place he wants to call home. In invoking a diasporic frame of reference—"Whylah Falls be a snowy, northern Mississippi, with blood spattered, not on magnolias, but on pines, lilacs and wild roses"—Clarke reminds his audience that scenes of racial violence and injustice haunt this nation too.

To be a witness, one need not be a member of a given community; one need only be brought into relationship with it. In summoning witnesses to its cause, a performance forges a community of those on the scene, a community that does not depend on belonging to a nation, an ethnicity, a particular gender or sexuality but creates a sense of belonging by bringing actors and audience together in relationship to the dramatic action. In the African-Nova Scotian plays I have been discussing, the dramatic action invariably raises the threshold of performance by summoning witnesses to events both historical and contemporary that disrupt familiar ways of imagining community. Exploiting the always doubled, "twice-behaved" (Schechner 35) quality of performance to foreground ambivalence, African-Nova Scotian playwrights intervene in normative models of citizenship and culture to restore the losses resulting from historic exclusions and ongoing injustice. Clearly, to the extent that it, too, "enact[s] crises of nationhood" (Filewod xvii), African-Nova Scotian theatre is not separate from other (African-)Canadian theatre, nor is it lacking in affinities with other theatres of the African diaspora. In bearing witness to events particular to African-Nova Scotian history, however, performances also forge a community that, if only through the act of witnessing, has ties to this place.

(2006)

Notes

1 I would like to thank George Elliott Clarke, David Woods, Addy Doucette and Kathleen Tudor for generously answering my questions and making scripts available to me.

2 Clearly, in the wake of the Canadian government's passing of the same-sex marriage bill, Canadian readers of Austin, not to mention of Parker and Sedgwick, will be aware of still more complex angles from which to approach the marriage example.

3 A community settled by black Nova Scotians in the 1850s on what was then the periphery of Halifax, Africville was subjected to encroaching commercial and industrial interests over the course of the twentieth-century: CNR tracks, an incinerator, a land-fill site. At the same time, the city refused Africville residents the sewers and water services other Haligonians took for granted. By the 1960s,

Africville had acquired a national reputation as a slum, and it was a "slum" situated on prime industrial real estate. So, in the name of progress, the city relocated Africville residents to public housing in the city's north end, and expropriated the land for industrial development—primarily expressways and container shipping. For a more extended analysis of the construction of Africville in African-Nova Scotian writing, music, theatre and the visual arts see my "Africville."

[4] Woods refers to Africville as "Coleville" in the play.

[5] I develop this argument about *Beatrice Chancy* more fully in "This History's Only Good for Anger."

[6] See Walker, *Black Loyalists*. While Boyd's play is out of chronological synch with the historical migrations of African-Nova Scotians to Sierra Leone—migrations that date to the late eighteenth century—his invocation of that historical trajectory in performance underscores the creative intervention that characterizes the performance of history, as Roach and Rokem emphasize.

Works Cited

Anderson, Benedict. *Imagined Communities: Reflections on the Origin and Spread of Nationalism.* London: Verso, 2003.

Bhabha, Homi. "Narrating the Nation." Introduction. *Nation and Narration.* Ed. Homi Bhabha. London: Routledge, 1990. 1–7.

Borden, Walter. *Tightrope Time: Ain't Nuthin' More Than Some Itty Bitty Madness between Twilight and Dawn.* Sears, Vol. 1. 477–554

Boyd, George. *Consecrated Ground.* Sears, Vol. 2. 397–483.

———. *Wade in the Water,* Toronto: Playwrights Canada, 2005.

Brydon, Diana. "Black Canadas: Rethinking Canadian and Diasporic Cultural Studies." *Revista Canaria de Estudios Ingleses* 43 (2001): 101–17.

Campbell, Lucky. *A World of Our Own.* Halifax: Orangestar, 1997.

Clarke, George Elliott. *Beatrice Chancy.* Vancouver: Polestar, 1999.

———. "A Dramatic Entrance." Foreword. Delisle 7–10.

———. "Making the 'Damn' Nation the Race's 'Salvation': The Politics of George Elroy Boyd's *Consecrated Ground.*" Sears, Vol. 2. 393–6.

———. "Walter Borden's *Tightrope Time,* or Voicing the Polyphonous Consciousness." Sears, Vol. 1. 473–76.

————. *Whylah Falls: The Play.* Toronto: Playwrights Canada, 1998.

Delisle, Louise. *Back Talk: Plays of Black Experience.* Lockeport, NS: Roseway, 2005.

Filewod, Alan. *Performing Canada: The Nation Enacted in the Imagined Theatre.* Kamloops, BC: Textual Studies, 2002.

Moynagh, Maureen. "Africville, an Imagined Community." *Canadian Literature* 157 (1998): 14–34.

————. "'This History's Only Good for Anger': Gender and Cultural Memory in *Beatrice Chancy.*" *Signs: A Journal of Women in Culture and Society* 28.1 (2002): 97–124.

Parker, Andrew and Eve Kosofsky Sedgwick. Introduction. Parker and Sedgwick, *Performance* 1–18.

————, ed. *Performance and Performativity.* New York: Routledge, 1995.

Roach, Joseph. "Culture and Performance in the Circum-Atlantic World." Parker and Sedgewick, *Performance* 45–63.

Rokem, Freddie. *Performing History: Theatrical Representations of the Past in Contemporary Theatre.* Iowa City: U of Iowa P, 2000.

Schechner, Richard. *Between Theatre and Anthropology.* Philadelphia: U of Pennsylvania P, 1985.

Sears, Djanet, ed. *Testifyin': Contemporary African Canadian Drama.* 2 vols. Toronto: Playwrights Canada, 2003.

Van Fossen, Rachael. "A Particular Perspective: (Re) Living Memory in George Boyd's *Wade in the Water.*" *African-Canadian Theatre.* Ed. Maureen Moynagh. Toronto: Playwrights Canada, 2005. 92–106.

Walker, James W. St. G. *The Black Loyalists: The Search for the Promised Land in Nova Scotia and Sierra Leone.* Toronto: U of Toronto P, 1992.

————. *Once.* Unpublished play, 1996.

————. *Part of the Deal. Sunday Matinee.* CBC Radio, 1992.

Crossing the River:
Zuppa Circus's *Penny Dreadful*

by Roberta Barker

In a kitchen in Victorian Halifax, young gentleman Harold Linden (Stewart Legere) enchants scullery maid Addy (Susan Leblanc-Crawford) with an account of his dangerous voyage across a mighty African river. Dour groundskeeper Charlie (Ben Stone) objects to "Harry's" use of the kitchen table as a bridge: "We have to eat off that!" But Addy ignores her companion's complaints, gazing with adventure-starved eyes as Harry transforms the site of her everyday labours into the territory of her dreams. At the end of her journey through Zuppa Circus Theatre's *Penny Dreadful* (2007), directed by Alex McLean, she will remember this moment. She will contemplate "the stuff in [people] that makes them wanna cross the river," and her eyes will light up for the last time as she herself lowers the table, now her path to the gallows.

The table/bridge and the imagined rivers it crosses are fitting images of Zuppa Circus's achievement in *Penny Dreadful*. The metamorphosis of ordinary objects into metaphors, not only for more exalted things but for the transformative power of imagination itself, has been intrinsic to their work since Stone co-founded the company with Sandy Gribbin ten years ago. But this particular image also speaks to a theme that distinguishes *Penny Dreadful* from Zuppa's earlier shows: the gulf between classes. Such subject matter is closely associated with classic realist dramas like those of Ibsen, whose *Ghosts* is one of *Penny Dreadful*'s key intertexts. And this, in turn, suggests the widest gulf crossed by *Penny Dreadful*: the chasm usually fixed between realist drama and physically driven, devised performance.

Realism mandates socially detailed settings, psychologically complex characters, and a narrative that mimes "real life." In the past, these have not ranked high among Zuppa Circus's priorities. Their work is distinguished by playful juxtapositions of physical action, found and new text, evocative objects and powerful live music (usually created by Halifax musicians Jason MacIsaac and David Christensen). The opening moments of *Penny Dreadful* feature just such a dance of performance elements, Clair Gallant's cello summons the performers into the space. The departed Addy visits her fellow servant from beyond the grave; but Leblanc-Crawford's forceful gestures are those of a living woman, and Addy's eager smile contradicts her declaration that she is as "sad" as the melancholy Charlie. We learn that she is notorious in the scandal rags, but that none of them can agree on her true nature. As she speaks, Charlie turns her slowly atop a fragile piano stool, giving the audience an ever-shifting perspective on her elusive identify. Then, a flurry of notes from Gallant's cello casts Addy and Charlie back to an earlier moment in their history, when both were servants in the Linden household. Clearly, we are neither in the tightly bound realm of realist character, nor in the linear flow of realist time.

We *are*, however, in the presence of realism's psychological complexity and "adult" themes. Addy unbuttons her blouse, offering her body to Charlie, then retreats into a fetal position when he tries—first timidly, then hungrily—to embrace her. Their subsequent argument culminates in a moving image as both collapse into chairs, facing in opposite directions. The normally reticent Charlie bursts into sobs; Addy takes his head in her arms and kisses it. Many of the actions, says Leblanc-Crawford, are condensed from the physical score of her first show with Zuppa Circus, the hypnotic *Nosferatu*. Here, they mesh with simple, everyday language—"It's alright, Charlie. We'll be OK"—to convey the unspoken longings of two troubled human beings.

Alongside such revelations of character emerge the secrets familiar from realist drama: sexual transgression, delusion, disease, illegitimacy. Addy was "pricked young," but was raised by nuns and believes herself blessed. Rakish Harry suffers from syphilis; in the boys' childhood, every sight of Charlie made Harry's mother weep. When Harry tells Addy that he "needs her help," the resulting tragedy recalls Zola's and Dostoevsky's tales of transgression and retribution as much as it does the sensational accounts of "true crime" that give *Penny Dreadful* its title.

Moreover, the story unfolds in a socially specific setting: 1863 Halifax. Place names litter the text of *Penny Dreadful* and inflect the identities of its characters ("Linden Street" is an address in Halifax's prosperous South End, while "Charles Street" is in the working-class North). Many of these details derive from the company's "Ministry of Information," a rehearsal-room table piled with research that enriches all aspects of the production. The production's Assistant Dramaturge, Claire Cuyer, describes searching period newspapers for accounts of public ceremony in Victorian Halifax. Her work contributed to the important sequence in which tensions between Addy, Harry and Charlie peak during celebrations in honour of the Prince of Wales's wedding.

This sequence shows how devised theatre can fold realist techniques into passages that go beyond the traditional limits of realism. Addy, Charlie and Harry prepare for a parade, decked in costumes that speak loudly of their classes and personalities. But they are joined onstage by Gallant, who, although a key performer in the show, by no means embodies a socially specific "character." As Gallant plays, Addy, Charlie and Harry greet individual spectators with friendly "hellos." The fourth wall crumbles; the citizens of 2007 Halifax appear as extras in the scrupulously researched world of their city's past.

A later section of the Parade sequence departs even further from realism. Text shared among the three performers conveys an apocalyptic vision of urban riot as Charlie sets mousetraps around a slowly circling Addy and Harry plays the piano. The effect is dreamlike, disturbing and potentially confusing for spectators accustomed to a straight through-line. Are we watching an event in the "real" world or a hallucination? If the latter, whose hallucination is it? As the show continues, we realize that Addy was wrestling with a fateful decision at this point, but we are not explicitly shown her moment of revelation.

Leblanc-Crawford describes the challenges of rehearsing this scene: "For a long time, I didn't know what I was doing." Eventually, McLean's suggestion that she look at every section of the audience clarified it for her; "Then," she says, "I had the action to support me." Bruce Barton, *Penny Dreadful*'s dramaturge and a frequent Zuppa collaborator, describes the company's process as one in which "the performers 'discover' (that is, *create*) the characters through action." When Addy fixes each spectator with her gaze as Charlie methodically surrounds her with traps, we are not offered realism's coherent unpacking of their motivations. Instead, we glimpse inner contradictions: Abby's disconcertingly bright gaze suggests both compassion and a hunger for violence, while Charlie's labour appears simultaneously orderly and obsessive. For Barton, such concrete actions offer Zuppa "an uncommonly articulate means of expressing the depths that so often remain repressed, abstract, and intimated in realist performance."

The ensemble also accesses these "depths" by mining their own personalities and relationships. McLean and Leblanc-Crawford describe an important source for the show: an improvisation by Leblanc-Crawford, Stone and guest artist Simon Henderson (creator of the role of Harry in the 2006 workshop of *Penny Dreadful*) during rehearsals for an earlier Zuppa production, *Uncle Oscar's Experiment*. The performers played themselves at a dinner party; Leblanc-Crawford calls it "one of the most realistic things we've ever done." The company returned to it as they began to create *Penny Dreadful*: its exploration of real-life personal dynamics, as well as its dark development, had a profound effect on the relationships in the final show.

Another example of the links between performers' personalities, collaborative process and the depiction of character lies in the "I wants" that punctuate *Penny Dreadful*. During rehearsals, McLean gave Stone and Leblanc-Crawford the task of creating lists of their own desires. These lists helped to shape the litanies that appear at pivotal moments in the show, opening direct windows on the characters' inner lives. "I want to sit on a purple velvet settee!" declares Addy; "I want to have a farm with a guard dog," counters Charlie; "I want to clean out my insides," cries Harry as he faces death. In many realist rehearsals, actors are encouraged to identify (and to identify *with*) their characters' objectives; these exercises are then hidden inside the final version of the show. In *Penny Dreadful*, personal exploration becomes onstage text, fusing process and performance.

Like Zuppa Circus' previous shows, *Penny Dreadful* hinges on a series of poetic images: Harry inviting Addy onto his imaginary bridge; a hooded Charlie, pursued by furies as his own mousetraps snap at his feet; Addy's slow procession through the traps on her way to the gallows, accompanied by an exquisite setting of the folksong, "Lord Ronald." These moments are enriched by a combination of social detail and psychological insight that opens up exciting vistas for Zuppa's future exploration. Like its characters, *Penny Dreadful* crosses the river, illuminating the ways in which devised theatre can use realist techniques to its own ends and achieve realist goals by its own means.

(2008)

Works Cited

Barton, Bruce. Email communication with the author. 20 February 2008.

Guyer, Claire. Personal interview with the author. 16 December 2007.

Leblanc-Crawford, Susan. Personal interview with the author. 20 December 2007.

Zuppa Circus Theatre. *Penny Dreadful.* Dir. Alex McLean. Perf. Claire Gallant (Cello), Susan Leblanc-Crawford (Adelaide Clem), Stewart Legere (Harold Linden), and Ben Stone (Charlie). Premiere Performance. North Street Church, Halifax, NS. 9 October 2007.

On the Edge of the Eastern World: John Barlow's *Inspiration Point* and Atlantic Canadian Aboriginal Theatre

by Len Falkenstein

> We have to draw a line in the sand somewhere. The Rez is on the edge of the world. Another mile and we'd be in the ocean. This is it. But that's not enough for them. They keep closing in. (John Barlow, *Inspiration Point* 87)

The Indian Island First Nation is situated on a small peninsula that juts into the Northumberland Strait at the midway point of the east coast of New Brunswick. In 2006, Statistics Canada placed the population of Indian Island at 97; John Barlow, a resident of the First Nation, during a recent interview placed it at just over 120. [1] Access to the tiny Mi'kmaq community is limited—a single road in and out—and the land the reservation occupies has historically been contested. Indian Island is situated in a part of the province where New Brunswick's three founding peoples—English, Acadian, and Aboriginal—live in close proximity, but in communities divided on linguistic/ethnic lines. The reservation's closest neighbours are the primarily Acadian towns of Bédec and Richibucto and the primarily Anglophone community of Rexton. The east coast region of the province is predominantly francophone Acadian, however, as the names of the roads surrounding the reservation attest: Chemin de la Pointe, Chemin Bédec. This confers another form of isolation on Indian Island, as according to Statistics Canada only ten residents of the reservation are bilingual, and none identify French as their mother tongue. Most residents of the community speak English at home, with a small number fluent in Mi'kmaq.

Linguistically, geographically, and ethnically/racially, then, Indian Island First Nation is a little world unto itself, a community that, despite its name, is not literally situated on an island but figuratively *is* one within the region, hemmed in by the sea on one side and surrounded by overwhelmingly white bi-cultural New Brunswick on the other. [2] For residents of the community, a sense of isolation, of being on the edge of the world and facing a constant struggle for cultural survival, is the daily reality.

Mi'kmaq playwright Barlow captures this sense of embattlement in *Inspiration Point* (2004). The play depicts life on a small Maritime reservation, (which, while never named, is clearly Indian Island) as poised between hope and despair. While intensely rooted in the specific culture, folklore, and geography of Indian Island, the play speaks to issues common to Aboriginal peoples elsewhere in New Brunswick and beyond: the complex and fraught history of relations between the Aboriginal and settler communities, particularly as played out at the level of control and ownership of land; anger at historic ills and the need of redress for injustices suffered by Natives at the hands of whites; the very basic struggle for survival of a community threatened by assimilationist forces, both external and internal; and the question of how best to move beyond the past and adapt for a future in which cultural legacy seems destined to be accorded less real-world value than technological proficiency and economic achievement.

In its portrayal of the challenges faced by a historically dispossessed and marginalized Maritime Native community, however, *Inspiration Point* also incisively portrays the day-to-day lived experience of a broader Maritime population, both Aboriginal and non-Aboriginal. Barlow's characters' sense of exclusion and disempowerment, their struggle to find a meaningful and sustaining means of making a living in an economically depressed region, and their ongoing debate over whether to stay in the home they love or seek greener pastures elsewhere are all metonymic of the plight of many Maritimers. As such, *Inspiration Point* dramatizes both the condition of a specific Atlantic Canadian community and that of the region as a whole. Few plays speak to what it means to live in the Maritimes with such a rare combination of wit, insight, and poignancy. What makes the play even more extraordinary is that it is the work of a rare type of writer, an Aboriginal Atlantic Canadian playwright.

When I asked him recently whether he was aware of other Native playwrights in Atlantic Canada, Barlow was unable to name one. When the same question was put to her, Yvette Nolan, Artistic Director of Toronto's Native Earth Performing Arts, and perhaps the person with the broadest knowledge of Aboriginal theatre in Canada, cited a handful of theatre artists from Nova Scotia, but no dramatists with an established body of work. Nolan added that in the twenty-two-year history of Weesageechak Begins to Dance, Native Earth's annual workshop showcase of new plays by Aboriginal dramatists from across Canada, the only play from Atlantic Canada to have been programmed is Barlow's *Inspiration Point.*

Any explanation for the dearth of Aboriginal playwrights in the region must consider demographics. Not only is the population of the region small, but the Aboriginal population is smaller as a percentage of total population than almost anywhere else in Canada. In the region's two largest provinces, Statistics Canada reports an "Aboriginal identity population" of 17,655 of 719,650 New Brunswickers and 24,175 of 903,090 Nova Scotians. The concentration of most of this population on small, isolated reservations and the lack of a significant urban Aboriginal population has led to a situation, in Nolan's words, where the Native population of the region is both small and "pretty invisible."

Just as important a consideration is the lack of a theatre tradition in the Native communities of Atlantic Canada. Barlow has indicated that theatre has had virtually no presence in Indian Island and that he had no significant exposure to it until he enrolled in a drama course at St. Thomas University in Fredericton. Given that aspiring Aboriginal playwrights lack artistic predecessors to act as inspirational models, and there is neither a critical mass in the Native community with an interest in theatre, nor a Maritime equivalent of an Aboriginal developmental company like Native Earth, it is not surprising that few Native playwrights have emerged from the region. In the words of Nolan, "if there's no community to be developing those voices, then those voices don't have a forum; they don't necessarily develop, or they move to somewhere like Toronto, where they will have an opportunity.... It takes a community to support a voice." The alternative to moving across the country is, of course, to seek out opportunities to create theatre in association with mainstream (predominantly white) companies in the region, an intimidating prospect for an emerging Aboriginal writer, who may at worst encounter indifference, cultural insensitivity, or hostility, or at least a limited ability to engage with the work across the cultural divide. This is the path Barlow has taken, fortunately with largely positive results.

· · ·

Inspiration Point began as an assignment for a university creative writing class. Barlow expanded the original play for submission in 2003 to the annual one-act playwriting contest sponsored by Fredericton-based NotaBle Acts Theatre Company, whose mandate is to develop and produce new plays by New Brunswick dramatists. Impressed by the work, NotaBle Acts decided to stage it as the feature main stage production of its 2004 summer theatre festival, where it premiered July 28, 2004. [3] Yvette Nolan became aware of the play during the casting process and decided to program it for that year's Weesageechak Begins to Dance festival. Barlow went to Toronto in October for a week-long workshop at Native Earth led by dramaturg Bill Lane, which culminated in a public staged reading on October 17, 2004. The following spring, *Inspiration Point* received another staged reading, this time as part of Moncton-based Acadian theatre company Théâtre L'Escaouette's Festival a haute voix. Within the space of a year, then, the play had been performed by three companies before three very different audiences: a primarily anglophone audience in Fredericton, a largely Aboriginal audience in Toronto, and a predominantly francophone audience in Moncton. Given its combustible mix of history, politics, and slice-of-reservation-life, the play, not surprisingly, generated different responses from these audiences. The play's subject matter and its compelling mix of entertainment and provocation are arguably key to understanding both these responses and the play's ability to appeal across what have traditionally been some very entrenched geographic, linguistic, and racial/ethnic divides.

The plot of *Inspiration Point* is relatively simple, centring on a trio of young Native men who are forced to confront the frustrations of their lives in a highly symbolic and politically charged location. The lights rise at the top of the play to reveal a truck buried up to its axles in mud in the otherwise pristine front lawn of an oceanfront cottage. The vehicle's occupants, a pair of Native men named Joseph and Paul, smoke one in a succession of several joints as they contemplate their predicament. As the play progresses, we learn that they are residents of a nearby reservation, and that the property on which they are stuck, known on the reserve as Inspiration Point, has been a popular party and makeout spot for residents of the Rez. The Point, however, has recently been bought by whites. As the set description indicates, the new owners, a yuppie Acadian lawyer couple, have symbolically claimed, fenced, and, through meticulous landscaping, "civilized" the property: the "well manicured lawn" is "ornamented with a flagpole that flies an Acadian flag, a park bench, and two signs: 'Please keep off grass' and 'Warning: Pesticide Use'" (1). The colonialist echoes of this seizure of a piece of land that was never owned by the First Nations residents of the reservation, but that had long been regarded as "theirs," are devastatingly reinforced by the building that the new owners have purchased and moved onto the property: a deconsecrated "former Catholic church, now converted to a summer cottage." [4]

For Joseph and Paul, whose return to the Point has been inadvertent—the result of losing control of their truck on the nearby highway while trying to avoid a raccoon—as for the other residents of the reservation, the loss of Inspiration Point is an outrage and a provocation. It represents the latest incident in a long history of colonialism, racism, and threatened assimilation, a history that the play suggests has not ended, contrary to what most Canadians might like to believe. The extent to which Inspiration Point serves as a metonym and symbol of the legacy of failed trust, broken promises, and animosity between Aboriginal and non-Aboriginal Canadians becomes increasingly apparent after the arrival of the play's third character, Peter. Older than Joseph and Paul and with a broader critical awareness of politics and history, Peter is something of a provocateur who challenges the other two to read their bummer of a minor traffic accident within a larger political and cultural context. As they do, the discussion about what the men need to do to solve both the immediate problem (how to get their truck out of the mud, the owners of the cottage being absent, as they almost always are) and the larger problem (the stasis of their lives) grows more heated, the stakes higher, and the connections to the historical legacy more explicit.

Viewed from this perspective, the men are brought to see the outside acquisition—effectively the colonization—of Inspiration Point as the final straw in a history of rapacious expansionism that has pushed the Mi'kmaq of the reserve to "the edge of the world. Another mile and we'd be in the ocean" (87). The men also comment bitterly on what they have come to understand as the sinister and racist motives behind the creation of the reservation system and its local land allotment practices. In Joseph's words,

> You know Benny has an old map that shows this place as a marsh. It reads, "No good for farmland" (*pause*), but in big red letters it reads, "Prime Indian land." You know, the perfect place to stash those little Red Devils. (57)

Placing the Native population on small parcels of undesirable land, Paul suggests later, was not merely a policy of benign neglect, but a form of quarantine with genocidal intentions: "They didn't put Indians on reservations for our own good, they put us here to die out" (72).

In Barlow's characters' understanding of history, Christianity was an active and willing partner in this genocidal project. In one of the darkest moments of the play, Joseph compares Christianity (Catholicism, more precisely) to the lethal Black Widow spider: "They're like those spiders that mate and then eat their partner… they fuck ya then eat ya. That's the Church, a nest of Black Widows. And that's what these fuckers used on us" (57). Placed in this context, the symbolism of the erection of a church on Inspiration Point cannot be overstated, especially when the characters' description of the Church's arrival at the Point explicitly invokes the originary colonial moment:

> **PAUL:** The church did look pretty cool though when it arrived.
> **PETER:** The church? They all look alike.
> **PAUL:** Naw man, when it came down on that truck.
> **JOSEPH:** Yeah, I guess it did. Looked like a big sail boat with that
>   cloud of dust following it; a big billowing cloud looking thing,
>   flying above the trees, moving along the river. I could almost
>   imagine what the Old ones thought when they saw that first ship
>   sailing into our river for the very first time.
> **PETER:** "Shit, there goes the neighbourhood." (50)

Several hundred years after that moment of first contact, the seemingly rather more banal invasion of the church via slow-moving tractor trailer effectively reinscribes and re-enacts the dispossession wrought by colonialism.

The reservation community's sense of betrayal at the loss of Inspiration Point is perhaps made especially acute in that it is perceived as another in a series of acts of aggression and threatened assimilation by the Acadian population, the Mi'kmaq's traditional allies. Barlow has noted that at the time of the British deportation of the Acadians, "Le Grand Dérangement" of 1755–63, the Mi'kmaq came to the aid of many Acadians, and a historic bond developed between the two peoples: "We sided with the French and the English just walked in…. [The Acadians] remember. It's a shared history. They remember that when they needed help, we helped them out." It is significant, therefore, that Acadians are depicted as the immediate threat in terms of the play's two most significant conflicts, that over the contested space of Inspiration Point and that which comprises the play's most prominent plotline: Joseph's agonizing over whether or not he should date Sylvie, an Acadian girl he is attracted to, but whom his parents reject for being non-Aboriginal.

With distinctions between anglophones and francophones elided, the perspective presented in the play is overwhelmingly one of a Native "us" in conflict with a homogenous white "them," a "them" that is both casually and overtly racist. During our interview, Barlow spoke of being acclimatized to incidents of racism growing up: race-related tensions erupting into fights "outside the bar on Saturday nights"; a gang of white kids who liked to gather on a bridge at Rexton and throw stones at Natives paddling upriver until one day a "crazy old Indian" who had had enough decided to blast them with a shotgun. In the play, Peter at one point parodies the type of white racist paranoia that Barlow perceives as commonplace: "Don't they know, we're crazy man, we're loco! We'll fucking rape your women and eat your babies!" (52). Disgusted by what he sees as the prevalence of these racist attitudes, Joseph, speaking of the many World War Two veterans from the reservation, observes, "Makes me wonder what ever convinced my Grandfather to help these bastards out in the war. To risk his life for people who threw rocks at him, who spit on him?" (25).

The degree to which the men feel excluded from, and even under attack by, mainstream white Canadian society is readily apparent in these comments. While Barlow admits that instances of overt racism have thankfully become much less common in recent years, it is clear that he and his community still feel embattled, continually fighting for their very survival, as a result of insidious racist, or at least race-based, policies. In particular, blood quantum, the complex set of genetically-based regulations deriving from federal legislation that legally defines who is a status Indian and to which band individuals belong—which has huge implications regarding treaty rights and the legal status of bands—has special relevance to the play. A contentious subject for Aboriginal people everywhere, blood quantum is particularly important for Native people in Atlantic Canada, given the small size of the Aboriginal population. The situation is magnified for tiny First Nations such as Indian Island, for whom a small number of people "marrying out" and/or leaving the reserve could seriously threaten the band's existence.

Considered in this light, the Joseph/Sylvie plotline presents an obvious parallel to the territorial neo-colonial incursions Barlow's characters feel threatened by. The three men discuss Joseph's dilemma extensively, with Peter suggesting that what he refers to (in admittedly crude and sexist fashion) as "white pussy" (39) is the new stealth weapon of white neo-imperialism, a contemporary equivalent to the missionary Christianity of colonial times. Echoing the logic of conspiracy theorists, he argues that media bombardment with highly sexualized images of white women has made them a highly valued commodity for Native men, threatening inevitable cultural extinction. Whether or not Joseph should date Sylvie is debated, thus, not merely as a matter of the heart, but as a choice with serious political overtones, one linked to the play's most dominant image, the lady slipper. When the conversation turns to "cool Indian names" (34), Joseph expresses a preference for "Lady Slipper" and tells the story of a white man who picked a stand of the flowers near the reserve, not realizing the consequences:

> we're just like lady slippers; you know, the things that're beautiful about us, our language and the other stuff... like culture, our songs.... Well, the beautiful thing about a lady slipper is the flower. It stands out, but if you pick the flower it doesn't grow back.... Ever.... The plant doesn't die, it just becomes like everything else in the woods, a green plant... nothin' special. (36)

The implication is that marrying Non-Aboriginals will result in a similar loss of Aboriginal identity and culture.

Significantly, however, after the men exhaustively discuss the perils of "marrying out," the play ends with Joseph calling Sylvie to ask her out. Joseph's somewhat surprising decision suggests the complexity of the issue and Barlow's unwillingness to either provide simple answers or retreat to uncomplicatedly essentialist positions.[5] Native actor Tim Hill, who played Joseph in both the Fredericton and Toronto stagings of *Inspiration Point*, explains the character's choice in this way: "I think as a young man, as a human being, without having to be a political puppet, he wants what he wants and in that moment he wants her and maybe consequences be damned."

Notably, the Joseph/Sylvie plotline reaches a conclusion that is markedly different in tone from that of the play's other major conflict, the men's anger at the loss of Inspiration Point. Channeling their rage over both the colonization of the property and the other injustices they have suffered, Peter finally convinces Joseph and Paul that some "next level shit" (82) is in order:

> We have to make a statement. If we don't make it we leave it up to some-
> one else to make it for us, then we lose control, and we'll end up being
> scenery in someone else's movie. We gotta scream at the top of our
> lungs, "I'm not dead!" "Don't bury me yet, I'm not dead!" Say it once and
> say it loud, I'm Red and I'm proud. We gotta let the world know, the red
> man ain't dead. (88)

Peter's plan is to call all their friends from the reserve to join them for a blowout party on the church lawn, reclaiming the Point. The party will feature a huge bonfire, he suggests, stoked by gasoline and Roman candles, a bonfire that might just get out of control and spread up the lawn to the church: "You see a church and I see kindling" (84). Joseph and Paul are initially reluctant, but Peter manages to convince at least the fearful Paul, and the play ends with the partiers on the way and Peter and Paul working feverishly to start a fire (the men have run out of matches and their inability to find a light to allow them to continue to work through their considerable cache of pot has become a running gag in the play). Peter has just managed to produce some sparks via the traditional ignition method of rubbing sticks together when Paul discovers a lighter he has had in a pocket the whole time. The stage lights darkened, the play's final image is of the men's faces illuminated only by the flame of Paul's lighter, which they stare at in wonder. "What are you waiting for, let's light this sucker up," says Joseph (99). It is a starkly ambiguous moment, the flame representing the spark of possibility and inspiration the men have been seeking throughout the play, but also the instrument of the church's (probable) destruction.

As such, it is a fitting conclusion to a play that bristles with indignation at historic injustices. "Like I keep sayin'," Paul quips at one point, "white folks, can't live with 'em, not allowed to kill 'em and scalp 'em anymore" (59). During our conversation, Barlow acknowledged the anger of the play, describing the writing of it as both a cathartic and necessary process:

> Everybody's got a certain play in them and you've almost got to get it out
> of your system... this is my bitching play. I've got to get all my bitchiness
> out of me, and throw it into a play and get it out of there. It's like
> cleaning house... this is me, I'm Native, this is what's going on and this

is what I'm fricking pissed off about and put it all into a play and spit it
out.

What Tim Hill calls the question of "the validity of the anger" in *Inspiration Point* and
other Native plays of its ilk has provoked widely divergent views, especially within
the Native community. Yvette Nolan echoes Barlow's words in her take on the play's
ending: "They have to burn down the church in order to let that go," suggesting that
the church represents baggage from the past that must be jettisoned. Hill's position is
different, however: "Do I think it's necessary for them to burn the church? No." While
acknowledging empathy for the characters' anger, he asserts, "Myself, I don't believe in
violence as a solution or as a means of solving problems," hastening to add, "but it
often does seem like only when you block a road or disrupt other people's lives do you
get any attention, do you get any reaction whatsoever."

In what some might regard as a surprising irony, the "validity" of *Inspiration
Point*'s anger seems to have been questioned more by the play's Aboriginal audience
than its white ones. My own perception as an audience member at the play's
Fredericton run was that the anger was accepted as justified by the predominantly
white, middle-class anglophone audience, and this also seems to have been true of the
mainly francophone audience at Théâtre l'Escaouette's staging. [6] On the other hand,
Barlow and Hill came away from the play's Toronto staging at Native Earth feeling that
the largely Aboriginal audience was less receptive to the play's tone (a perception not
shared by Nolan, however). In conversation with me, both suggested that for the many
audience members who were well-steeped in Native theatre practice from across
Canada, the play may have trod ground that was too familiar—that the audience was
not necessarily unsympathetic to the issues of the play, but that it had seen them, and
that anger, on stage too many times. In Hill's words, "Here in Toronto people have
heard the angry young Native man. They've heard the call to action; they've heard the
frustration that these three characters all face in the script. I don't think that negates
it or diminishes its impact or importance."

To write the play off as a case of "same old, same old," however, would be to
unfairly fail to acknowledge Barlow's near total isolation from the Canadian Native
theatre community, as an Aboriginal playwright from the Maritimes writing his first
play. As Hill puts it, "Certainly I think that in Fredericton and for John Barlow it's
the first time these things are being addressed and being spoken out loud to an
audience.... For him it's the first time, it's a fresh story." To dismiss the play in this way
also would be to overlook its specifically local relevance and its rich depiction of life
as it is lived in an Atlantic Canadian Native community, something that has never
been seen on stage before. Two of the most hilarious stories in the play concern Paul's
disastrous attempt to use a lobster claw as a roach clip and Peter's epic description of
his life and death battle with an angry crane that attacked him while he was on a
nighttime eeling expedition on the river. *Inspiration Point* is steeped in such local,
Mi'kmaq, and personal detail—descriptions of flora, fauna, and geography, and tales
from Barlow's family lore. [7]

Perhaps even more importantly, to read *Inspiration Point* simply as an "angry" play that engages primarily in confrontational finger-pointing at whites over the ills Aboriginal people have suffered would be to fail to recognize the play's considerable joy, humour, and optimism, and to overlook how frequently the play's finger of blame is pointed at the Native community itself. Peter, Paul, and Joseph are not stuck just literally in the Acadian couple's front lawn, but stuck metaphorically as well—stuck in a lifestyle that is uninspired, limited both by lack of opportunities and their own failure to imagine, or take action to create, more fulfilling lives. Unemployed, or at least underemployed, Paul and Joseph spend their days partying, smoking pot, and shooting the shit, placing them, as Barlow has acknowledged, uncomfortably close to the "lazy Indian" of racist stereotype. [8] Joseph, as typified by his soul-searching over Sylvie, is paralyzed by indecision, while Paul, highly religious and superstitious, and afraid of ghosts, bears, and the dark, is paralyzed by fear. When Peter arrives, he reprimands them for their feeble efforts to get their truck out of the mud. Unknowingly directly contradicting Paul's earlier words to Joseph, "Man, wouldn't it be cool if someone would drive down that road and get us out of here?" (15), Peter scolds, "Look at you guys. You get stuck in the mud and you sit around until the truck, what? Miraculously drives itself out? It's not gonna happen, man" (69).

Responsibility for the malaise afflicting the Aboriginal community, *Inspiration Point* suggests, lies not only at the individual level with those like Joseph and Paul who are unable or unwilling to imagine solutions, but at the collective level, as manifested in the loss of Native languages and traditional knowledge, both lamented in the play, with fire-starting one example: Peter comically charges Paul with telling those en route to the party to make sure they "don't forget a light; wouldn't that be a nice sight, fifty Indians standing around not able to light a camp fire" (78). Native leaders and band politics also come under attack for failing to respond effectually to the needs of their communities, as personified by the local chief, "Walking Eagle" so called because he's "so full of shit he can't fly" (34).

In response to this collective failure of will, especially as it is manifested in Paul's particular handicap, fear, Peter counsels, "Fear is nothing more than the imagined future. You're scared of what you can't see. You can't change the fact that you can't see the future, but you can learn not to be afraid of it" (89). For Peter, there is a solution, a way to move beyond fear and get unstuck, which he proposes in words that represent a direct rebuttal to any charges that the play merely rehashes old grievances: "I know one thing for sure, anything's gotta be better than sitting around and listening to the same old stories. We need to get inspired, make some new stories" (64).

Indeed, this is a process that the play suggests is already well under way. Alongside its anger, soul-searching, and confrontation, *Inspiration Point* provides moments of optimism that suggest great confidence about what the future holds for Native peoples, none more telling than this early exchange:

> JOSEPH: Who knows, look at us, we're starting a new century, technological Indians.
> PETER: Cyber Indians.
> PAUL: Can you imagine? I bet the arseholes who signed those treaties with us never thought we'd still be around, let alone educated and actually understand what we signed way back in the day. I mean, around the last time we celebrated a turn of the century, they slaughtered over three hundred Indians at Wounded Knee.
> PETER: We've come a long way, baby.
> JOSEPH: In a hundred years we will be the story. (24)

The play's final tableau, which features Joseph finally managing to inch the truck out of its mud hole, Peter starting a fire by traditional means, and Paul doing the same with a modern white invention, the lighter, is a triumphant moment that indicates that diverse, culturally heterogeneous solutions to the men's problems have been within their power the whole time. To draw a parallel between the optimism of the ending and Barlow's personal narrative, it is significant that the dramatist, who admits that he left the reserve for university in large part out of anger and "frustration" with his life there, has chosen, in the years since *Inspiration Point* was written, to return to become a part of the solution, and is now working for his band as an economic development officer:

> Once I got my education is when I got my sense of responsibility to my reserve, to my first nation, to my family. My mom always used to tell me, John, get the hell out of here because there's nothing here; there never was and there never will be.... It's like my mom saying, John, get out of here, this place is going to burn and none of us is going to make it out alive, good luck to you. Do I want to leave my mom in a burning building? Hell no, man, I gotta find a way out of there. I gotta get crafty, creative, and I gotta save us.

In conversation about his work for the band, Barlow brims with optimism about the future, even as he cannot put aside fears about the demographic, political, and cultural issues that threaten the survival of his people.

In addressing these issues, the play speaks by extension to concerns that are common to all Atlantic Canadians. The dispossession of Barlow's characters, the sense in which they feel powerless and voiceless, has a clear parallel in the way that Eastern Canadians often feel marginalized and alienated from the economic, media, and political power centres of the country. Consider these remarks, in which Barlow discusses the situation of his community *vis a vis* the province of New Brunswick and the Atlantic region:

> We have a lot to contribute to this country. We have a lot to contribute to this economy, this culture. We have a lot of smart people with good ideas and we've been held back.... You know what? We want our own little economy; we want to be self-sufficient; we don't want to depend on

anything and we don't want anyone to look down on us because we're lazy and ignorant. We're not lazy and ignorant, we're very industrious, very educated, but we do live in a frickin' depressed part of the country and we don't think it should be depressed anymore.

Barlow is, of course, using "we" to refer to Native people in Atlantic Canada, but what is remarkable here is how easily one might substitute "Atlantic Canadians" for Barlow's "we" to derive an apt summary of popular sentiment in the region regarding Atlantic Canada's relationship to the rest of Canada. Atlantic Canadians have long been stereotyped as lazy handout-seekers dependent on equalization payments from more prosperous regions of the country. These stereotypes have generated considerable anger—witness how Stephen Harper's infamous description of the region as suffering from a "culture of defeat" continues to rankle in Atlantic Canadians' collective memory. Viewed in this context, Barlow's characters can be described as experiencing a double marginalization, a double stereotyping as Natives *and* Atlantic Canadians, that renders their isolation even more profound.

The single issue in *Inspiration Point* that would resonate most strongly for a general Atlantic Canadian audience is the conflicted feelings Barlow's characters experience regarding their home. For Peter, Paul, and (especially) Joseph, leaving the Rez is an ever-tantalizing option, offering an escape from what they see as the stagnation and close-mindedness of their small community and the promise of better opportunities. Balanced against the impulse to leave is their sense of loyalty to their culture and people and their deeply rooted love of home. Barlow's own words on the subject are passionate and telling:

> I grew up in my community. My grandfather is buried down the road from me. My friends are buried beside my grandfather.... I know all the swimming holes. I know all the channels of the river. I know where the moose cross. I know where to pick sweetgrass. I've cut wood all around there. I've built the houses there. I live in the house that I built. My parents are there; my family's there; my friends are there; my memories are there. Everything's there. Why would I leave? Do I leave all that simply so that I can look like I made it to somebody else?

One need only spend a short time with young Maritimers to realize how often the subject of leaving for the (possibly) greener pastures of Ontario or Alberta is agonizingly debated, and how often those who do leave return some months or years later. Almost always, the type of fierce attachment to home Barlow expresses weighs heavily in the decisions both to emigrate and to return.

Commenting further on the question so many Aboriginals confront of whether to stay on the reserve or not, Barlow adds,

> I think if I stay there and I thrive, I make it better for me and I make it better for the person next to me. Then I've made it. It's easy to run from a problem; it's easy to run from anything. Staying and standing up, that's the hardest thing.

Barlow's decision to stay on his reservation and in his province, his determination to pursue progress through his work in the political and economic realm despite the struggles and setbacks that threaten his community, and his commitment as a dramatist to remain at home to create work inspired by the direct experience of his people despite the many challenges that artistic isolation presents can all be seen as integrally related to this larger desire to make home a better place, and in the process tell new, important, and honest stories from the edge of the Eastern world.

(2010)

Notes

[1] Throughout this essay, when I quote Barlow directly, the reference is to the recent personal interview. When I quote from his play, the reference is to *Inspiration Point*.

[2] According to 2006 figures, less than 2% of the provincial population belonged to visible minority groups (Statistics Canada).

[3] In the interests of full disclosure, I should note that I am currently Artistic Director of the NotaBle Acts Theatre Company, and was Co-Artistic Director in 2004 when *Inspiration Point* was staged by the company.

[4] Somewhat incredibly, none of these details are fictional: Barlow based the play and its setting on his favourite party spot, a lookout across the bay from Indian Island that he and his friends christened "Inspiration Point"; as in the play, the Point was purchased by a white family that moved a former Catholic church onto the site as a cottage.

[5] That this issue is both delicate and personal became clear during our interview when Barlow suggested he had some hesitation about how he approached the "marrying out" issue in the play, given his close relationship with his sister, who is married to a white Acadian man.

[6] Université de Moncton English and drama professor Glen Nichols, who attended the reading, suggested to me that the play "seemed warmly received. There was interest and appreciation for the piece."

[7] Barlow admits to having had apprehensions about his right to use family stories.

[8] Barlow indicated some discomfort with how these characters are depicted because of the stereotype concern, but suggests that he based them on his own perception of himself as a younger man and that he is "very sympathetic" to the characters' condition of stasis: "I don't want to fall on clichés and stereotypes and portray my people in a bad light. But at the same time there are some damn lazy Indians out

there. And some of them are doing pills and some of them got nothing better to do than smoke dope in the back of a pickup truck. And I have smoked dope in the back of a pickup truck and I've gotten a pickup truck stuck so I understand." Notably, one white reviewer called the play "a challenge because it puts straight in our face every uncomfortable stereotype and fantasy, every comfortable fallacy and prickly home truth, about… indigenous people" (Hunt).

Works Cited

Barlow, John. *Inspiration Point.* Typescript. 2007.

———. Personal interview. 3 October 2009.

Hill, Tim. Telephone interview. 16 November 2009.

Hunt, Russ. Rev. of *Inspiration Point.* NotaBle Acts Theatre Company. July–Aug 2004. http://www.stu.ca/~hunt/reviews/inspoint.htm. 18 October 2009.

Nichols, Glen. Email interview. 27 November 2009.

Nolan, Yvette. Telephone interview. 23 October 2009.

Canada. Statistics Canada. *2006 Community Profiles—Census Subdivision.* http://www12.statcan.gc.ca/census-recensement/2006. 10 October 2009.

Suggested Further Reading

Anthologies and Special Issues

Barton, Bruce, ed. *Marigraph: Gauging the Tides of Drama from New Brunswick, Nova Scotia, Prince Edward Island.* Toronto: Playwrights Canada, 2004.

———, ed. *Shifting Tides: Atlantic Canadian Theatre Yesterday, Today, and Tomorrow.* Spec. issue of *Theatre Research in Canada.* 26.1–2 (2005).

Burnett, Linda, ed. *Theatre in Atlantic Canada.* Spec. issue of *Canadian Theatre Review* 128 (2006).

Knowles, Ric[hard Paul], ed. *Atlantic Alternatives.* Spec. issue of *Canadian Theatre Review* 48: (1986).

———, ed. *The Proceedings of the Theatre in Atlantic Canada Symposium.* Sackville, NB: Centre for Canadian Studies, Mount Allison University, 1988.

Lynde, Denyse, ed. *Voices from the Landwash: 11 Newfoundland Playwrights.* Toronto: Playwrights Canada, 1997.

Peters, Helen, ed. *The Plays of CODCO.* New York: Peter Lang, 1992.

———, ed. *Stars In The Sky Morning: Collective Plays of Newfoundland and Labrador.* St. John's: Killick, 1996.

Secondary Sources

Ayers, Peter. "Learning to Curse in Iambics: Shakespeare in Newfoundland." *Shakespeare in Canada: A World Elsewhere?* Ed. Diane Brydon and Irena R. Makaryk. Toronto: U of Toronto P, 2002. 192–211.

Barton, Bruce. "Redefining 'Community': The Elusive Legacy of the Dramatists' Co-Op of Nova Scotia." *Theatre Research in Canada* 21.2 (2000), 99–115.

Bell, John. "The Nova Scotia Theatre Archives: A Report." *Canadian Drama* 5 (1979): 257–58.

Belliveau, George. "Daddy on Trial: Sharon Pollock's New Brunswick Plays." *Theatre Research in Canada* 22.2 (2001): 161–72.

———. "Glace Bay to Hollywood: A Political Journey." *Theatre Research in Canada* 22.1 (2001): 46–57.

Blagrave, Mark. "Temperance and The Theatre In The Nineteenth Century Maritimes." *Theatre Research in Canada* 7.1 (1986). 23–32.

Bondar, Alanna F. "'Life Doesn't Seem Natural:' Ecofeminism and the Reclaiming of the Feminine Spirit in Cindy Cowan's *A Woman from the Sea*." *Theatre Research in Canada* 18.1 (1997): 18–26.

Borden, Walter. "Black Theatre in Nova Scotia: In Search of a Sustainable and Viable Presence." *Canadian Theatre Review* 118 (2004): 41–43.

Brookes, Chris. *A Public Nuisance: A History of the Mummers Troupe*. St. Johns: Institute of Social and Economic Research, Memorial University, 1988.

Buchanan, Roberta. "Newfoundland: Outport Reminders." *Canadian Theatre Review* 43 (1985): 111–18.

Clarke, George Elliott. "'Must All Blackness Be American': Locating Canada in Borden's *Tightrope Time*, or Nationalizing Gilroy's *The Black Atlantic*." *African-Canadian Theatre*. Ed. Maureen Moynagh, Toronto: Playwrights Canada, 2005. 11–28.

———. "'Symposia' in the Drama of Trey Anthony and Louise Delisle." *Theatre Research in Canada* 30.1–2 (2009): 1–16.

Cowan, Cindy. "Message in the Wilderness." *Feminist Theatre and Performance*. Ed. Susan Bennett. Toronto: Playwrights Canada, 2006. 1–10.

Dalton, Mary. "The Mummers Troupe, The Canada Council, and the Production of Theatre History." *Theatre Research in Canada* 19.1 (1998): 3–34.

Filewod, Alan. "Dissent on Ice: The Mummers Enact the Public Sphere." *Performing Canada: The Nation Enacted in the Imagined Theatre*. Kamloops, BC: U College of the Cariboo, 2002. 59–82.

Glaap, Albert-Reiner. "Family Plays, Romances and Comedies: Aspects of David French's Work as a Dramatist." *On-Stage and Off-Stage: English Canadian Drama in Discourse*. Ed. Albert-Reiner Glaap and Rolf Althof. St. John's: Breakwater, 1996. 161–74.

Gross, Konrad. "Looking to the Far East? Newfoundland in David French's Mercer Trilogy." *Down East: Critical Essays on Contemporary Maritime Canadian Literature*. Trier: Wissenschaftlicher Verlag, 1996. 247–63.

Gygli, Karen L. "A 'Brave' New Newfoundland: *Jacob's Wake* by Michael Cook and the Significance of Past and Place." *McNeese Review* 35 (1997): 62–78.

Heiland, Donna. "George Elliott Clarke's *Beatrice Chancy*: Sublimity, Pain, Possibility." *Postfeminist Gothic: Critical Interventions in Contemporary Culture*. Ed. Benjamin A. Brabon and Stéphanie Genz. Basingstoke, Hampshire: Palgrave Macmillan, 2007: 126–39.

Jewinski, Ed. "Jacob Mercer's Lust for Victimization." *Canadian Drama* 2 (1976): 58–66.

Jones, Heather. "Rising Tide Theatre and/in the Newfoundland Cultural Scene." *Canadian Theatre Review* 93 (1997): 38–41.

Keiley, Jillian and Robert Chafe. "An Introduction to Artistic Fraud of Newfoundland." *Theatre Research in Canada* 26 (2005): 105–13.

Knowles, Ric[hard Paul]. "Guysborough, Mulgrave and the Mulgrave Road Co-op Theatre." *People and Places: Studies of Small Town Life in the Maritimes.* Frederiction/Sackville: Acadiensis/Mount Allison, 1987. 226–44.

———. "Halifax: the First Atlantic Theatre Conference." *Canadian Theatre Review* 44 (1985): 126–27.

———. "Neville's Neptune." *Canadian Theatre Review* 31 (1981): 125–27.

Larson, Katherine. "Resistance from the Margins in George Elliott Clarke's *Beatrice Chancy.*" *Canadian Literature* 189 (2006): 103–18.

Lynde, Denyse. "Newfoundland Drama: An Ever Changing Terrain." *On-Stage and Off-Stage: English Canadian Drama in Discourse.* Ed. Albert-Reiner Glaap and Rolf Althof. St. John's: Breakwater, 1996. 83–96.

———. "Writing and Publishing: Four Newfoundland Playwrights in Conversation." *Canadian Theatre Review* 98 (1999): 28–46.

Morrow, Jim. "Mermaid Theatre and Its Place in Canadian Puppetry." *Canadian Theatre Review* 95 (1998): 13–16.

Moynagh, Maureen. "'This History's Only Good for Anger': Gender and Cultural Memory in *Beatrice Chancy.*" *Signs: A Journal of Women in Culture and Society* 28.1 (2002): 97–124.

Mullaly, Edward J. "Canadian Drama: David French and the Great Awakening." *Fiddlehead* 100 (1974): 61–66.

Munday, Jenny. "Guysborough-Mulgrave Road Co-op Theatre: The View from Inside to Electrolux." *Canadian Theatre Review* 71 (1992): 88–91.

Newman, Shelley and Sherrill Grace. "Lill in Review: a Working Bibliography." *Theatre Research in Canada* 21 (2000): 49–58.

Nothof, Anne. "David French and the Theatre of Speech." *Canadian Drama* 13.2 (1987): 216–23.

O'Neill, Patrick B. "Jacob Bailey: Nova Scotia's Loyalist Playwright." *Canadian Drama* 15.2 (1989): 202–54.

Overton, David. "A Festival by Any Other Name: Eastern Front's On the Waterfront Festival Goes Super Nova." *Canadian Theatre Review* 138 (2009): 24–27.

Peake, Linda M. "Establishing a Theatrical Tradition: Prince Edward Island, 1800–1900." *Theatre Research in Canada* 2.2 (1981): 117–32.

Perkyns, Richard. "Michael Cook's *Jacob's Wake* and the European Tradition." *On-Stage and Off-Stage: English Canadian Drama in Discourse*. Ed. Albert-Reiner Glaap and Rolf Althof. St. John's: Breakwater, 1996. 108–17.

———. "Two Decades of Neptune Theatre." *Theatre Research in Canada* 6.2 (1985). 148–86.

Peters, Helen. "Theatre in Newfoundland." *Down East: Critical Essays on Contemporary Maritime Canadian Literature*. Trier: Wissenschaftlicher Verlag, 1996, 237–46.

Smith, Mary Elizabeth. "English Drama in New Brunswick." *A Literary and Linguistic History of New Brunswick*. Fredericton: Fiddlehead Poetry Book & Goose Lane Editions, 1985. 166–91.

———. "Shakespeare in Atlantic Canada during the Nineteenth Century." *Theatre Research in Canada* 3 (1982): 126–36.

Smyth, Donna E. "Getting the Message: The NAAGs of Halifax." *Feminist Theatre and Performance*. Ed. Susan Bennett. Toronto: Playwrights Canada, 2006. 32–40.

Stanlake, Christy. "Blending Time: Dramatic Conventions in Yvette Nolan's *Annie Mae's Movement*." *Journal of Dramatic Theory and Criticism* 14.1 (1999): 143–49.

Tyson, Brian. "'Swallowed up in Darkness': Vision and Division in *Of the Fields, Lately*." *Canadian Drama* 16.1 (1990): 23–31.

Van Fossen, Rachel. "A Particular Perspective: (Re)Living Memory in George Boyd's *Wade in the Water*." *African-Canadian Theatre*. Ed. Maureen Moynagh. Toronto: Playwrights Canada, 2005. 92–106.

Vingoe, Mary. "Janis Spence: A Playwright Who Lives and Works in Newfoundland." *Women on the Canadian Stage: The Legacy of Hrotsvit*. Ed. Rita Much. Winnipeg: Blizzard, 1992. 13–20.

Wagner, Vit. "Playwright Daniel MacIvor: Down the Road and Back Again." *ARTSatlantic* 53 (1995): 34–36.

Walker, Craig Stewart. "Elegy, Mythology and the Sublime in Michael Cook's *Colour the Flesh the Colour of Dust*." *Theatre Research in Canada* 15.2 (1994): 191–203.

———. "Ship of Death: Eschatology in Michael Cook's *Quiller*." *Theatre Research in Canada* 16.1–2 (1995): 69–80.

Wallace, Robert. "Technologies of the Monstrous: Notes on the Daniels's Monster Trilogy." *Canadian Theatre Review* 120 (2004): 12–18.

Wilson, Ann. "*Beatrice Chancy*: Slavery, Martyrdom and the Female Body." *Siting the Other: Re-Visions of Marginality in Australian and English-Canadian Drama*. Ed. Marc Maufort and Franca Bellasi. Bruxelles: PIE-Peter Lang, 2001. 267–78.

Notes on Contributors

Roberta Barker is Associate Professor and Chair in the Dalhousie Theatre Department, where she has taught since 2001. She is the author of *Early Modern Tragedy, Gender, and Performance, 1984–2000: The Destined Livery* (2007) and editor of a facsimile edition of the anonymous Elizabethan play *Common Conditions* (2004). Her articles on early modern and modern drama in performance have appeared in *Shakespeare Quarterly, Shakespeare Survey, Modern Drama, Early Theatre, English Studies in Canada, Early Modern Literary Studies, Canadian Theatre Review,* and *Literature Compass,* as well as in a number of edited collections.

Bruce Barton teaches playmaking and dramaturgy at the University of Toronto. He has published in numerous scholarly and practical periodicals and essay collections, and his book publications include *Developing Nation: New Play Creation in English-Speaking Canada* (2009); *Collective Creation, Collaboration and Devising* (2008); *Reluctant Texts from Exuberant Performance: Canadian Devised Theatre* (2008); *Imagination in Transition: David Mamet Moves to Film* (2005); and *Marigraph* (an anthology of Canadian Maritimes playwriting, 2004). Current research includes a three-year study on dramaturgies of the body in physically-based devised theatre and intermedial performance. Current creative practice includes writing, directing, and dramaturgy for multiple devised theatre projects and the creation of aerial-based interdisciplinary performance.

George Belliveau is Associate Professor in the Faculty of Education at the University of British Columbia, where he teaches undergraduate and graduate courses in Theatre/Drama Education. His research interests include research-based theatre, drama and social justice (bullying), drama across the curriculum, and Canadian theatre. His work has been published in journals such as *International Journal of Education and the Arts, Arts and Learning Research Journal, Canadian Journal of Education, English Quarterly, Theatre Research in Canada, Canadian Theatre Review,* among others. His co-authored book with Lynn Fels, *Exploring Curriculum: Performative Inquiry, Role Drama and Learning* (2008), was published by Pacific Educational Press.

Linda Burnett spent many years in Nova Scotia, a place she thinks of as home still, but now lives in northern Ontario and teaches in the Department of English and Fine Arts at Algoma University. She was the editor of *Canadian Theatre Review* 128: *Theatre in Atlantic Canada* (Fall 2006). Recent research projects include an essay on Margaret Cavendish's re-vision of John Ford's *'Tis Pity She's a Whore* and an essay on skepticism in the work of Donne and Shakespeare. Her essay "'Redescribing a World:' Towards a

Theory of Shakespearean Adaptation in Canada" has been reprinted in *Canadian Shakespeare*, Volume 18 of Critical Perspectives on Canadian Theatre in English.

George Elliott Clarke (O.C., O.N.S., Ph.D.) hails from Windsor, Nova Scotia, and is the inaugural E.J. Pratt Professor of Canadian Literature at the University of Toronto. A prizewinning poet and novelist, Clarke is also revered for his plays, opera libretti, and literary scholarship. His honours include The Archibald Lampman Award for Poetry (1991), The Portia White Prize for Artistic Excellence (1998), a Bellagio Center (Italy) Fellowship (1998), The Governor-General's Literary Award for Poetry (2001), The Dr. Martin Luther King, Jr. Achievement Award (2004), The Pierre Elliott Trudeau Fellowship Prize (2005), The Dartmouth Book Award for Fiction (2006), and The Eric Hoffer Book Award for Poetry (2009).

Michael Devine (B.A., M.F.A., Ph.D.) has directed more than thirty professional productions in seven languages, including productions for national theatres in Canada, Serbia, Kosovo, Romania, and Hungary. His plays have been produced in Serbia, Kosovo, Hungary, and Canada. Trained as an actor in London, England, New York, NY, and at York University, his internationally recognized acting methodology, BoxWhatBox, has been featured in fourteen countries. Devine was the Artistic Director of Theatre Newfoundland from 1997–99 and Founding Artistic Director of the Gros Morne Theatre Festival. He is the founder of the Centre for Alternative Theatre Training, an international organization dedicated to accessible intercultural theatre training. Currently Associate Professor of Theatre at Acadia University in Nova Scotia, Michael's website can be found at found at http://www. michaeldevine.org or http://www.boxwhatbox.org.

Len Falkenstein is Director of Drama at the University of New Brunswick in Fredericton, where he teaches playwriting, theatre, and drama. His plays, which include *Doppelgänger* (published in *Ryga* Vol. 1), *Futures, Free/Fall,* and *Happy City,* have been produced at the Summerworks Theatre Festival and Fringe Festivals across Canada. He is Artistic Director of the NotaBle Acts Theatre Company, whose mandate is to develop and produce new plays by New Brunswick dramatists, as well as Bard in the Barracks, Fredericton's outdoor summer Shakespeare festival. His academic work includes essays and reviews on Canadian and Irish drama in *Canadian Theatre Review, Canadian Literature,* and *The Canadian Journal of Irish Studies.*

Alan Filewod is Professor of Theatre Studies at the University of Guelph. His books include several anthologies of plays, as well as *Collective Encounters: Documentary Theatre in English Canada* (1987), *Performing "Canada": The Nation Enacted in the Imagined Theatre* (2002), and, with David Watt, *Workers' Playtime: Theatre and the Labour Movement since 1970* (2001). He is a past president of the Association for Canadian Theatre Research and of the Association for Canadian and Quebec Literatures/Association des littératures canadienne et québécoise, and is a former editor of *Canadian Theatre Review.*

Ric Knowles is Professor of Theatre Studies at the University of Guelph, editor of *Canadian Theatre Review,* and general editor of Critical Perspectives on Canadian

Theatre in English. His books include *The Theatre of Form and the Production of Meaning, Shakespeare and Canada, Reading the Material Theatre,* and *Theatre & Interculturalism.*

Graham W. Lea is a graduate student at the University of British Columbia. He has presented and published on research-based theatre, theatre and additional language learning, Prince Edward Island theatre history, and Shakespeare in elementary classrooms, and has been involved in the creation and production of four research-based theatre productions. He has extensive experience as a theatre practitioner, both on and off the stage. Research interests include research-based theatre methodology, integration of science and art in education, international education, and Prince Edward Island theatre history.

Denyse Lynde is a Professor at Memorial University of Newfoundland, where she teaches in theatre and media. Her research interests lie in the theatre and drama of Newfoundland and Labrador.

Bryden MacDonald is a playwright, director, and teacher. His published plays are *Whale Riding Weather, The Weekend Healer,* and *Divinity Bash/nine lives.* His latest play, *With Bated Breath,* premiered at Centaur Theatre this season. He has created and directed theatrical interpretations of the words and music of Leonard Cohen (*Sincerely a Friend*), Carol Pope & Rough Trade (*Shaking the Foundations*), and Joni Mitchell (*When All the Slaves Are Free*). Other directing credits include *Cat on a Hot Tin Roof, What the Butler Saw, Seduced,* and *Entertaining Mr. Sloan* (Neptune Theatre); *The Business of Living* (Mulgrave Road); *Glace Bay Miners' Museum* and *Albertine in Five Times* (Theatre Antigonish); and *Of The Fields, Lately* (Live Bait). He has taught at The National Theatre School of Canada and McGill University, and has conducted workshops or been artist-in-residence or guest artist at a number of theatres and festivals across the country.

Maureen Moynagh teaches postcolonial literature and the literature of the African diaspora at St. Francis Xavier University. She is the editor of *African-Canadian Theatre* (Playwrights Canada Press, 2005), and her most recent book is *Political Tourism and its Texts* (U of Toronto Press, 2008). She is currently editing a documents book on transnational collaboration among first-wave feminists, and doing research in the area of hemispheric American studies.

Glen Nichols teaches drama and Canadian literature in Moncton. He has published articles on Acadian theatre, theatre translation, and theatre history. In 2003, Playwrights Canada published *Angels and Anger,* a collection of five modern Acadian plays Nichols translated and edited.

Robert Nunn taught dramatic literature and theory and theatre history at Brock University until his retirement in 2000. He has published numerous essays on Canadian plays and playwrights, including Hrant Alianak, David Fennario, David French, Sharon Pollock, Judith Thompson, and Drew Hayden Taylor, on whose work he recently edited a collection of essays. He was co-editor of *Theatre Research in Canada/Researches théâtrales au Canada* from 1993 to 1996.

Brian Parker is Professor Emeritus in the department of English, University of Toronto, where he served as founding director of the Graduate Centre for the Study of Drama, director of Graduate English Studies, and Dean and Vice-Provost of Trinity College. His scholarly publications are divided between the early modern and the modern periods, including Canadian drama where, with Cynthia Zimmerman, he covered "Theatre and Drama" for *The Literary History of Canada*, volume 4.

Mary Elizabeth Smith is a retired Professor of English at the University of New Brunswick in Saint John. She is author of *'Love Kindling Fire': A Study of Christopher Marlowe's* The Tragedy of Dido Queen of Carthage, and *Too Soon the Curtain Fell: A History of Theatre in Saint John 1789–1900*. As well as articles on Renaissance theatre she has published extensively on the theatre history of Atlantic Canada. More recently she has written about iconography in early Christianity and apocalyptic images in art and literature.

Donna E. Smyth taught English and Creative Writing at Acadia University, Wolfville, Nova Scotia, and worked as a playwright with Mermaid Theatre in Wolfville. Her one-woman play celebrating the life and work of the poet Elizabeth Bishop, *Running to Paradise*, was produced by the Studio Group in Wolfville and Halifax in 1998 and published by Gaspereau Press in 1999. Her two-act play, *Sole Survivors*, was produced by the Ship's Company Theatre in Parrsboro, Nova Scotia, in 2000, and published by Broken Jaw Press in 2003.

Jerry Wasserman is Professor of English and Theatre and Head of the Department of Theatre and Film at the University of British Columbia in Vancouver. He is an actor, critic, and theatre historian, and he has published widely on Canadian plays and playwrights. His *Modern Canadian Plays* is soon to appear in its 5th edition.

Josh Weale is a writer/performer from Prince Edward Island with numerous theatre credits to his name as an actor, director and playwright. He originally co-presented a version of "TheatrePEI: The Emergence and Development of a Local Theatre" at the 2004 Shifting Tides conference. He has studied at both University of Prince Edward Island and York University, and he currently resides in Toronto where he works as a media analyst.